Using **WEB** and **PAPER** *Questionnaires* for Data-Based Decision Making

3/97

UNIVERSI

WITHDRAWN

To Stan, whose support and encouragement made this book possible.

Using **WEB** and **PAPER** *Questionnaires* for Data-Based Decision Making

From Design to Interpretation of the Results

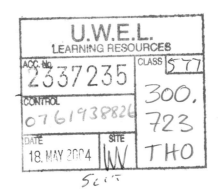

U.W.E.L.
LEARNING RESOURCES

ACC. No. 2337235

CLASS 577

CONTROL 0761938826

300. 723

DATE 18. MAY 2004

SITE W

THO

Scit

SUSAN J. THOMAS

CORWIN PRESS
A Sage Publications Company
Thousand Oaks, California

Copyright © 2004 by Corwin Press

All rights reserved. When forms and sample documents are included, their use is authorized only by educators, local school sites, and/or noncommercial entities who have purchased the book. Except for that usage, no part of this book may be reproduced or utilized in any form or by any means, electronic or mechanical, including photocopying, recording, or by any information storage and retrieval system, without permission in writing from the publisher.

For information:

Corwin Press
A Sage Publications Company
2455 Teller Road
Thousand Oaks, California 91320
www.corwinpress.com

Sage Publications Ltd.
1 Oliver's Yard
55 City Road
London EC1Y 1SP
United Kingdom

Sage Publications India Pvt. Ltd.
B-42, Panchsheel Enclave
Post Box 4109
New Delhi 110 017 India

Printed in the United States of America

Library of Congress Cataloging-in-Publication Data

Thomas, Susan J.
Using web and paper questionnaires for data-based decision making: From design to interpretation of the results / Susan J. Thomas.
　　　p. cm.
Includes bibliographical references and index.
　ISBN 0-7619-3882-6 (Cloth) — ISBN 0-7619-3883-4 (Paper)
1. Social surveys—Methodology. 2. Internet questionnaires. 3. Questionnaires.
4. Decision making. I. Title.
HM538.T49 2004 300′.72′3—dc22　　　　　2003025626

This book is printed on acid-free paper.

04　05　06　07　10　9　8　7　6　5　4　3　2　1

Acquisitions Editor:	Rachel Livsey
Editorial Assistant:	Phyllis Cappello
Production Editor:	Diane S. Foster
Copy Editor:	Linda Gray
Typesetter:	C&M Digitals (P) Ltd.
Proofreader:	Scott Oney
Indexer:	Will Ragsdale
Cover Designer:	Michael Dubowe
Graphic Designer:	Lisa Miller

Contents

Preface

Increasingly more often, educators (teachers, school administers, counselors, school board members, and other school leaders) are asked to gather information on which to base decisions. Questionnaires can be an effective means to gather such information. But creating a questionnaire that asks the right questions at the appropriate level for the intended audience can be a challenging task. Four years ago, I wrote *Designing Surveys That Work! A Step-by-Step Guide* to provide support to educators who need to create a high-quality questionnaire. Since that time, I've worked on several survey projects and advised on many others. What I learned was that educators need more examples, more details on how to use the information gathered from questionnaires to make data-based decisions, and more guidance on how to present the results to a variety of audiences. I also learned that educators need to know how to disaggregate data from questionnaires so they can make meaningful comparisons among subgroups based on demographic (e.g., gender, race/ethnicity) or experiential variables.

Web-based questionnaires are much more widely used now than they were four years ago. As I worked with my colleagues to create Web-based questionnaires for our own projects, we consulted many different resources and learned by trial and error. We also found that many of the methods used for paper-based questionnaires need some adapting to work well with Web-based questionnaires—and this was not always clear in the resources we consulted.

On the basis of these experiences, I created this book. I know that you are busy—and that collecting information is most likely not your full-time job. I also know that you have many challenging decisions to make and you need good data to guide your decision making. The reporting requirements of the No Child Left Behind (NCLB) Act will mean that you'll need to gather data—and then disaggregate the results so you can examine the impact of various interventions on the racial/ethnic groups within your school and your district.

◆ WHAT IS THE PURPOSE OF THIS BOOK?

The main purpose of this book is to support the decision-making processes of educators as they collect and use data from questionnaires to make data-based decisions. But more than that, there's guidance for all phases of a survey project, beginning with the question of whether you really need a questionnaire to gather information for making decisions to reporting the results and recommendations to a variety of audiences. The book focuses on what's important to educators—from planning the administration of the questionnaire around the school calendar to using a variety of data sources to make important decisions.

I want you to be successful. I want you to be able to conduct a high-quality survey project, get the information you need, and have confidence that your questionnaires will be interesting to those who receive them and will yield accurate data to guide your decisions.

◆ WHO SHOULD READ THIS BOOK?

Although this book was developed primarily for school administrators, teachers, counselors, and other school leaders, anyone who is considering creating a questionnaire to gather information will find this book very useful. Data from questionnaires can be used for many purposes, such as describing behaviors, identifying preferences, and determining needs. This book, however, focuses on using the data gathered from a questionnaire to make data-based decisions.

◆ WHAT ARE THE UNIQUE FEATURES OF THE BOOK?

This book is designed to be a user-friendly how-to book, thanks to the feedback from the teachers, school administrators, school leaders, counselors, and other practicing professionals who took my research classes and used my early materials as they were developed. I also received useful feedback from several readers of the first book. The unique features of this book include the following:

Sequential Arrangement of Chapters. The chapters in this book follow the steps necessary to conduct a successful survey project. Each chapter presents the details of each phase of a survey project.

Easy to Read. This book is written in an informal style to help the reader understand the information easily. The writing style is engaging and conversational. Icons signal important points, such as the major steps in a survey project and helpful hints.

Examples. Each chapter contains examples of the points being made in the chapter. In addition, a case study of a survey project is developed throughout the book.

Samples. Sample cover letters, invitations, and parental permission forms are included, as are planning templates.

Web-Based Questionnaire Guidelines. In each chapter, information about how to apply the ideas and concepts in that chapter to a Web-based questionnaire are included and are identified with an icon.

Checklists. Each chapter concludes with a checklist containing the key activities included in that chapter. Readers are urged to use these checklists to ensure that they are ready to proceed to the next step in the process of creating their survey project.

Activities. Several chapters contain activities to check your understanding of the points made in that chapter. Answers to these activities are provided at the end of the chapter.

Icons. Icons are used to call out several special pieces of information. These include hints, parts of the case study, and the 16 steps to a successful survey project.

Resources. The full Web-based questionnaire for the case study appears at the end of the book, followed by a bibliography of useful sources and the reference list containing the sources cited throughout the book.

◆ WHAT'S IN EACH OF THE CHAPTERS?

There are five major components to a successful survey project:

1. Planning

2. Creating the questionnaire

3. Gathering the data

4. Analyzing the results and making decisions

5. Communicating the results

Planning. Chapter 1 focuses on planning, including identifying the purpose of the survey project and creating objectives to guide the development of the questionnaire, identifying the people who will respond to your questionnaire, determining whether a paper-based or Web-based survey is appropriate, and gaining the necessary approvals to conduct the survey project.

Creating the Questionnaire. Chapters 2, 3, and 4 provide guidance for creating the questionnaire, including writing the questions and carefully crafting the response choices and formatting the questionnaire.

Gathering the Data. Chapters 5, 6, and 7 provide information about gathering the data, including selecting the sample, creating cover letters, pilot testing everything, producing the questionnaire, and using it to gather the data.

Analyzing the Results and Making Decisions. Chapter 8 shows how to analyze the results from a questionnaire and provides examples of how data from questionnaires were used to make data-based decisions.

Communicating the Results. Chapter 9 provides examples of reports of survey projects for different audiences.

◆ THE CASE STUDY OF A SURVEY PROJECT

To help you get a better sense of how to develop a survey project, a case study of a survey research project is developed throughout the book. The focus of the case study is parents' involvement in their child's school. The purpose of gathering the data is to determine parental awareness of activities available in their school in which they can participate, their satisfaction with these activities, suggestions for other activities, barriers to their participation in these activities, and whether they would be likely to participate in some of these activities if the barriers were removed. Data from the questionnaire will be used to develop activities designed to support school-family partnerships based on identified needs rather than perceived ones, thus increasing the likelihood for success of a new parent involvement program.

When you see this symbol and shaded text, you'll know that it's part of the case study—and that these are "pieces" of the survey project. Throughout the book, the case study builds; you'll find the complete questionnaire for the case study in the Resource section at the end of the book.

◆ ICONS IDENTIFY SPECIAL FEATURES IN THE BOOK

Other icons will alert you to specific kinds of information. For example, electronic or Web-based questionnaires are becoming increasingly popular. More and more people have e-mail and Web access. Some school districts have Web sites and post questionnaires there on a regular basis. Although many of the basic steps are the same whether you use a paper-based questionnaire or an electronic questionnaire, there are some important differences. This computer indicates special considerations for Web-based questionnaires.

Throughout the book, you'll find hints and reminders—things to remember as you create all the pieces of your survey project. Each of these hints has a light bulb icon.

There are 16 major steps in a successful survey project. Each time one of these steps is discussed, you'll see this icon to remind you. Table 1.2 in Chapter 1 describes these steps.

◆ HOW SHOULD THE BOOK BE USED?

The guidelines and activities included in this book are meant to help anyone creating any type of questionnaire—whether paper-based or Web-based, whether for a large survey project involving hundreds or even thousands of respondents or for a small survey project that focuses on gathering information from a relatively small target audience. The case study shows a relatively large project involving many interested stakeholders and multiple schools. Your survey project may be much smaller and less complex than this one.

A survey project can be conducted by one to two individuals. The attention to detail and to quality is the same for all survey projects.

LET'S GET STARTED!

Acknowledgments

Four reviewers provided insightful suggestions for making this book more user-friendly and more useful to educators. These include Mildred Murray Ward, Ph.D., Associate Dean, California Lutheran University, Thousand Oaks, CA; Mike Harmon, Ph.D., Program Manager, Test Administration, Georgia Department of Education, Atlanta, GA; Chester H. McCall, Professor of Research Methods, Pepperdine University, Culver City, CA; and Lillian Biermann Wehmeyer, Ph.D., Chair, Azusa Pacific University, Azusa, CA. Their thoughtful suggestions are gratefully acknowledged.

Long-time good friend, colleague, and mentor Howard Stoker, Ed.D., provided encouragement throughout the writing process, wisdom and wit, and access to his archives for some needed references.

Special thanks to Sandra Stein, Ph.D., Professor of Education at Rider University, a colleague and friend who encouraged me to put the first book together and then provided excellent comments and suggestions based on feedback from her students (who are teachers, counselors, and school administrators) so that this book will be even better and more useful.

A big thank-you to Tiffany Scheel, Instructional Designer and good friend, who provided formatting and editing suggestions for the entire manuscript and identified resources for some of the sections on Web-based questionnaires. Her suggestions on what's practical and realistic for Web-based questionnaires made these sections even more useful.

About the Author

Susan J. Thomas is Managing Consultant with IBM Business Consulting Services, Human Capital Solutions. She works with a variety of clients and companies to provide consulting services in the areas of skills competency analysis (which includes different types of questionnaires), certification test development and skills assessment, questionnaire development (both paper-based and Web-based), and training evaluation. She also assists clients with data-based decision making by helping them design questionnaires and by performing statistical analysis and data mining to help them make recommendations and create action plans.

Prior to joining the IBM Corporation, she was a measurement statistician and test development specialist with the Educational Testing Service. She was also an adjunct professor at Rider University, where she taught graduate courses in research methods (including questionnaire design), testing and measurement for teachers, basic statistics, and authentic assessment.

Previously, she was a faculty member at the University of Illinois, Urbana-Champaign, and Florida State University, where she taught courses in measurement, research design, and various areas of educational and developmental psychology. She has directed numerous funded research projects, has presented extensively at the annual meetings of the American Educational Research Association and the National Council for Measurement in Education, and has served as a Divisional Vice President of the American Educational Research Association.

She has published several journal articles, as well as *Evaluation Without Fear* with coauthor Roger Kaufman, and *Designing Surveys That Work!*, a predecessor to the current book. She conducts workshops for teachers on topics related to assessment and has developed many training guides for these workshops. She did her undergraduate work at the University of Wisconsin–Eau Claire and received her Ph.D. from Purdue University.

1

Launching Your Survey Project

Wen you want information from someone, how do you usually go about getting it? Often, you ask questions. In a conversational setting, you can ask questions of someone to gain the information you need. A structured version of these conversations is called an interview. But for many reasons—mostly cost and resources—we're usually not able to talk with a great number of people in person. If data collection is limited to a few people, that information may not represent the views of the larger group to whom we want to generalize the results. Decisions based on such data may be misleading or even erroneous. A practical way of gathering information from a large number of people is to use a questionnaire.

Asking questions, getting responses, and using that information is what survey research is all about. *Survey research* or a *survey project* denotes the process of gathering information from members of a particular group using an interview or a questionnaire. The focus in this book is on creating and using questionnaires.

A *questionnaire* is a tool used to gather information in a survey project using either paper-based or Web-based modes of delivery.

A *survey project* consists of the tasks and activities required to plan and create a questionnaire and use it to gather information.

◆ WHEN ARE QUESTIONNAIRES USED?

Questionnaires are used as data collection tools for many types of survey projects, including fact-finding questionnaires; determining opinions, perceptions, and attitudes; identifying interests and experiences; conducting needs assessments; and so on.

Survey research using a questionnaire is an appropriate method of data collection when . . .

- Existing information is not available to answer the questions posed
- A questionnaire is the best means to provide the information required (rather than interviews, an experiment, or observations)
- A sponsor and resources (staff and budget) are available to complete the survey project
- There is a plan in place to *use* the results of the survey project

Using Questionnaire Results for Data-Based Decision Making

A well-done survey project provides high-quality data. In many cases, results of questionnaires are used to inform decisions. For high-stakes decisions, you should use other sources of information in addition to the responses from a questionnaire. A high-stakes decision is one that takes significant resources to implement and one for which the consequences of being wrong are great. For example, data from questionnaires may be used to guide important decisions such as recommending the location of a new school, determining the need for a charter school, or creating special programs in response to requirements from the No Child Left Behind (NCLB) Act. In all these situations, significant time and resources are required to implement decisions—and there's a high cost associated with making a wrong decision.

If your decision has low stakes—for example, selecting a topic for the spring one-day inservice session—then results from a carefully constructed questionnaire administered to an appropriate target audience will most likely provide the information you need to make your decision. The more important the decision, the better— and more varied—your sources of data must be.

Depending on the decision you need to make, you may need to *disaggregate* your data to explore potential differences among subgroups.

Disaggregating your data means that you create subsets of your data for purposes of analysis. For example, for data gathered in response to requirements from the NCLB Act, it's important to gather information on ethnicity/race and gender so you can make comparisons of responses among these groups.

A caveat: Sometimes people who respond to a questionnaire don't tell the whole truth, or they give only partial information. That's why it's important to validate the information from a questionnaire with other information and common sense.

Using a questionnaire to gather data to make a decision has several benefits:

- Involving a wide range of constituents in the decision-making process
- Gathering a range of viewpoints—ensuring that many people are heard
- Determining support for proposed projects or actions (Avoid hindsight!)

Following are some examples of data-based decisions:

Problem: Many students who rode their bikes to school were not using helmets, resulting in a number of injuries.

A school district noted that one in three of its elementary and middle school students were riding bicycles without helmets, ranging from zero in one school to 83% in another. This district has a high unemployment rate and a high proportion of the population below the national poverty level. A questionnaire to parents indicated that the primary reason for their children not wearing helmets was the cost of the helmet. The district held a series of bicycle safety awareness workshops and publicized these in the community. As a result, over 500 helmets were donated, and the use of helmets rose significantly over a two-year period as documented by a follow-up questionnaire.

Note that another means of gathering information about helmet use following the donation of the helmets would be observation: Are all or most of the children wearing their helmets? The observational data would corroborate the results of the questionnaire.

Problem: Informal reports by teachers suggested the presence of bullying in the elementary school, but there were no hard data on the types of bullying or their prevalence.

Several school districts worked together to create a questionnaire that was distributed to all fourth graders. Students were asked how safe they felt at school, whether bullying happened to them (specific behavioral examples were used), and if so, what they did. Questionnaire results indicated that nearly one-quarter of the students reported being bullied, albeit of a mild nature such as teasing. However, 25% of these students reported serious bullying, including being kicked, hit, or pushed on a frequent basis. Most often the bully was a boy from a higher grade level. The results of this questionnaire were used to create awareness and support programs to lessen the incidence of bullying at school.

Another data source to validate the results of this questionnaire would be observations in the school, interviews with teachers, and reports of bullying by students and teachers. All these data sources can be used in planning an intervention program.

In these examples, a questionnaire provided information to make data-based decisions. In the bicycle helmet study, the questionnaire revealed that the reasons children did not wear helmets had nothing to do with understanding the need for wearing them.

For the school districts focusing on making the school environment a safer place, data on the incidence of bullying, and the types of bullies and their actions led to the development of an intervention program.

Using Questionnaire Results
for Planning, Describing, and Identifying

Results of questionnaires can be used for many purposes, including the following:

- Identifying needs (needs assessments)
  - What are the technology needs of the district—and what training must be provided for that technology to be used effectively?
- Determining opinions, attitudes, and beliefs
  - What are parents' attitudes about charter schools?

- Identifying interests
  - What is the level of interest among parents in participating in activities in their child's classroom?
- Identifying feelings and perceptions
  - How do parents perceive the value of magnet schools?
- Describing behaviors
  - What kinds of reading-related activities do parents of early-elementary students use with their children?

◆ WHAT QUESTION DO YOU WANT TO ANSWER?

You've learned about uses of questionnaire data and how those data need to be a part of the evidence for high-stakes decisions. You've also learned about other uses of data from questionnaires, such as planning or describing interests or preferences. So now, here are some questions to consider: What question do you want to answer? Who needs the information (project sponsor or decision maker)? How will that information be used?

Table 1.1 describes some goals for survey projects, as well as uses of the results from the questionnaires. For some, the data will be used to make a decision, while for others, the information will be used to plan activities or understand perceptions.

Questionnaires are used to gather data, and they require resources and commitment from many people, including those who are providing you with the data (the respondents). The results of questionnaires must be *used!* That does seem obvious, but on occasion, questions will be included on a questionnaire that do not need to be there. For example, will the data from all demographic questions be used in the analyses? If not, why are they being asked? Sometimes questionnaires contain questions that were added because someone was curious but there were no specific plans to use the data. Careful planning can avoid this—and perhaps shorten the questionnaire.

◆ WILL A SURVEY PROJECT PROVIDE YOU WITH THE INFORMATION YOU NEED?

A strange question, especially when you are reading a book about how to create a great survey project! But let's be sure that's what you need. Following are some types of research studies that provide data and information to support decision making—but they use different methods of doing so.

Experimental Research Studies

An experimental research study is one in which a variable is manipulated and outcomes are measured to evaluate the effect of the manipulation. For example, the effect of a new curriculum on student understanding of mathematics may be investigated. Experimental research is characterized by careful controls in the design of the study to help ensure that you are able to measure the effect of the intervention—in this example, the new mathematics curriculum. Questionnaires can be used before and after the experimental intervention to gather information. The experimental

Table 1.1   Examples of Survey Project Goals

Group Sponsoring Survey Project	Goal of Survey Project
Parent-Teacher Organization (PTO)	To determine the current level of parent involvement among parents of students in different grade levels for the purpose of developing outreach programs to be more inclusive for all parents (This questionnaire could be administered at different times to look for trends in participation.)
School board	To gather information on salaries, benefits, and working conditions in similar districts in the state to assist the board in making decisions relative to collective bargaining
Group of school librarians in the district	To identify best practices for public and school libraries working together to support academic success to guide the development of new districtwide library programs
School alumni office	To describe alumni outcomes for the purpose of identifying role model graduates to encourage students to stay in school until they graduate
Community group	To gather information about citizen involvement with the district and its schools for the purpose of identifying ways to increase citizen involvement (This questionnaire could be administered at different times to look for trends in participation.)
Teacher inservice committee	To determine teacher reactions to a series of several different workshops delivered during the school year for the purpose of determining what works best
School district	To gather information about perceptions regarding the district, its schools, and the quality of the education it provides to students—for the purpose of designing an effective communication plan

research question is as follows: What is the effect of the new mathematics curriculum on student achievement in mathematics? Additional details about experimental research can be found in research textbooks (e.g., Fraenkel & Wallen, 2002; Gall, 2002; Johnson & Christensen, 2000; Mertler & Charles, 2001).

Action Research Studies

Action research is similar in some ways to experimental research in that an activity or a program is implemented and its effect or outcome is measured. The goal is to find out why something happened or why something worked as it did. Action research does not use a random sample of participants, is not designed to be generalized to other groups or to other settings, and has no control or comparison group. Action research studies are on a much smaller scale than are experimental research studies, focus on questions of immediate interest to teachers and other educators who conduct these studies, and often seek to answer a specific question that will guide specific actions. Both questionnaires and observations may be used to gather the data.

For example, a middle school teacher observed that in her third-period computer class, some of her students were acting as peer tutors and helping other students who were challenged by some of the features and functions of the computer programs they were using. These peer tutors were working with their classmates during study hall. She observed that the tutored students became proficient in using the computer program much faster than students in some of her other classes where there were no peer tutors. She decided to try peer tutoring in another of her classes and identified three students who were interested. After two weeks, the students who received the peer tutoring were able to use the computer programs proficiently.

The action research question is as follows: What is the effect of using peer tutors to increase the proficiency level of students using a particular computer program? Further information about action research can be found in sources such as Arhar, Holly, and Kasten (2000), McLean (1995), or Mills (1999).

Questionnaires can be used to gather information in experimental and action research studies, as well as in survey projects. But the difference here is that the survey projects described in this book focus on gathering information to make a data-based decision.

◆ CREATING A SURVEY PROJECT

Let's begin the process of creating your survey project. Survey projects come in all sizes—from an individual school leader creating a questionnaire to administer to a small group of teachers to large districtwide, statewide, or even national survey projects. Much of the discussion in this book is geared to larger survey projects because they have more people involved. But all points made in this book will work for any size survey project.

Table 1.2 provides a summary of the steps of a successful survey project. For each step in the process, the critical success factors are identified—those things that must be done *during this step in the process* to help ensure that your survey project is successful. The table also indicates in which chapter each step is discussed.

Table 1.2　A Summary of the Steps and Critical Success Factors in a Survey Project

Step	*Critical Success Factor*	*Find More Information in Chapter*
1. Conduct the initial planning.	• Identify the sponsors and stakeholders and garner their support in all phases of the initial planning. • Get buy-in and sponsorship at the right levels within the organization. • Identify the audiences for the final report. • Identify sources of information you can use to help you with the project.	1 – Launching Your Survey Project
2. State the guiding question and create clear, concise, and unambiguous objectives.	• Have a clear guiding question and clear and unambiguous objectives.	1 – Launching Your Survey Project

Step	Critical Success Factor	Find More Information in Chapter
3. Identify the target audience: the people who have the information you need.	• Carefully define the target audience to ensure you'll get the information you need.	1 – Launching Your Survey Project
4. Determine the mode of data collection that's appropriate for your target audience.	• Tailor the mode of data collection (paper-based or electronic questionnaire) to the skills and needs of the target audience.	1 – Launching Your Survey Project
5. Create a detailed project plan.	• Create realistic schedules and timelines. • Create detailed project plans and resource assignments. • Create reasonable, realistic budgets and stick to them. • Create a plan for analysis, including disaggregating your data so that you'll know what demographic questions to include.	1 – Launching Your Survey Project
6. Gain needed approvals to contact members of the target audience and to conduct the survey project.	• Plan for and obtain needed approvals from the school district, the Institutional Review Board, or other oversight organization at the beginning of the project.	1 – Launching Your Survey Project
7. Write the questions.	• Write questions that map to the guiding question and the objectives. • Have enough questions to meet the objectives of the survey project, but not so many that respondents quit or feel so overwhelmed that they do not even begin the questionnaire. • Use response scales that are appropriate to the question, are clear and complete, are appropriate to the target audience, and require no interpretation. • Tailor the types of responses to the level of understanding of the respondents.	2 – Asking the Right Questions 3 – Creating Response Choices for Rating Scales
8. Create the questionnaire.	• Create directions that are clear and complete. • Format the questionnaire so that it is easy for respondents to understand.	4 – Putting the Questionnaire Together

(Continued)

Table 1.2 (Continued)

Step	Critical Success Factor	Find More Information in Chapter
	• Produce a questionnaire that is professional looking, useful, and functional. • Plan for and build in reliability and validity.	
9. Select the sample and plan the method to contact and gain cooperation from participants.	• Create a detailed plan for contacting your target audience. • Determine how many respondents you need so you'll have the data to make your decisions. • Identify the gatekeepers and gain needed permission to contact members of the target audience.	5 – Identifying and Contacting Respondents
10. Create cover letters or invitations.	• Make good use of their one minute to reach your audience. • Create powerful invitations and cover letters that will convince participants to become respondents.	5 – Identifying and Contacting Respondents
11. Conduct a thorough pilot test of all aspects of the survey project.	• Try out everything—from the wording of the questions to the directions and format to the data coding and analysis.	6 – Pilot Testing the Questionnaire
12. Use the information from the pilot test to make revisions.	• Use the information gathered in the pilot test to make needed revisions— even if it takes a bit of extra time.	6 – Pilot Testing the Questionnaire
13. Produce the questionnaire and gather your data.	• Send prenotifications to participants selected for your study. • Send out your questionnaire at a time in the lives of your target audience that will maximize your response rate. • Conduct follow-up contacts to increase your response rate. • Send reminder notices halfway through the time period the questionnaire is available.	7 – Maximizing Your Response Rate: Collecting the Data

Step	Critical Success Factor	Find More Information in Chapter
14. Analyze the data.	• Code the responses carefully and conduct frequent checks on the reasonableness and quality of your data. • Use appropriate analyses for the type of data provided by the questionnaire. • Back up your data set.	8 – Analyzing the Data and Making Data-Based Decisions
15. Use the data to make decisions.	• Consider other sources of information in addition to the data from the questionnaire to make data-based decisions.	8 – Analyzing the Data and Making Data-Based Decisions
16. Create the reports of the results and recommendations.	• Create reports that match the needs of the audiences for information.	9 – Communicating the Results

 # STEP 1: CONDUCT THE INITIAL PLANNING

Who Needs the Information?

Who are the sponsors and stakeholders in the survey project? A sponsor is the person who needs the information.

A sponsor may be any of the following:

- A school district gathering information about salaries and benefits for teachers and administrators
- A community group seeking input on school facilities planning, including building or remodeling schools in the district
- A vocational high school curriculum committee wanting to ensure that its graduates have the skills, knowledge, and competencies required for successful performance on the job
- A school guidance counselor who needs information about student interests in career planning workshops

Sponsors have different expectations based on their own experiences. It's important to understand the sponsor's expectations of the results of the survey project. For example, does he prefer using qualitative or quantitative data to make decisions? Or perhaps a combination of both? What are her expectations for the final report? Details, as in a technical report, a high-level overview such as a presentation, or both?

A word of caution: Watch out for possible biases that could creep into a survey project, such as when a sponsor has an ax to grind or a controversial point that she or he wants to demonstrate has support. As discussed later (Chapter 2, "Asking the Right Questions"), the wording of questions is critically important: Questions must be free of biases to ensure that fair and accurate data are gathered.

HINT: Make sure you know as much as possible about the sponsor's preferences and design for them.

How do you identify stakeholders in the survey project? Answer these questions:

- Who needs the information?
- Who makes the decisions based on the results of the questionnaire?
- Who has an interest in the outcome of the questionnaire results?
- Whose "turf" might be affected?
- Who controls the funding?
- Who might be interested in the survey project not being completed?
- Who needs to be included in the planning?

HINT: Garner support from a variety of stakeholders.

For our case study, the sponsor is the Parent-Teacher Organization (PTO). Stakeholders include school administrators, teachers, and school staff members who will implement parent involvement programs and parents who will partic-ipate in these programs.

Who Are the Audiences for the Final Report?

Who will be interested in the results? Audiences for the final report can include the sponsor, stakeholders, and members of the target audience. Other potential audi-ences could include researchers, members of the community, or members of selected professional associations. Each audience requires a different type of report in terms of the amount of detail, particularly of the analyses.

For our case study survey project, the primary audience for the final report is the sponsor, the PTO. We'll need to provide a detailed report to the PTO Steering Committee and a presentation for the PTO membership.

What Existing Information Is Available for Your Survey Project?

As you plan your survey project, consider other sources of information that may be available. When you are gathering data to make a high-stakes decision, it's important to have information from other sources, such as interviews, observations, and depending on the type of decision you're making, perhaps results from statewide assessments. When you have data from several sources, and if the data from the different data sources support the results from your survey project, then you have strong evidence for your decision. This process is called "triangulating the information."

Following are some suggested activities to identify available information to help you create your survey project:

- Determine the data requirements for the decision you need to make—what data do you need to make a decision?
- Determine what data and information already exist. If there is some, determine how much is available and usable for your study. You want to avoid asking for information that's already been gathered. Depending on the information you need, here are some suggestions:
  - If you're working in a school district, check with staff members who may know about studies that have been completed in the past three to five years.
  - Check with other similar organizations, such as school districts in the same state.
  - Check on the Internet. There are numerous reports of questionnaires and survey project results on the Web. Use a search engine such as Google to find information about completed survey projects.
  - Check reports of completed survey projects in journal articles, in sources such as ERIC, and on the Web (e.g., alumni outcomes, salary and benefit packages). Your school or district may also have some completed survey projects. Some data may be appropriate for your project.
  - Review sources of questionnaires such as *Dissertation Abstracts, Buros Mental Measurements Yearbook, Pro-Ed Test Critiques,* and *Tests in Print.*
- Identify similar survey projects that can help you formulate your objectives clearly and provide ideas for questions for your questionnaire.

STEP 2: STATE THE GUIDING QUESTION FOR THE SURVEY PROJECT AND CREATE CLEAR, CONCISE, AND UNAMBIGUOUS OBJECTIVES

Think about the information you need—whether it be to make a decision or for other uses. The data can be points of view, opinions, a needs analysis, facts, behaviors, or activities. The guiding question indicates why the survey project is being done—and the uses that will be made of the results of the questionnaire.

Write Your Guiding Question

Your guiding question will assist you in creating the questionnaire that will provide information you need. A carefully constructed questionnaire can provide information for many uses.

- Identifying needs (needs assessments)
  - What kinds of strategies will increase parent involvement in the schools in our district?
  - What types of sports programs will parents and the community support?
  - What are the technology needs of the district—and what training must be provided for that technology to be used effectively?
- Determining opinions, attitudes, and beliefs
  - What are parents' attitudes about charter schools?
  - How do teachers view parent involvement in their classrooms?
  - What are parents' opinions of the teacher strike in the district?
- Identifying interests
  - Which class activities should be kept and which should be changed?
  - What is the interest level of sophomores in participating in community service activities?
  - What is the level of interest among parents in participating in activities in their child's classroom?
- Identifying feelings and perceptions
  - How do students feel about homework assignments that require Internet-based research?
  - How do parents perceive the value of magnet schools?
  - How satisfied are parents with their child's overall school experience?
- Describing behaviors
  - How often do students use various school facilities, such as the library, resource center, computer lab, sports equipment, and pool?
  - What kinds of reading-related activities do parents of early-elementary students use with their children?
  - What kinds of volunteer activities have parents participated in during the current school year?

The guiding question for the case study that is developed throughout the book is as follows:

What kinds of strategies will increase parent involvement in the elementary schools in our district?

After you have written your guiding question, it's time to create the specific objectives that will guide the development of the questionnaire.

Develop Objectives Based on Your Guiding Question

An *objective* is an idea or concept you want to measure. Objectives flow from the guiding question and provide specific guidance to create the questions for your questionnaire. Questionnaire objectives must be clear, concise, and measurable.

◆ GUIDELINES FOR WRITING CLEAR OBJECTIVES

1. Focus each objective on one concept or idea.

2. Do not use the word *and.* If one of your objectives uses *and,* it probably is really two objectives.

3. Tie each objective to the guiding question.

Objectives for our case study survey project include the following:

- Determine parental awareness of opportunities the school currently provides for parents to be involved in their child's school.
- Identify current levels of parent participation in the available activities.
- Determine parent satisfaction with the parent participation activities currently available.
- For parents who do not participate in these activities, identify reasons and barriers.
- Identify types of parent involvement activities preferred by parents.

Each of the preceding objectives will guide the creation of a set of questions.

HINT: The clearer and more focused your objectives, the more likely you are to gather the information you will need to make your decision.

STEP 3: IDENTIFY YOUR TARGET AUDIENCE

Although Chapter 5, "Identifying and Contacting Respondents," provides greater detail on the target audience, here we will identify the target audience. The reason for considering this aspect of the survey project at this time is that it will help you to determine how the data will be collected. Will you use a paper-based questionnaire? Will you use a Web-based questionnaire? What are the features, benefits, advantages, and disadvantages of each of these modes of data collection?

For our case study survey project, we'll need input from parents from all three elementary schools in the district.

Let's look at some of the guiding questions provided earlier as examples and identify appropriate target audiences. Table 1.3 provides this information.

Table 1.3   Examples of Guiding Questions and Target Audiences

Guiding Question	Target Audience
What types of sports programs will parents and the community support?	Parents at the school plus a sample of members of the community who are not parents at the school
Which class activities should be kept and which should be changed?	Students and teachers
How do students feel about homework assignments that require Internet-based research?	Students
What kinds of reading-related activities do parents of early-elementary students use with their children?	Parents of early-elementary students

 ## STEP 4: DETERMINE THE MODE OF DATA COLLECTION THAT IS APPROPRIATE FOR YOUR TARGET AUDIENCE

Begin by considering the following questions:

- Who is the target audience?
- What is the best way to gather information from this audience?
- What must you consider as you decide on the mode of data collection?

The mode of data collection (mail, telephone, e-mail, Web) might depend in part on what kind of access you have to the target audience as well as their access to, and level of comfort with, computers.

Paper-Based Questionnaires

Most people are familiar with paper-based questionnaires they receive in the mail. But unless the potential recipient receives prenotification or a very persuasive cover letter, the questionnaire might be lost in a pile of unsolicited mail. Some studies show that people are more honest with an anonymous paper-based questionnaire.

A disadvantage of a mailed questionnaire is time: Data collection usually takes two to four weeks—sometimes longer. In addition, data must be entered into the computer for analysis, requiring additional time.

For questionnaires distributed in person, or sent home with students, the time period usually is shorter.

Electronic Questionnaires

There are three major types of electronic questionnaires:

- E-mail questionnaire
- E-mail invitation linked to URL (Web "address")
- Questionnaire on a Web page

 Electronic questionnaires are being used more often with many target audiences, including teachers, administrators, parents, and students and in many communities. If you don't have good technical skills and want to use an electronic questionnaire, you'll need to work with a consultant who has those skills. But the survey project team must complete many activities, whether a paper-based or electronic questionnaire is used. Throughout this book, the computer indicates additional details about electronic or Web-based questionnaires—and we'll refer to all of these types of electronic questionnaires as "Web-based."

E-mail questionnaires are contained within an e-mail. They are usually limited to plain text because many e-mail services cannot handle graphics or grid-type responses. (Details about grid-type responses are in Chapter 4, "Putting the Questionnaire Together.") They are sent to a specific list of people for whom you have e-mail addresses. The respondent uses the "reply" e-mail function and answers the questions—and the respondent's e-mail address is usually a part of this reply. There are ways to block a person's e-mail address from the response, depending on the software you use. If you choose not to block the respondent's e-mail address on the response, then promise confidentiality of the data.

E-mail invitation link to URL (or Web address) questionnaires invite the participant to respond to the questionnaire by either clicking on an embedded URL or copying and pasting the URL into their Web browser. The participant responds to the questionnaire on the Web.

Web page questionnaires are those posted on an organization's Web site. A variety of ways are used to contact potential respondents and direct them to the Web page to complete the questionnaire. A Web questionnaire resides on a Web server and is accessed via an organization's home page or a link to another site from the home page. Advantages include the use of multimedia, graphics, and video. You can use grid-type responses and can program filters and skip patterns. (See Chapter 4 for examples of these kinds of questions.) A program can check for consistency of responses—and if certain patterns of inconsistency are noted, the respondent can be prompted to reconsider a response. Other advantages include a cost that is often lower than for a paper-based mail questionnaire, quick turnaround time to receive data, and a greater variety of response formats than are possible with a paper-based or e-mail questionnaire.

For both e-mail and Web-based questionnaires, members of the target audience need access to and familiarity with computers. In our case study example, this statement leads us to the question: Are Web-based questionnaires useful for the K-12 audience, including teachers and parents? The answer is a qualified "yes—it depends." The greatest dependency is whether teachers, administrators, parents, students, and community members have access to the Web. Some school districts currently have their own Web sites, and others are exploring the options for going online.

There are many advantages for schools to move toward Web-based data gathering. For example, a secondary school may collect data from parents, students, and other community members about their satisfaction with different facets of school activities and policies. Some districts conduct follow-up studies of former students about the adequacy of their preparation, either for a job or for college. More school districts are moving toward total quality strategies as they plan organizational improvements—and Web-based questionnaire methodology is a realistic alternative in terms of efficiency of data collection and conserving financial resources.

Disadvantages include the software and skills required to program or load a questionnaire, although many companies can do this for you. Another disadvantage is the process used to contact members of the target audience to invite them to come to the Web site to respond to the questionnaire. Chapter 5, "Identifying and Contacting Respondents" and Chapter 7, "Maximizing Your Response Rate: Collecting the Data" provide some suggestions for distributing Web-based questionnaires. Other disadvantages include computer access to the questionnaire and various technology-related issues.

Despite these limitations, the use of Web-based questionnaires will continue to grow, and within a decade their use is likely to surpass the use of paper-based questionnaires. There will continue to be a variety of methods of gathering questionnaire data, including face-to-face interviews, telephone interviews, paper-based questionnaires (mail and in-person), and electronic questionnaires (e-mail and Web-based).

> **The most important consideration in selecting which mode to use is to know the capabilities of your target audiences and determine which mode of delivery best matches their capabilities for responses and your project's capabilities in terms of resources.**

What about mixed mode? Can you use both Web-based and paper-based questionnaires in the same project? The answer is a qualified yes, since this is an area where the measurement implications are being explored. Initial results of research where multiple modes of responding to the questionnaire were available found that although some respondents switched modes of response when offered the chance, overall the response rate did not change. However, it may be possible to increase response rate by using a different mode of delivery in the follow-up, such as offering a Web-based questionnaire to persons who have not responded to a paper-based questionnaire (Dillman, 2000; Matz, 1999).

Comparing Paper-Based and Electronic Questionnaires

Important advantages of using electronic questionnaires include low cost and speed of getting the questionnaires to the participants and the responses back into your database. Unlike paper-based questionnaires, inviting additional participants to respond to a Web-based questionnaire has a very low incremental cost. An important advantage is that the responses can be automatically transferred to a database so there is no need to code the information and enter the data into your computer for analysis. It is also possible to include a wider geographic representation—including respondents from outside the United States—at a very small incremental cost (unlike the hefty costs of international postage for a paper-based questionnaire).

As an example, after the questionnaire has been created and the target audience identified, a Web-based questionnaire can provide data in approximately five days after participants receive access to the questionnaire, compared with two to four weeks for a mailed paper-based questionnaire. In terms of cost, a Web-based questionnaire sent to 2,000 participants costs little more than sending the questionnaire to 200 participants. However, for a paper-based questionnaire, if you provide a postage-paid return envelope, you'll need to use 2,000 stamps, plus the costs of printing and copying the questionnaires and cover letters, stuffing the envelopes, paying outgoing postage, and entering the data into your database when the completed questionnaires come back.

Expenses associated with a Web-based questionnaire include loading the questionnaire onto the Web (which may involve some programming skill or using a commercially available Web questionnaire package) and server access costs (unless the organization has its own Web site).

For our case study survey project, we will use a Web-based questionnaire on the school district's Web site.

Now that you've created your guiding question, developed your objectives, and identified your target audience and the mode of data collection, let's focus on creating a detailed project plan.

 ## STEP 5: CREATE A DETAILED PROJECT PLAN

Successful projects—whether they are survey projects, curriculum development projects, or long-range instructional development projects—are all characterized by carefully developed project plans. It is possible to conduct a survey project without detailed planning, but the results may not be useful or credible, and the resources used will not have been well spent.

Table 1.4 describes some planning activities to consider as you create your project plan, which serves as a foundation for your project.

HINT: Use a software tool such as Microsoft Project to create your timeline, resource deployment (people and dollars), tasks, and milestones.

Now let's look in more detail at each of these components of your detailed project plan.

Table 1.4 Activities in a Project Plan and Their Importance

Activity	*Why Is This Important?*
1. Identify the deadline and the time and resource requirements for all questionnaire development activities required to meet that deadline.	• Tasks almost always take longer than planned. • It will help avoid surprises later in the project and ensure that the final results will be available when you need them.
2. Plan the processes needed for data collection, contacting participants, producing the questionnaire, conducting the analyses, and producing the report.	• Most likely you'll need to work with other departments or groups, so you'll need to do more than identify the resources needed. • You may want to identify specialists to help you in these areas.
3. Plan how you will contact members of your target audience.	• You'll need to allow time for contacting these people.
4. Plan for and gain approvals to conduct the survey project and to contact members of the target audience.	• Ensuring that you have the right approvals at the beginning of the project will save time and headaches later.
5. Plan the data analysis so that you are sure the results of the questionnaire can be analyzed in a way that provides the information needed to make the decisions.	• Planning the analyses up front will help you identify the demographic data you'll need to gather in the questionnaire so you can disaggregate your data to identify potential differences among subgroups.

Determine When You Need the Results of the Questionnaire

When you plan the timeline, start at the end: When do you need the results? If you find the date is too close to do a good job, consider alternatives: Push the decision date out, conduct focus groups while you're developing the questionnaire to provide preliminary input, or create a process for staged decision making so that some decisions are made based on preliminary data and validated when the rest of the information is gathered.

A *focus group* is a group of 8 to 12 people who represent the target audience. They can provide initial input while the survey project is being completed.

Focus groups are also useful for gaining the insights, opinions, and support of stakeholders. See Chapter 6, "Pilot Testing the Questionnaire," for details on how to organize and conduct focus groups.

Staged decision making consists of making a series of decisions as the information becomes available rather than waiting until the end of the survey project. For example, suppose a group of school librarians in the district is interested in providing a wider range of services to support academic success. They carefully plan a survey project, which they project will take approximately eight months to complete. However, they want to identify and implement some best practices from other libraries. They could conduct focus groups and telephone interviews to gather some initial information and perhaps devise a pilot test of one or two of these best practices. Then when their survey project is complete, they can consider a broader range of ideas and best practices and select those that will best fit the needs of their library users. By using staged decision making, they will not have to wait nearly a year to identify and try out some new ways of providing library services.

Planning for a Web-based questionnaire requires several tasks related to the production of the questionnaire that must be included in the planning. Will you use a Web questionnaire service to load your questionnaire on the Web and host it? Such a service handles many of the details and logistics; you provide the questionnaire, and the service loads the questionnaire onto a Web site and provides you with a data set. Another option is to use questionnaire software, but you'll need a Web site to host the questionnaire. Do a search on the Web using a search engine such as Google, with the search terms "Web-based surveys" and "Web-based questionnaires." If you use Google's advanced search feature, you'll get only those entries that have the phrases in them. You'll find resources, vendors with software, and some reports of Web-based survey projects. Evaluate your options for getting your questionnaire onto the Web so you can include this activity in your timeline.

> We'll use the case study to create a timeline with estimates of the time required for each task. We'll also share assumptions we made as we created the timeline.

The following example is for our case study:

> We need the information by the end of October—so we start with this end date and plan backward. But as you will see, working in a school district means there are many other considerations in addition to the number of months the project will take.
>
> We estimate that the work will take approximately six months, but the timing of the distribution of the questionnaire is critical. It must be available for distribution at the end of the first month of school, around October 1, with the results available by the end of October. That way, parents will have some knowledge of their child's school, teachers, and the kinds of activities available to them to become involved in their child's school. So allowing two weeks for the data collection and one week for the data analysis and report writing, the results would be ready for the decision makers by the end of October.
>
> Counting back six months means starting around the first of May. But that's a really busy time in most schools. So we'll start in the middle of January with the planning process and devise a schedule so that all contact with teachers, parents, and community members who will give input to creating the questionnaire can be completed by the middle of April.
>
> As you can see, even creating a timeline is not straightforward. We need to consider the environment in which we'll be working.

Create a Timeline Based on the Major Steps of a Survey Project

Table 1.2 listed the 16 major steps required in a survey project. We'll use these major steps to create the project timeline for our case study survey project. Note that our case study project is more extensive than are many survey projects. You may be able to complete yours in three to four weeks.

The following steps are for the case study survey project:

1. Conduct initial planning. (6 weeks)
   - Work with sponsors to identify stakeholders, hold focus groups to get their input and support, determine resource requirements, and create a high-level project plan.
   - Identify the needs of decision makers to plan analyses.
   - Gather information from the Web, research literature, and other school districts to determine whether similar work has been done.
   - Gather detailed information about what activities for parent involvement are currently available in each school in the district.
   - Get buy-in from the school administration to gather information from parents using a questionnaire.

2. Write the purpose of the survey project, create the guiding question, and write detailed objectives, including gathering appropriate reviews. (1 week)

3. Identify the target audience. (1 week—overlaps with Step 4)

4. Determine the mode of data collection. (1 week—overlaps with Step 3)

5. Create the detailed project plan. These are the processes necessary to make everything happen, such as determining the sample size, selecting and contacting participants, and producing the paper or electronic questionnaire. (1 week)

6. Gain needed approvals to conduct the survey project and to contact members of the target audience from school administrators.

7. Write questions that link to the objectives, and use response scales appropriate to the target audience. Include reviews by sponsors and stakeholders. (3 weeks)

8. Create the questionnaire: Format the questions and response scales; work with the Web developer to plan loading the questionnaire on the Web. (1 week)
   - Load the questionnaire on the Web and perform quality checks.

9. Select the sample and plan the method to contact participants.
   - Send the prenotification—advance notice that the person will be invited to respond to the questionnaire. Because of the timeline for our case study, we'll send prenotices out while the pilot test is being conducted.

10. Create the invitation to respond to the questionnaire and develop follow-up processes. (1 week)

11. Pilot test the questionnaire, make necessary revisions, and produce the final version. (2 weeks)

12. Use the information from the pilot test to make revisions to any elements of the survey project. (1 week)

13. Gather the data and post the questionnaire on the school's Web site, including prenotices and follow-up notes. (2 weeks)

14. Analyze the data. (1 week)

15. Use the results to make the decisions, make recommendations, and begin to make plans to implement the decisions. (2 weeks)

16. Create the final report. (2 weeks)

Figure 1.1 provides a graphic timeline for the case study survey project.

You might want to set up this template in a project management tool such as Microsoft Project if there are several people on the survey project team. If you're working alone or with one or two other people, a paper version of the timeline and plan is probably sufficient.

The detailed planning just described seems like a lot of work, and it is. But the most common mistake in planning is to underestimate the time needed by making a global estimate rather than considering each of the steps required. Activities can be overlapping, but consider which tasks have dependencies—tasks that must be completed before other tasks can start.

 HINT: Plan the schedule and timeline collaboratively with all those who will work on the project. Post the schedule where all team members can see it.

Identify the Resources Needed to Complete the Tasks

Now that we've created the timeline, we need to consider the people and budget needed to complete the survey project. There are three elements to identifying the people needed. The first is to determine what types of skills are needed, the second is to identify who has those skills, and the third is to decide how to obtain that person for your project.

As you plan your people resources, consider the following:

- Who will handle communications with the sponsor and stakeholders?
- Who will create the objectives that will guide the development of the questionnaire?
- Who will work on gaining the needed approvals and permissions?
- Who will gather the detailed content information required to create the questions?
- Who will create the questions and response scales?
- Who will handle all aspects of production?

Figure 1.1 Timeline for the Parent Involvement Case Study Survey Project

Weeks	1	2	3	4	5	6	7	8	9	10	11	12	13	14	15	16	17	18	19	20	21	22
Initial planning	▓	▓	▓	▓	▓	▓																
Write purpose, guiding question, objectives							▓															
Identify target audience								▓														
Determine mode of data collection									▓													
Create detailed project plan										▓												
Gain administrative approval											▓	▓	▓									
Write questions												▓	▓									
Create questionnaire													▓									
Select the sample														▓								
Write invitation													▓									
Send prenotices															▓							
Pilot test the questionnaire																▓						
Revise the questionnaire																	▓					
Gather the data																		▓	▓			
Analyze the data																				▓		
Create the reports																					▓	
Use results to make decisions																						▓

NOTE: The vertical line between weeks 14 and 15 denotes the "break" in the calendar from the end of May until the school year starts in September.

- Who will do the statistical analysis and report writing?
- Who will present the results to the sponsor?

Who will do the work? Note that some small survey projects are conducted by individuals or by a team of two persons. In that case, the one or two persons conducting the survey project will be responsible for all of the activities listed here.

Create a Budget for Your Survey Project

Resources include more than people, as indicated in the budget factors identified in the following list. Let's look at some of the factors to consider as you create your budget plans:

- Staff time for planning the study and steering it through the various stages, including time spent with the sponsor in refining data needs
- Sample selection costs, including office staff labor and costs to identify members of the target audience
- Staff and materials for pilot testing (Pilot testing might need to be done more than once if there are many revisions.)
- Staff and expenses for contacting participants: prenotices, cover letter or invitation, and follow-ups for nonrespondents
- Staff and material costs for getting information from the questionnaire into a computer file, unless you're using a Web-based questionnaire, in which case the data flow directly into a database
- Staff and material costs for hosting a Web-based questionnaire—for example, software, technical support, Web site
- Cost of spot-checking the quality of the process of computerizing the paper questionnaires or verifying the data files for a Web-based questionnaire
- Analyst costs for preparing tabulations and special analyses of the data
- Staff time and material costs for statistical analyses of the data and report preparation
- Telephone charges, postage, reproduction, and printing for the questionnaire as well as the report

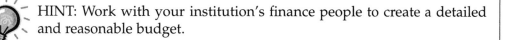 HINT: Work with your institution's finance people to create a detailed and reasonable budget.

Plan the Activities to Support Your Survey Project

All survey projects need data analysis and reporting, and some will need a communication plan. For these activities, you might need to work with members of other groups or departments to obtain these resources, particularly during the production and data analysis portions of the project. But each project is different, and your survey project team might have all of these skills.

If you are using a Web-based questionnaire, be sure you have detailed plans for getting the questionnaire posted on the Web site and for receiving the data. Unless you have very good technical skills and can handle the technology work yourself, you need to make sure that you have made all the arrangements for this part of the work. If there are challenges with a survey project using a Web-based questionnaire, they are often here. Be proactive in planning to ensure that all aspects of this part of the project go smoothly.

Plan the Data Analysis to Identify Needed Demographic Data

Use your guiding question and your objectives to guide your plans for the data analysis, particularly your plans for disaggregating the data for reporting purposes—and identify the demographic questions you'll need to ask. For many analyses of school-based data, you'll need, at a minimum, demographic information about gender and race/ethnicity so you can disaggregate the data for reporting purposes. For school districts gathering data for the NCLB Act, it's important to have the appropriate demographic data for your analyses.

> *Demographic information* is descriptive information about the respondents, such as gender, ethnicity, age, prior experience of some kind, or level of education. The specific demographic information you will need depends on your purpose and the kinds of information you need to make your data-based decision.

We'll use the case study as an example to plan the analyses at a high level and identify the demographic data we'll need to gather.

For our case study survey project, the demographic information we will need for each objective is described in the following and summarized in Table 1.5.

For our case study, we want to increase parents' involvement in their child's classroom and in their child's education. And for our data analyses, we plan to disaggregate the data by race/ethnicity of parents, working status of parents, and previous experience volunteering in the school. We also need demographic information to describe the respondents, including which school their child attends, the number of children attending an elementary school in the district, grade levels of their children, and gender of parent who is responding to the questionnaire.

The first objective, *"Identify parental awareness of opportunities the school currently provides for parents to be involved in their child's school,"* focuses on determining parental awareness of the activities currently available in the school. So we'll need to know the following information:

Which of the three elementary schools each child attends

The number of children attending this school

The grade levels of each of their children

We will gather gender information from parents to determine the participation of fathers and mothers in the various activities available in the school as well as employment information—if one or both parents is employed outside the home—and we'll also ask for ethnicity. This information will allow us to disaggregate the data by gender and race/ethnicity. Our data analyses can then include subgroup analyses for each of the three schools as well as comparisons about parent awareness of opportunities based on the number of children they have attending the elementary schools, gender and race/ethnicity of responding parent, and employment outside the home.

The second objective, *"Identify current levels of parent participation in the available activities,"* asks parents to indicate in which of the school's activities they have participated during the previous school year. No additional demographic data will be needed for analyses of the results of these questions. Data analyses include comparison of participation in the three schools and comparisons of participation of parents with differing numbers of children in the schools, by gender, race/ethnicity, and employment status of respondent.

The third objective, *"Determine the level of satisfaction with the activities currently provided to parents,"* requires no additional demographic data for analyses of the results of these questions. Data analyses include comparison of participation in the three schools and comparisons of participation of parents with differing numbers of children in the schools, by gender, race/ethnicity, and employment status of respondent.

The fourth objective, *"For parents who do not participate in these activities, identify reasons and barriers,"* focuses on understanding the reasons that some parents do not participate in these parent volunteer activities—in particular, what barriers exist for encouraging parents to become involved in their child's classroom and education. Demographic information needed here includes working status of parents, gender, race/ethnicity, and parents' previous experience in classroom activities in the past year. Analyses will be done for subgroups, comparing participation of parents who work outside the home full-time, part-time, or not at all and comparisons by gender and race/ethnicity of respondent as well as by number of children in the school.

The fifth objective, *"Identify types of parent involvement activities preferred by parents,"* seeks input from parents about what activities they would like to have available and how likely they are to participate in the activities currently available, if the barriers were removed. No additional demographic information will be needed in addition to what has already been identified earlier. Analyses will include subgroups based on child's grade in school, parental working status, school, number of children in school, gender, and race/ethnicity.

Table 1.5 summarizes the demographic information needed for analyses for each objective.

The results of these analyses will inform decisions about the strategies that will increase parent involvement in the elementary schools in the district.

The demographic variables will be used to disaggregate the results and compare responses from several subgroups such as race/ethnicity of parents, working status of parents, and previous experience volunteering in the school. In addition to the data from the questionnaire, other sources of information will be used in the decision-making process, including interviews with teachers and school staff members and observations of parent involvement at selected activities.

Table 1.5   Demographic Information Needed for Analyses for Case Study Survey Project

Objective	Analyses	Demographic Data[a]
1	Descriptive statistics, profiling parents who are aware of opportunities and those who are not; disaggregating the data by race/ethnicity and working status of parents	1, 2, 3, 4, 5, 6
2	Descriptive statistics, searching for differences in parents who participate; examine relationship of awareness of opportunities with satisfaction and participation; disaggregating the data by race/ethnicity of respondents and working status of parents	1, 2, 3, 4, 5, 6
3	Descriptive statistics, searching for differences in parents who participate; examine relationship of awareness of opportunities with satisfaction and participation; disaggregating the data by race/ethnicity of respondents and working status of parents	1, 2, 3, 5, 6
4	Descriptive statistics, examine relationship between reasons and barriers and working status of parents, number of children in school, gender, and race/ethnicity of respondent, previous experience volunteering in schools	1, 2, 3, 4, 5, 6
5	Descriptive statistics, examine relationship of preferred activities, previous experience, and parent characteristics	1, 2, 3, 4, 5, 6

[a]Codes for demographic variables:
1 = School
2 = Number of children attending an elementary school in the district
3 = Grade levels of children attending elementary schools in the district
4 = Working status of parents (e.g., full-time, part-time, at home)
5 = Gender of parents
6 = Race/ethnicity of parents

STEP 6: GAIN NECESSARY APPROVALS TO CONTACT MEMBERS OF THE TARGET AUDIENCE AND TO CONDUCT THE SURVEY PROJECT

Depending on your target audience, you may need to obtain permission to contact them to invite them to respond to your questionnaire. For example, if your target audience is made up of students, you'll need permission from parents or guardians. You'll need permission from the principal and perhaps others at the school or the central office to contact parents. And if there's an Institutional Research Review Board (IRRB), you'll need their permission as well.

An *IRRB* is an oversight body that safeguards the rights and welfare of people participating in a research study, including a survey project. This group reviews the ethical appropriateness of the proposed study in terms of potential risks to participants in light of hoped-for benefits. Most survey projects will fall into the "exempt" classification—that is, they do not require review by the full IRRB. For additional details, see a research textbook such as Johnson and Christensen (2000) or Gall (2002). Each school district is different and has different requirements, processes, and timelines required for the approvals. Be sure you understand exactly what you need to do and when you need to do it so you can conduct your survey project in the timeline you have planned.

For our case study survey project, we must obtain permission from the school administration and district office before we can contact parents. Then we will send a note home with the students and post a notice on the district's Web site.

There's been a lot to do in this chapter—as noted earlier, careful planning is critical to the success of your survey project. Before you continue with Chapter 2, complete the following checklist.

Checklist for Launching Your Survey Project

Use the following checklist to make sure you've completed all the activities necessary to begin the detailed planning process described in Chapter 1.

❑ Have you identified the audiences for the final report?

❑ Does the guiding question capture the essence of your concern, interest, or need for information?

❑ Do the objectives clearly link to (and flow from) the guiding question?

❑ Will the information gathered from these objectives provide the data to support the decision you need to make?

❑ Does the target group you've identified have the information required to provide valid and useful information?

❑ Does the mode of data collection match the access capabilities of the target audience?

❑ Have you identified the end date of the survey project—when the final report will be due?

❑ Have you created a detailed timeline to meet the target end date?

❑ Have you identified the resource requirements for the survey project activities?

❑ Have you developed a realistic budget for the project?

❑ Did you identify appropriate demographic questions to include on your questionnaire so you can disaggregate the data in your analyses?

❑ Do you have the necessary approvals and support for moving forward with the project?

2

Asking the Right Questions

A good question will provide the information you need. The way you phrase a question can change the answers you get. The single greatest source of error in a survey project is poorly worded questions. The question writer's greatest challenge is to translate the ideas and concepts contained in the objectives into clear and concise questions so that those responding to the questionnaire will understand each question as it was intended. People are doing you a favor to respond to your questionnaire, so respect their time by wording your questions clearly and asking only for the information you will use.

In this chapter, you'll learn to create useful questions that will provide you with the information you'll need to make your decisions, to describe preferences, to determine needs, and so forth. The chapter presents the different types of questions and provides guidelines and examples to help you write good questions. It also offers suggestions for designing questions for Web-based questionnaires.

STEP 7: WRITE THE QUESTIONS

Step 7 is a big one and involves many activities discussed in the next two chapters. This chapter provides guidance for writing high-quality questions that link to your guiding question and objectives, and Chapter 3, "Creating Response Choices for Rating Scales," details information about creating response scales for rating scale types of questions.

Let's start by looking at some objectives and the questions that have been written for these objectives.

◆ MAP QUESTIONS TO YOUR OBJECTIVES

Following are some examples of objectives with questions linked to those objectives.

Objective: To determine the adolescent's attitudes toward the use of computers in composition writing.

1. I prefer to do my writing at the computer.
2. Using the word processor makes it more difficult for me to revise my work.

Objective: To describe parental perceptions of the academic performance of their child with ADHD who is on medication.

1. My child can focus better on homework when he or she is on medication.
2. My child's teacher has noticed a positive change in my child's academic performance since he or she started the medication.

Objective: To determine how middle school teachers perceive the effect of peer-assisted instruction on achievement in the classroom.

1. Peer-assisted instruction helps adolescents to be more successful in school.
2. Students participating in peer-assisted instruction receive higher grades than do students not participating in this program.

 HINT: Ask a colleague to review your questions before you begin the pilot test—looking in particular for questions that might not be necessary to the objectives of the survey project.

Now that we've looked at some examples of questions linked to objectives, let's start the question writing by considering what the content of the questions will be.

◆ DETERMINE QUESTION CONTENT

Writing good questions consists of more than structure. Using the appropriate content is critical! The first consideration in creating questions is to ensure that they link to your guiding question and the specific objectives. But depending on your role on the project team, you may be asked to create questions about a topic for which you have limited understanding. One way to gather background information is to immerse yourself in the research literature. Another way is to gather information from similar projects—and determine what you can reuse or revise for your project. If neither of these approaches is feasible, a cost-effective and efficient means of gathering this information is to use a focus group.

Using Focus Groups to Identify Content for Your Questions

Focus groups can provide information about a topic before constructing the questions—to learn how people think about a topic, their understanding of general concepts or specific terms, or their opinions about the sensitivity or difficulty of questions. Results from focus groups are qualitative and cannot be compared in the strict quantitative sense. However, conducting several focus groups before beginning a large project can give insight into differing views. The project team can then use this information to create the questions.

In a focus group, the facilitator's role is to keep the discussion moving and on topic, but not to express opinions that might bias the discussion. Questions for a focus group should be clear and sequenced in a logical way, usually going from general to more specific (Jayanthi & Nelson, 2001; Krueger & Casey, 2000).

The ideal size of a focus group is from 8 to 12 persons. If the group is too small, 1 or 2 people are likely to dominate the group. If it's too large, the group is likely to break into side conversations.

Focus groups excel at providing in-depth qualitative insights gathered from a relatively small number of people. They do not provide quantitative data as a questionnaire does but, rather, offer an opportunity to collect a breadth and depth of information so you have the detailed information you need to create your questions. For additional information on how to conduct a focus group, see Jayanthi and Nelson (2001).

◆ TYPES OF ITEM FORMATS

Responses to questions (items) on a questionnaire can be a series of choices (fixed response) or an opportunity to create a response (open response). Both types of items and response modes can be used in a questionnaire, depending on the information required. All these types of items can be used in paper-based as well as Web-based questionnaires.

- Fixed- and open-response items provide somewhat different types of information.
- Fixed-response items provide choices to respondents, who must select one or more of the choices that you provide. Several fixed-response formats are described in the following discussion.
- Open-response items ask the respondent to create an answer. Toward the end of the chapter is a description of the process of creating high-quality open-response items.

> HINT: Use open-response questions sparingly. Respondents often perceive them as burdensome to answer—and the analyses are a lot more work!

Fixed-Response Formats for Questionnaire Items

Fixed-response items can be checklists, ranking formats, rating scales, or semantic differential scales. The type of items you include in your questionnaire (and the type of responses that go with these questions) will depend on your guiding question: What do you want to know? Depending on the length of the questionnaire, the audience, and the type of information you need, you may want to use more than one type of item format in your questionnaire.

The discussion of fixed-response formats begins with a brief overview of each type.

Adjective Checklist. Adjective checklists are used to gather information about respondents' affective reactions to a topic, experience, or concept.

Behavior Checklist. Behavior checklists are used to determine what experiences the respondents have had, what activities they have participated in, or what activities they are interested in trying.

Other Types of Checklists. A list of categories is provided and the respondent selects those that apply to him or her. An example follows:

How did you learn about Gilchrist Elementary School's homework policies? (Select all that apply.)

a. Parent handbook
b. Parent orientation meeting
c. Monthly newsletter to parents
d. My child's homework calendar
e. My child's assignment notebook

f. The school's homework hotline
g. Special information sheet
h. Teacher conference
i. Gilchrist's Web site
j. Other (specify) _____

Ranking Format. Respondents are asked to rank-order items based on a common feature, such as preferences, interests, usefulness, importance, and so forth.

Fixed-Sum Questions. A type of ranking question, the fixed-sum format requires respondents to weight items based on some criterion, such as importance, degree of interest, or time spent.

Semantic Differential Scale. A semantic differential scale measures respondents' reactions to concepts through ratings on a 7-point bipolar rating scale, with pairs of opposite words (antonyms) anchoring the scale points.

1.   Interesting ____:____:____:____:____:____:____ Uninteresting

Rating Scales. Rating scales provide a means to gather information about the degree to which the respondent finds something interesting, satisfying, helpful, and so forth.

Likert-Type Rating Scale. One type of rating scale is the Likert-type rating scale, which is a summated rating scale consisting of several related items designed to measure the same idea or same construct. The ratings on the related items are summed to yield a total score for each respondent (e.g., Johnson & Christensen, 2000; Nunnally, 1978; Shaw & Wright, 1967).

Now let's look at each item format more closely. We'll start with the three types of checklists. For all three types, a list of response categories is provided, and respondents select those that apply to them.

Adjective Checklists

Adjective checklists can be used to gather information about respondents' affective reactions to proposed activities such as the charter school in the following example. In some cases, the affective reactions captured by an adjective checklist provide insight into the reasons for a person's responses to other questions on your questionnaire.

Respondents indicate their feelings about a topic, experience, or concept by circling or underlining the appropriate adjectives. Following is an example:

Circle each word that describes how you feel about establishing a charter school in your community.

Unnecessary	Elitist	Needed	Stimulating
Inconvenient	Important	Frustrating	Unpleasant
Practical	Useful	Worthless	Interesting

Adjective checklists are relatively simple to construct and consist of directions and a list of 12 to 16 adjectives. There should be an equal number of negative and positive adjectives. If you are having some challenges coming up with a list of adjectives, you might consider using a focus group to help you.

Adjective checklists can be used at different points in time to look for trends. For example, feelings are often quite strong regarding privatization of public schools. Debates about whether to do this can last for many months. Using a questionnaire containing an adjective checklist can take the "pulse" of the community at different points in time and trends can be identified. Is the community moving toward or against support of privatizing the schools?

 Adjective checklists can be used with Web-based questionnaires. There are slight differences in the directions. Respondents record their choices by clicking on a radio button (a circle next to their preferred response) rather than circling or underlining a response.

Following is an example of an adjective checklist formatted for Web delivery.

Click on the button next to each word that describes how you feel about establishing a charter school in your community. If you change your mind, click on that button again and it will be deselected.

Unnecessary ⭕	Elitist ⭕	Needed ⭕	Stimulating ⭕
Inconvenient ⭕	Important ⭕	Frustrating ⭕	Unpleasant ⭕
Practical ⭕	Useful ⭕	Worthless ⭕	Interesting ⭕

Scoring Adjective Checklists

Scoring is done by counting the number of times each adjective is chosen. This can be done for the total group of respondents. You can also determine "scores" for an individual respondent by counting the number of positive and negative adjectives circled.

Advantages of the adjective checklist:

- Easy to create
- Can be used in a variety of settings and for many different topics
- Can be used with many different target audiences: Carefully constructed adjective checklists can be used with young children as well as older students and adults.

Limitations of the adjective checklist:

- Respondents cannot express degree of feeling about a topic.
- The list of adjectives may be incomplete.

Guidelines for Writing an Adjective Checklist

1. State the directions clearly.

2. Indicate the subject about which the respondent is to express feelings.

3. Indicate how the responses are to be made (circling, underlining, checking, etc.).

4. Use 12 to 16 adjectives.

5. Use an equal number of positive and negative adjectives.

6. Arrange the adjectives in random order.

Behavior Checklists

Behavior checklists are used to determine what experiences respondents have had, what activities they've participated in, or what activities they are interested in trying. Here's an example:

When your district began planning its After School Scholars Program, which of the following activities, if any, did you do? Please check all that apply.

____ Visited afterschool programs in other communities
____ Explored grant opportunities for potential funding
____ Conducted a needs analysis with our school's parents

Behavior checklists used in Web-based questionnaires are very similar in format and directions to the paper-based questionnaires. A similar format can be used—the only difference is that rather than checking responses, the person responding on the Web clicks on radio buttons.

An important difference between adjective checklists and behavior checklists is that in the behavior checklist, respondents indicate what they have done rather than what their feelings are about something. Knowing whether people have done certain activities is often important, but we know only whether they've participated in the activity . . . not how often, how much they enjoyed the activity, or whether participating in the activity helped them accomplish some goal.

Scoring Behavior Checklists

Behavior checklists are scored similarly to adjective checklists: Count the number of times each response was chosen. Like adjective checklists, behavior checklists can be used to describe responses at a particular point in time, or by administering the checklist at different times, it can indicate changes in behavior over time. Results are often reported as percentages or as tables or graphs.

Advantage of the behavior checklist:

- It provides information about the respondent's experiences.

Limitations of the behavior checklist:

- No information is provided about the frequency of the behavior, whether the respondent enjoyed the activity, and so forth.
- Some relevant behaviors may be missing.

Guidelines for Writing a Behavior Checklist

1. State the directions clearly.

2. Indicate the general behavior or activity being studied.

3. Specify the time period for the responses in the directions.

4. Describe each behavior or activity in concrete, specific terms.

Other Types of Checklists

In addition to the adjective checklists and behavior checklists described earlier, there are more general kinds of checklists. These are used for many different purposes, such as gathering information about how people learned about an activity, whether they have had certain experiences, and so on. (This format is used for one of the questions in the Questionnaire on Bullying in Chapter 8, "Analyzing the Data and Making Data-Based Decisions.") The following question is from that questionnaire.

What types of bullying have you experienced this year at school? (Please select all that apply.)

___ I've been called names.

___ I've been physically threatened.

___ I've been shoved.

___ I've been physically hurt.

___ Something of mine has been stolen.

Another example of an "other" checklist follows:

How did you learn about Gilchrist Elementary School's homework policies? (Select all that apply by circling the letter next to your choice[s].)

a. Parent handbook

b. Parent orientation meeting

c. Monthly newsletter to parents

d. My child's homework calendar

e. My child's assignment notebook

f. My child's assignment notebook

g. Special information sheet

h. Teacher conference

i. Gilchrist's Web site

j. Other (specify) _____

 Checklists used in Web-based questionnaires are very similar in format and directions to the paper-based questionnaires. A similar format can be used—the only difference is that rather than checking responses, the person responding on the Web clicks on radio buttons.

Scoring Other Types of Checklists

The other types of checklists are scored similarly to the behavior checklists and adjective checklists: Count the number of times each response was chosen. Like adjective checklists and behavior checklists, the other checklists can be used to describe responses at a particular point in time, or by administering the checklist at different times, it can indicate changes over time. Results are often reported as percentages or as tables or graphs. In the example question from the questionnaire on bullying, the responses could be compared before and after a school "safe zone" had been implemented.

Advantage of other checklists:

- They provide information about the respondent's experiences.

Limitations of other checklists:

- No information is provided about the relative importance of each of the sources of information, experiences, and so forth.
- Some relevant information sources (or other variables measured) may be missing.

Guidelines for Writing Other Types of Checklists

1. State the directions clearly.
2. Indicate the general experience or other type of information being studied.
3. Specify the time period for the responses in the directions.
4. Describe each experience or other type of information in concrete, specific terms.

Ranking-Format Items

Asking respondents to rank items based on a common feature allows educators to learn about preferences, interests, opinions, usefulness (of something), importance, and so forth. The following example illustrates:

Please rank your perception of the effectiveness of the following activities in making your school safer. Use "1" to indicate the activity you believe will be most effective, "2" for the next most effective, through "5," the least effective.

____ Having a police presence in the school
____ Enforcing the school's discipline code
____ Providing counseling to students identified as "bullies"
____ Implementing a peer mediation program
____ Providing positive parenting classes

Asking respondents to rank items forces them to indicate priority. In the example given, respondents rank the perceived effectiveness of each activity by indicating which activity they believe will be most effective, next most effective, and so on, until all items are ranked.

A ranking format can be used whenever you want information about the respondent's perception of the relative standing of a set of items, activities, interests, and so forth. However, limit the list of things to be ranked. It's probably not reasonable to ask a person to rank more than six or seven things.

Scoring Ranking-Format Items

Determine the median[1] ranking for each activity. In the preceding example, the lowest median indicates the respondents' perceptions of the most effective means of improving school safety, because the respondents used "1" to indicate which activity would be most effective.

Advantages of the ranking format:

- It can determine the relative position or ranking of something.
- Lists of things to rank are relatively easy to create.

Limitation of the ranking format:

- It does not permit the determination of intensity of feelings or beliefs. For example, among the activities listed, the respondent may not believe that any will be particularly effective—so the one ranked as the first choice may be the one he or she thought least likely to fail.

Fixed-Sum Items

Another type of ranking format is the fixed-sum item. With this type of question, respondents indicate a percentage or a weighting that sums to 100. This item format is useful when you want to understand how a person allocates time or importance among a group of activities. With a ranking format, we cannot know how much actual difference the respondent perceives between the rankings. The fixed-sum format affords the respondent such as opportunity.

For the following five activities, please divide 100 points among them, giving the highest number of points to the activity you perceive to be the most effective in making your school safer. Assign the points based on your perception of the relative effectiveness of each activity. Be sure your points sum to 100!

____ Having a police presence in the school
____ Enforcing the school's discipline code
____ Providing counseling to students identified as "bullies"
____ Implementing a peer mediation program
____ Providng positive parenting classes

Fixed-sum questions are more useful with Web-based questionnaires because the totals can be automated. The respondent can see how many "points" are left to allocate. With a paper-based questionnaire, there is no guarantee that the respondent's math is correct!

Scoring Fixed-Sum Items

Calculate the mean weighting for each activity. The activity with the highest mean in the preceding example is the most effective.

Advantages of the fixed-sum format:

- It can determine the relative position or ranking of something.
- Lists of things to weight are relatively easy to create.

Limitations of the fixed-sum format:

- With paper-based questionnaires, there is no guarantee that the respondents can do the math correctly so the weight sum equals 100%!

- Respondents must be fairly sophisticated. For example, children can do simple ranking, but not the fixed-sum weighting. Some adult populations may also be challenged with this format.

Guidelines for Writing Ranking Questions

1. State the directions clearly.
2. List the elements (such as activities or interests) to be ranked in specific terms.
3. Limit the list of elements to be ranked to six or seven.

 HINT: If you are unsure about whether to use a fixed-sum format, test it out in the pilot test. (See Chapter 6, "Pilot Testing the Questionnaire," for details.)

Semantic Differential Scale

The semantic differential scale, developed by Osgood and his associates (Osgood, Suci, & Tannenbaum, 1957), is a combination of the adjective checklist (described earlier) and rating scale (described in the following section). In this format, the single concept to be rated is written above the scale. Under the concept are a number of 7-point scales, with opposing adjectives (or antonyms) or short phrases at each end. In the following example, the project team was interested in understanding respondents' feelings about the availability of a computer-based chat room to work on a project that was assigned to students in a research methods class.

Computer-based chat room

Check the appropriate space on each scale.

Interesting	___ ___ ___ ___ ___ ___ ___	Uninteresting
Confusing	___ ___ ___ ___ ___ ___ ___	Clear
Useless	___ ___ ___ ___ ___ ___ ___	Useful
Efficient	___ ___ ___ ___ ___ ___ ___	Time-consuming

To construct a semantic differential scale, identify the concept about which you want opinions or feelings. Then identify 8 to 16 adjectives that can describe the concept. Write the opposite of each of the adjectives. Randomly arrange the direction of the pairs of adjectives to help ensure that the respondent reads each adjective pair carefully before responding.

 HINT: Many word processors have a thesaurus tool that can help you identify some antonyms.

Scoring a Semantic Differential Scale

To score a semantic differential scale, assign the values of 1 through 7 to the pairs of adjectives with the positive adjective on the right, and the values of 7 through 1 to the pairs of adjectives with the negative adjective on the right. The assumption is made that the intervals representing each response are equal, so the numbers can be summed. (See Chapter 8, "Analyzing the Data and Making Data-Based Decisions," for more details on assumptions made about the kinds of data gathered from different types of response scales and the ways to analyze these responses.) Sum the total number of points to obtain the score for each respondent (Johnson & Christensen, 2000; Osgood et al., 1957).

Advantages of a semantic differential scale:

- A semantic differential scale is similar to an adjective checklist in that it provides the respondent an opportunity to report feelings.
- It allows for more detailed information in that the respondent indicates the degree of feeling.

Limitation of a semantic differential scale:

- It measures feelings or opinions about only one concept.

Guidelines for Writing a Semantic Differential Scale

1. Identify a concept that is related to one of your objectives.

2. Write 8 to 16 adjectives that can describe the concept.

3. Write the opposite of each of these adjectives (so you'll have 8 to 16 pairs).

4. Randomly order the pairs of adjectives, with half having the positive adjective on the right and half having the negative adjective on the right. (For example, alternate negative and positive adjectives on the right.)

5. Separate each pair of adjectives with a seven-point scale.

6. Write the directions for the respondent.

Rating Scales

Rating scales are useful for the following:

- Gathering information about the degree to which a person finds something interesting, satisfying, or helpful (or some other adjective)
- Measuring attitudes, opinions, perceptions, and beliefs
- Determining how frequently a person participates in certain activities

An important advantage of a rating scale is that it permits a person to respond on a continuum rather than completely endorsing (or not endorsing) something.

If you are measuring agreement, satisfaction, or a concept for which you use several items to measure the concept, then a Likert-type rating scale may be appropriate. To use a Likert-type rating scale, all items must measure the same concept. In the next chapter, see the Feelings Scale, page 65 as an example. All items were constructed to measure a student's feelings about things that happen in school. These questions were written to measure a construct of a child's feelings, much along the same lines as a self-concept measure (e.g., Johnson & Christensen, 2000; Nunnally, 1978).

If you are measuring frequency, agreement, intensity, or a similar concept, then a rating scale is appropriate. Items from a rating scale should by analyzed using frequencies, percentages, charts, and graphs. Examples of rating scales with these types of responses are provided in the next chapter.

Ranking or Rating?

An important difference between ranking-format items and rating scales is that ranking provides information about relative standing, whereas rating scales provide information about intensity, frequency, degree of interest, degree of agreement, and so on. If the information about the potential effectiveness of activities to make schools safer were gathered using a rating scale, we might learn that the respondents did not think that any of the activities listed would be effective in their school.

Likert-Type Rating Scales

Many years ago, a psychologist named Rensis Likert developed a rating scale for use in measuring attitudes (Likert, 1932). His scale had five points ranging from *strongly agree* to *strongly disagree*. Other researchers have built on his work, using more (or fewer) than five rating points, and other rating anchors, such as *satisfaction, frequency, similarity to self,* and so on. Today, the number of response choices may vary from 4 to 11 (Nunnally, 1978). Rarely should more than seven scale points be used—respondents may be challenged in making very fine distinctions. Rating scales with four points are not as reliable as those with five or more rating points (Nunnally, 1978).

An important characteristic of a Likert-type rating scale is that several questions are written for each objective in a way that these responses can be summed. Depending on what you are measuring, you may have a total score or subscores for each of your objectives. More detail in how to score rating scales is provided in Chapter 3, "Creating Response Choices for Rating Scales."

A rating anchor provides definitions of each of the scale points. The words following each of the letters below are the "anchors" for the scale in this example. You may use different anchors if you wish. These are the anchors used by Likert in his original work.

A = Strongly agree
B = Agree
C = Undecided
D = Disagree
E = Strongly disagree

Because both rating scales and Likert-type rating scales are widely used, here's more detail about the construction of these scales.

> Items for rating scales contain two parts. The stem asks a question or provides a statement to which the participants respond, and the choices are the possible response choices (for rating scales) or scale anchors (Likert-type rating scales) to the stem.

In this chapter, we'll focus first on writing great stems, and in Chapter 3, "Creating Response Choices for Rating Scales," we'll consider how to create response choices that are appropriate for the target audience and to the information you need to gather to make your data-based decision.

10 Guidelines for Writing Great Stems

Avoid double-barreled statements by writing statements that contain one thought or concept. Don't ask the respondent to answer two questions with one answer!

1. Parents are notified immediately when their child is having academic difficulties and receive specific suggestions to help their children become successful in school.

2. Parents are notified immediately when their child is having academic difficulties.

3. Parents receive specific suggestions to help their children become successful in school.

Statement 1 asks two things: about notifying parents about academic difficulties *and* receiving information and helping their children. Statements 2 and 3 are better; the respondent can rate, independently, whether parents are notified about their child's academic difficulties and whether they receive suggestions about helping their child become successful in school.

Ask for the level of detail that is reasonable for the respondent to remember.

1. How satisfied were you with the program held at the PTO meeting, held on Tuesday, October 5?

2. How satisfied are you with the programs provided by the PTO over the past school year?

A questionnaire was sent to parents in May to gather information about the programs that had been provided by the PTO during the past school year. Statement 1 asks for a level of detail few parents are likely to remember—unless the program was very outstanding and memorable. Statement 2 asks a more general question about which parents are likely to have an opinion. If you want information about a specific program, it's better to gather that information at the end of the program!

Write short, concise statements; a questionnaire item should not be a measure of reading skill!

1. When I'm reading a story, sometimes I get confused, and then I go ask the teacher to help me with the words I don't know, and then I can understand the story.

2. When I don't understand something I read, I ask the teacher to explain the story so that I can understand it better.

Statement 1 is very wordy! It will take the respondent extra time to sift through all those words and figure out what you're asking. Statement 2 uses familiar words and is much clearer.

Write statements at the appropriate reading and understanding level for the respondents.

The following is from a questionnaire for third graders:

1. I am dependable.

2. My friends can count on me.

In Statement 1, the word "dependable" may be unfamiliar to some third graders. Statement 2 is preferred.

Avoid stereotyping.

1. The principal provides clear examples when he communicates with teachers.

2. The principal provides clear examples when communicating with teachers.

Statement 1 implicitly assumes that principals are male. Statement 2 is gender neutral.

Don't leave terms or concepts to the respondent's interpretation.

1. Our school board provides the necessary resources for schools to serve our community well.

2. Our school board provides the necessary resources (equipment, dollars, feedback) for schools to serve our community well.

Statement 1 is ambiguous and requires respondents to interpret "resources." Statement 2 defines what resources are being provided. If there are terms with precise or technical definitions, provide these so everyone understands the terms in the same way.

Avoid leading questions or other subtle forms of bias.

1. Community-minded citizens plan to vote for the school bond. Do you?

2. How likely are you to vote for the school bond in the upcoming election?

Statement 1 suggests that all community-minded citizens will vote for the school bond and confounds the question of whether a person plans to vote for the school bond with whether the person perceives himself or herself as community minded. Statement 2 simply asks whether the respondent plans to vote for the school bond.

Define acronyms used in stems.

1. PAI increases the academic success of adolescents.

2. Peer-assisted instruction (PAI) increases the academic success of adolescents.

Statement 1 uses an acronym that respondents might not know. Statement 2 provides both the definition and the acronym. Some respondents may know the concept by the acronym, whereas others know only the full name.

Avoid double negatives in questions.

1. I work hard to avoid not turning in my homework late.

2. I work hard to turn my homework in on time.

Statement 1 is very confusing—what's being avoided? Turning the homework in late or not turning it in late? Statement 2 is straightforward and clear.

Ask for information or opinions that the respondent is likely to have.

From a questionnaire to students of a neighborhood school who walk to school:

1. Long rides on the school bus each day make it difficult for me to stay awake in class.

2. When I stay up late at night to watch TV, I have trouble staying awake in class the next day.

The questionnaire author wanted to find out why students were sleepy and lethargic in class—but did not consider the type of school for the target population when she wrote Statement 1. Statement 2 is appropriate for both neighborhood and commuting schools. Students at the neighborhood school don't ride school buses, so they do not have the experiences required to respond to Statement 1.

See Table 2.1 for practice in identifying flaws in questions.

Positively and Negatively Worded Stems

For Likert-type rating scales where you are summing the responses from several questions, you may want to reverse the wording on one-third to one-half of the questions to avoid a response set.

A *response set* may occur when a person selects the positive answer for all or most questions, possibly without reading each question carefully.

Table 2.1   Practice Activity: Identifying Flaws in Questions

Complete the following activity to see how well you can identify flaws in these item stems. Compare your work with answers at the end of the chapter.

Question Stem	Flaw
A. How often do you consider ROI when you select a teaching activity?	
B. Using scaffolding to present new concepts facilitates high levels of student comprehension because it builds on what they know and students can learn more confidently.	
C. A school superintendent can best communicate with parents when he is active in community events.	
D. I find the subject interesting and would recommend the class to a friend.	
E. I verbalize my comprehension strategies when I read aloud in class. (to a second grader)	
F. Parents who are interested in their child's education find time to volunteer in the school. How often do you volunteer in your child's school?	
G. Homework assignments requiring Internet research help prepare students for college work. (to parents, most of whom do not have computers at home)	
H. A good teacher does not fail to give homework assignments prior to long weekends.	
I. Privatization of the schools will save money for the taxpayers.	
J. In the past year, how many times did your child attend soccer practice?	

Following are some questions from a Likert-type rating scale on stress and burnout:

1. I feel stressed when I have tight deadlines.

2. When I feel overwhelmed, I take a few minutes for myself to "catch my breath."

3. I worry about how much I have to do and how little time I have to complete the tasks.

4. I can openly talk with a person I trust about what is bothering me.

The respondent used a 5-point response scale to indicate to what degree each behavior was typical of him or her. A higher score was interpreted as meaning the person was feeling a higher level of stress.

The directions encouraged the respondent to read each statement carefully. But to ensure that they were reading carefully, half the items were worded negatively so that the respondent had to *disagree* with the negative statement in order to show a low level of stress and burnout.

In the preceding example, Questions 2 and 4 are positively worded, but Questions 1 and 3 are reversed, or negatively worded.

Scoring Rating Scales and Likert-Type Rating Scales

The scoring can be either straightforward or more complicated, depending on a variety of factors. More detail on coding rating scales and scoring Likert-type rating scales is provided in Chapter 3, "Creating Response Choices for Rating Scales."

Advantages of rating scales and Likert-type rating scales:

- Members of most target audiences are familiar with this format.
- The many types of response scales provide great flexibility.

Limitations of rating scales and Likert-type rating scales:

- Good questions are time-consuming to write.
- The questionnaire designer must have in-depth knowledge of the topic to write good questions.
- Question-writing guidelines must be followed carefully to avoid flaws in the questions.
- For the Likert-type rating scale, there must be enough items from the same domain so that the summed score is reliable and meaningful. (See Chapter 4, "Putting the Questionnaire Together," for more information on evaluating the reliability and validity of questionnaire data.)

Table 2.2 summarizes fixed-response format item types.

Open-Response Questions

An open-response question permits the respondent to provide a response rather than select one. Open-response questions can be used to measure attitudes, interests, beliefs, opinions, preferences, experiences—in short, just about any topic about which you want to gather information.

Open-response questions are used when . . .

- There could be a wide range of responses.
- You would like to know the respondent's thinking about some topic, including reasons or details unavailable with a fixed-response item format.
- You want more in-depth information than a fixed-response item format question can provide.

An often-cited reason for using open-response questions is to capture information that the team had not thought about when the questions were written or the response options created. This reason is valid for a focus group you might use to gather information to create the questionnaire, but not for your major data collection efforts.

Table 2.2   Review of Fixed-Response Formats

Format	Advantages	Limitations
Adjective checklist	• Easy to create • Can be used in many situations and for many topics • Can be used with many different target audiences	• Respondents cannot express degree of feelings.
Behavior checklist	• Provides information about respondents' activities or behaviors	• Provides no information about frequency, enjoyment, satisfaction with the activity.
Other types of checklists	• Provide information about respondents' experiences, how they learned something, and so forth	• Provide no information about the relative importance of the experiences, etc.
Ranking format	• Can determine relative position or ranking of something • List of things to rank relatively easy to create	• Cannot determine intensity of feelings or beliefs.
Fixed-sum questions	• Can determine the relative position or ranking • Lists of things to weight are easy to create	• Respondents must be fairly sophisticated to use this response format.
Semantic differential scale	• Allows respondent to report feelings • Can provide detailed information about a concept	• Each set of scales is limited to one concept.
Rating scale	• Provides for a means to gather information on many different topics • Most respondents are familiar with this type of question	• Responses cannot be summed and are reported using percentages, charts, and graphs.
Likert-type rating scale	• Provides for a range of responses with a variety of anchors • Provides numerical score • Can be used to obtain information on many topics • Most respondents are familiar with this type of question	• Scores in the middle range may be difficult to interpret.

Open-ended questions present unique challenges. Some respondents don't want to take the time to write out an answer—but they will select one. Persons who are less interested in the questionnaire are likely to skip opened-ended questions—or to stop responding when they encounter the first open-ended question. In addition, including open-ended questions lengthens the time required to respond to the questionnaire—another possible way to lower your response rate.

The responses need to be analyzed. Qualitative analyses provide very useful information—but consider the time and expense required to get that information. Is there any other way to do this? You might consider using focus groups or interviews, depending on the information you require. But you will need to plan to analyze and summarize the information.

 On Web-based questionnaires, the responses will be in text format in the database, and depending on the qualitative analysis software you have, you may be able to automate a part of the data analysis.

No matter what delivery medium you use, limit the use of open-ended questions. Some questionnaires have one opened-ended question at the end—for additional comments. Responses to such questions often provide interesting insights and seldom affect response rates.

Open-response questions are relatively easy to construct but require careful thought about the amount of time required of the respondent to provide a response. The questions must be carefully worded to ensure that they will provide the information you need.

Sample open-response questions:

- What types of parent involvement activities would you participate in if they were available at your child's school?
- In what ways can the workshop about preventing bullying at your school that you just attended be improved?
- What ways of structuring parent-teacher conferences do you find to be particularly effective?

Scoring Open-Response Questions

Scoring open-response items is a lot of work! Each response must be read, categories formed, and then each response must be assigned to a category. Sometimes categorizing the responses requires judgment: Are two respondents saying essentially the same thing but using somewhat different words?

Following are 10 responses to the question about improving the workshop about preventing bullying:

Raw data:

1. The handouts were hard to follow—the workshop leader should tell us what part of the handouts to look at.
2. The workshop leader did not follow the agenda he provided.
3. When a person asked a question, the workshop leader gave a very long answer and never got back to the original topic he was discussing before the question was asked.

4. The room was too cold—it was hard to pay attention.

5. There was a lot of noise in the hallway outside the room, and it was hard to hear the speaker part of the time.

6. Two people behind me were talking about other things.

7. The speaker spent too much time talking about kinds of bullying behaviors and not enough time telling us what to do about these behaviors.

8. I didn't like the room we were in.

9. I had to come to this workshop, and I don't have time for this kind of thing.

10. We don't have bullies at our school, so this workshop was a waste of time.

Steps to code the responses:

1. Read over each response to get an idea of the types of categories that you might use.

2. Identify three or four categories and place responses in these. Then see what responses you have left.

3. We'll start with the following categories:
   a. Workshop materials
   b. Presenter
   c. Physical facilities

4. Here's how we assigned the responses to the categories:

Response Category	*Responses*
Workshop materials	1
Presenter	2, 3, 7
Physical facilities	4, 5, 8

5. Using these three categories, we were able to categorize 7 of the 10 responses. We have the following responses left:

   (6) Two people behind me were talking about other things.

   (9) I had to come to this workshop, and I don't have time for this kind of thing.

   (10) We don't have bullies at our school, so this workshop was a waste of time.

Response 6 might be listed in the presenter categories because it suggests he did not engage all members of the audience. But the other responses in the "presenter" category are specifically about the presenter's behaviors.

Responses 9 and 10 don't offer suggestions for improvement but, rather, indicate the feelings of the participants about coming to the workshop. These would be categorized as "Other" or perhaps "Relevance to the participant."

Advantages of open-response format:

- Can be used to gather a wide range of information
- Permits respondents to express feelings, ideas, or reactions without being limited to preset categories

Limitations of open-response format:

- Amount of time required to summarize the responses
- Amount of time that may be required for respondents to provide the information you need
- Requires that respondents be fairly verbal (so this format is not appropriate for young children)

Guidelines for Writing Open-Response Items

The guidelines for creating good open-response items are very similar to those for creating good statements for Likert-type rating questions. Comparative examples follow for several of these points.

Do not ask leading questions.

1. Don't you agree that involving parents in classroom planning activities creates too much extra work for the teacher?

2. What role do parents have in planning activities in your classroom?

Question 1 suggests that having parents be a part of planning makes extra work for the teacher; Question 2 is more neutral. If parental involvement in planning does create extra work, respondents can so indicate, but they are not "led" to think in this direction.

Do not use loaded words or phrases that suggest approval or disapproval.

1. Many teachers believe their workload is unfairly increased with the assignment of recess and lunchroom duty. What additional assignments have you been given this year?

2. What responsibilities do you have in addition to teaching?

The word *unfairly* in Question 1 is loaded; it suggests that responsibilities beyond teaching are unfair. Question 2 is neutral and asks for information.

Avoid social desirability in the questions.

1. Successful teachers have found workshops such as the one we held today to be very useful. How much did you like today's workshop?

2. What was your reaction to today's workshop?

Question 1 suggests that because successful teachers liked the workshop, those teachers who consider themselves successful will also like the workshop. Question 2 is neutral.

Avoid suggesting a response.

1. How should teachers provide opportunities to students to make up tests they miss due to extended family vacations?

2. What provisions, if any, do you make for students who miss tests due to extended family vacations?

Question 1 suggests that teachers should provide these opportunities; so a teacher may feel it necessary to create such provision. Question 2 allows for the possibility that teachers have chosen not to allow makeup tests.

Encourage critiques by sharing a concern.

Some parents have suggested that their children have too much homework. How do you feel about the amount of time your child spends on homework each evening?

The question helps set the stage by indicating it's OK to have concerns.

Ask for information the respondent is likely to have.

What is your opinion of the school district's plan to include online interactive education two days per week?

The structure of this question is good—*if* the respondent is aware of the school district's plan and has sufficient knowledge to provide a response.

Write items at the appropriate reading and understanding level of the respondents.

1. How do you use scaffolding when you begin to study new ideas and new information?

2. What do you think about as you begin to study new ideas and new information?

Question 1 has a term (scaffolding) that is most likely unfamiliar to many people. Question 2 gets at the same idea—an understanding of how the respondent uses prior knowledge to learn about new ideas.

In addition, the following three guidelines from fixed-response formats are also relevant:

- Communicate clearly to the target audience.
- Create clear and concise questions.
- Clearly address one of the objectives you've created for the project.

◆ DETERMINE THE LENGTH OF THE QUESTIONNAIRE

This chapter has provided information to help you create great questions for your questionnaire. The focus has been on helping you ensure that your questions link to your objectives and that you ask for only the information you'll need to make your decision. But how many questions is enough? How many questions should you use?

As few as possible—both in number of questions and the time required to answer the questions! Try to limit the time required to respond to 15 to 20 minutes. If your questionnaire is longer, you run the risk of a lower response rate—unless the topic is very interesting or very meaningful to the respondent.

Ask only those questions that are necessary to gather the information you need to make your decision. Questions must be meaningful and interesting to the respondent—and each question must link to one of your objectives.

Don't add an extra question just because you're curious. The respondent's time is valuable—respect it!

All other things being equal, shorter questionnaires tend to have better response rates. One exception is that if the topic is very interesting to respondents, they will complete questionnaires that are 10 or more pages in length! To give you an idea of the number of questions and time needed, most respondents can answer questionnaires with 25 to 35 questions in 15 to 20 minutes if the questions are straightforward.

One way to use respondents' time efficiently is with skip patterns. (See Chapter 4 for details on how to use skip patterns.) Web-based questionnaires handle skip patterns particularly well because the "skip" is automatic, based on the person's responses.

Now that you've begun to create the questions for your questionnaire, use the following checklist to check your progress. Following the checklist is Table 2.3, Answers to the Practice Activity: Identifying Flaws in Questions.

Checklist for Asking the Right Questions

Use the following checklist to ensure that your questions meet the guidelines for good questions.

- ❑ Were the appropriate types of questions created to match the purpose and topic of the questionnaire?
  - ○ Does the stem of each item contain only one idea?
  - ○ Is the stem of each item clearly written?
  - ○ Are there any grammatical clues in the stem or choices to suggest the preferred or intended answer?
    - ▪ If yes, how can you revise the questions to remove these clues?
  - ○ Do any of the items appear to be biased in terms of race or ethnicity, age, and so on?
    - ▪ If yes, how can you revise the question to remove the potentially biasing terms?
  - ○ Does any item contain two negatives?
    - ▪ If yes, how can you revise the question to make it more clear?
  - ○ Do any of the items require the respondent to calculate something, such as percentage or average?
    - ▪ If yes, are the instructions clear—and is it reasonable for the respondent to do this calculation?
- ❑ Were the appropriate types of items created for the target audience (consider age, reading level, and knowledge base of the target audience)?

❏ Is every question linked to an objective?

❏ Is there a specific plan to use all the data you will collect?

❏ Do your open-response questions follow the guidelines for good questions?

❏ Have you created scoring guidelines for the open-response questions?

❏ Have you reviewed the questions with peers and colleagues?

Table 2.3 Answers to the Practice Activity: Identifying Flaws in Questions

Question Stem	Flaw
A. How often do you consider ROI when you select a teaching activity?	Define acronyms
B. Using scaffolding to present new concepts facilitates high levels of student comprehension because it builds on what they know and students can learn more confidently.	Question should be short and concise
C. A school superintendent can best communicate with parents when he is active in community events.	Stereotyping
D. I find the subject interesting and would recommend the class to a friend.	Double-barreled
E. I verbalize my comprehension strategies when I read aloud in class. (to a second grader)	Reading level is not matched to target audience
F. Parents who are interested in their child's education find time to volunteer in the school. How often do you volunteer in your child's school?	Leading question
G. Homework assignments requiring Internet research help prepare students for college work. (to parents, most of whom do not have computers at home)	Asks for information respondents may not have
H. A good teacher does not fail to give homework assignments prior to long weekends.	Double negative
I. Privatization of the schools will save money for the taxpayers.	Uses terms and concepts that may not be clear to members of target audience
J. In the past year, how many times did your child attend soccer practice?	Requires remembering too much detail

Note

1. A median is the 50th percentile, or the middle point in an ordered set of numbers. See Chapter 8 for details.

3

Creating Response Choices for Rating Scales

In this chapter, you'll learn to create response choices for different types of rating scales and scale anchors for Likert-type rating scales. The distinction between these two types of rating scales is based on the kind of information you want from the question as well as how you analyze the data. The Likert-type rating scale provides a summed score—that is, you can add the responses from several questions relating to a particular construct or topic to get a score for each respondent. Data from rating scales are category data that are best analyzed using percentages, charts, and graphs. (See Chapter 8, "Analyzing the Data and Making Data-Based Decisions," for examples and more details.)

In this chapter, we continue with Step 7, "Write the Questions." The responses are a part of questions, but given the number of decisions you need to make about the type of rating scale and responses you'll use, all this information needs a separate chapter.

◆ WHAT TYPE OF RATING SCALE IS APPROPRIATE?

That depends on what you want to know and how you will use the information. If you create several items related to a single concept to measure—for example, agreement or satisfaction—then a Likert-type rating scale may be appropriate. In a Likert-type rating scale, all items must measure the same concept. Later in this chapter, you'll see the Feelings Scale as an example. All items were designed to measure a student's feelings about things that happen in school. These items were written to measure a single construct, much along the same lines as a self-concept measure (e.g., Johnson & Christensen, 2000; Nunnally, 1978).

Using a satisfaction or an agreement scale does not necessarily mean that you have a Likert-type scale. Figure 3.1 provides an example. The questionnaire was designed to gather information about parent satisfaction with various aspects of the school climate by asking how much they agree (or disagree) with statements about the school climate. Read over each item carefully. Each item relates to some aspect of satisfaction with the school climate but from different perspectives. Item 1 is about the parents' perception of how safe their child is at school, whereas Item 2 focuses on the parents' feeling of being welcome to visit the school. Both are aspects of satisfaction but are different enough that combining all these items into a total score does not make sense. In this example, the appropriate way to report the results is to use percentages, charts, and graphs.

Figure 3.1   Example of a Rating Scale

Rating Scale for School Climate

(Excerpt)

Please indicate your feelings about the climate in your school by circling the letter corresponding to your choice.

A = Strongly agree

B = Agree

C = Neither agree nor disagree

D = Disagree

E = Strongly disagree

1. My child is safe while at school.	A	B	C	D	E
2. I feel welcome at my child's school.	A	B	C	D	E
3. Student discipline rules are enforced consistently.	A	B	C	D	E

In most cases, you'll decide on the type of responses you plan to use when you create your objectives and develop the stem of your question. For example, you may want to measure agreement, satisfaction, or frequency. Depending on how the questions are worded, these might be either rating scales (where you cannot sum the responses) or Likert-type rating scales (where you can sum the responses). But be sure to plan for the appropriate kinds of analyses.

Likert-type rating scales (and some other rating scales) have scale anchors. An anchor is the definition of a point on the response scale. This is an important point to remember, so it's highlighted as follows.

A scale anchor is the definition of a point on your response scale.

Most response scales will have definitions (anchors) for each scale point, but some scales will not. For example, the semantic differential scale described in Chapter 2 ("Asking the Right Questions") has anchors only at the ends of the response scale. Another example is a graphical rating scale that does not provide scale anchors for each scale point. An example follows:

Very Satisfied			Somewhat Satisfied			Not At All Satisfied
___7___	___6___	___5___	___4___	___3___	___2___	___1___

Rating scales can also use response choices that are a series of responses that look like a multiple-choice question. In these rating scales, responses must be analyzed using frequencies and percentages. Responses to questions with response choices such as these cannot be summed.

Match the Response Choices in Your Rating Scale to the Needs of Your Target Audience

Have you ever responded to a questionnaire and thought the response choices weren't quite right for you? And you selected the response that was "least inaccurate"? Many other respondents probably did the same thing, resulting in data that did not provide accurate information.

Determining the scale anchors or response choices for rating scales is a very important element of creating the items. They need to match the ability of the respondents to differentiate. You can also gather information about the effectiveness and utility of your response scales in the pilot test. (See details on pilot testing in Chapter 6, "Pilot Testing the Questionnaire.")

10 Guidelines for Writing Useful and Appropriate Response Scales

If you are measuring frequency, such as frequency of a behavior, avoid relative terms such as "frequently" so the respondents do not have to infer what you mean.

1. How often do you walk 30 minutes or more for exercise?
   - ☐ Often
   - ☐ Occasionally
   - ☐ Seldom
   - ☐ Rarely
   - ☐ Never

2. How often do you walk 30 minutes or more for exercise?
   - ☐ Daily
   - ☐ 4 to 5 times a week
   - ☐ 2 to 3 times a week
   - ☐ 4 to 6 times a month
   - ☐ 2 to 3 times a month
   - ☐ Never

The response choices in Question 1 require respondents to define what each response choice means, and they may interpret these differently. In Question 2, the meaning of each response choice is clear.

Use a full range of response choices.

1. Approximately how many cups of coffee do you consume in a typical day?
   – 1 to 5 cups
   – More than 5 cups

2. Approximately how many cups of coffee do you consume in a typical day (but not the weekend)?
   – None; I do not drink coffee
   – 1 to 3 cups
   – 4 to 5 cups
   – More than 5 cups per day

In Question 1, there is no way for people who do not drink coffee to respond, so they will most likely skip the question. But you won't know that this is the reason they skipped the question. In addition, the categories are very broad, and you would not be able to determine those who drink a few cups of coffee (1 to 3 cups) from those who drink a lot.

Think of what level of detail you need from your respondents. You can aggregate data from Example 2 to determine the percentage of respondents who drink 1 to 5 cups of coffee a day, but you cannot disaggregate data from Example 1 to determine how many respondents drink from 1 to 3 cups of coffee per day. (For example, you can add the responses together for 1 to 3 cups and 4 to 5 cups if you use two response choices, but if you use only 1 to 5 cups, you cannot disaggregate this data.)

But don't overdo it by using too many response choices! You don't want to annoy or confuse the respondent! Following is an example of too many categories—and all are left to the respondent's definition of what the term means!

Never	Fairly often
Almost never	Often
Rarely	Almost always
Occasionally	Always

In this example, there are too many choices, and some choices are very much alike. For example, what is the difference between "Often" and "Almost always"? This distinction is left to the interpretation of the respondent—and different people may interpret these anchors differently.

A good suggestion is that you not use "Always" and "Never" as choices. There are few things that a person never does or always does. A better option is using "Almost never" and "Almost always." Depending on the stem of your question, you may be better off providing more specific categories, such as number of times respondents did that activity or performed that behavior.

Do not use overlapping response choices.

1. How many students typically enroll in your department's advanced writing class each semester?
   - ☐ 10 to 15
   - ☐ 15 to 20
   - ☐ 20 to 25
   - ☐ 25 to 30
   - ☐ More than 30

2. How many students typically enroll in your department's advanced writing class each semester?
   - ☐ Less than 15
   - ☐ 15 to 20
   - ☐ 21 to 25
   - ☐ 26 to 30
   - ☐ More than 30

In Question 1, if there were typically 15 students enrolling in the advanced writing class, which response choice should you select? 10 to 15 or 15 to 20? In Question 2, the response choices do not overlap.

 HINT: Make sure the response scales are nonoverlapping (mutually exclusive) and comprehensive.

If you have questions about how the respondents may interpret the response choices, provide detail.

1. How prepared are you to use the Web page development skills you learned in the seminar?
   - ☐ Completely prepared
   - ☐ Somewhat prepared
   - ☐ A little prepared
   - ☐ Not at all prepared

2. How prepared are you to use the Web page development skills you learned in the seminar?
   - ☐ Completely prepared; I can design my own Web page.
   - ☐ Somewhat prepared; I can design a simple Web page but may need help with more complex designs.
   - ☐ A little prepared; I need some guidance to get started.
   - ☐ Not at all prepared; I don't know where to begin.

The response choices for Question 2 provide detail about what each response means. You can have more confidence that the respondent interpreted the response choice as you intended, and you'll have more accurate data to make your data-based decision.

Do not use jargon in the response choices. Respondents may understand the response choices differently than you intended.

1. Which of the following best describes the risk behavior used by your manager?
   ☐ Takes bold strides
   ☐ Takes calculated risks
   ☐ Is somewhat risk-averse
   ☐ Is completely risk-averse

2. Which of the following best describes the risk behavior used by your manager?
   ☐ Takes action without regard to consequences
   ☐ Weighs risks before proceeding
   ☐ Avoids risks whenever possible
   ☐ Will not take risks

For Question 1, the response choices "bold strides" and "calculated risks" might be interpreted differently by some of the respondents, resulting in inaccurate data. The second set of response choices is clearer and will help the respondent understand better what you are asking.

Agreement scale anchors can cause confusion among some respondents. Some scales range from "Strongly agree" to "Strongly disagree." For some respondents, "strongly" may be an overstatement of their feelings or beliefs.

Strongly agree	Agree
Agree	Tend to agree
Disagree	Tend to disagree
Strongly disagree	Disagree

If you are unsure about which set of agreement anchors will work best for your target audience, try both sets in your pilot test and ask the participants which is clearer and which they think will be more appropriate. (See Chapter 6, "Pilot Testing Your Questionnaire," for guidance on how to evaluate the scale anchors you plan to use.)

For scales of agreement or satisfaction, be sure you are providing the full range of response choices so there is no potential bias.

Example 1	Example 2
Strongly agree	Satisfied
Agree	Somewhat satisfied
Tend to agree	Somewhat dissatisfied
Do not agree	Quite a bit dissatisfied
	Very dissatisfied

In both examples, the scale anchors are not balanced and provide a biased set of response choices. In the agreement set of scale anchors, there are three choices for agreement but only one for disagreement. The message to respondents might be that they are expected to "agree." The second example, the satisfaction scale, has a bias toward dissatisfaction. Be sure your scale anchors are balanced.

Following is an example of a balanced set of scale anchors:

Strongly agree

Agree

Tend to agree

Tend to disagree

Disagree

Strongly disagree

Be sure the scale anchors match your questions and provide the information you need.

In the following example, a scale of importance was used.

How important is the inclusion of creative writing in the language arts curriculum?
☐ Very important
☐ Moderately important
☐ Of low importance
☐ Not important

But a series of questions about aspects of the curriculum might have everyone rating everything as very important. If the purpose of the questionnaire was to determine not only the importance of elements of the curriculum but also what's most important, using just the "importance" scale is not enough. In this case, a combination of rating and ranking could be used. For example, you could ask respondents to rank those elements of the curriculum that they rated as "Very important."

 A Web-based questionnaire is the optimum vehicle for this type of format. The programming logic can be set to create a list of all the aspects of the curriculum a respondent rated as "Very important" and then to provide the respondent with this list and ask the respondent to rank order these aspects of the curriculum he or she had rated as "Very important."

Be sure respondents have the experience and knowledge of the topic to make the distinctions among the scale anchors you provide.

For example, high school students have a lot of experience with teachers, courses, and homework assignments. They are experts! So a course evaluation can use five, six, or seven scale points; students should be able to make distinctions this fine—as long as there are clear scale anchors for each rating point.

On the other hand, a brief questionnaire to parents about plans to attend various school activities could have four scale points, as in the following example.

How likely are you to attend the Parent Orientation Meeting in September?

a. Very likely
b. Somewhat likely
c. Somewhat unlikley
d. Not at all likely

The number of choices depends on both the experience and knowledge of the respondent, as well as on what you need to know.

Rating Scales for Young Children

Rating scales can be used with children in the early elementary grades if the items are carefully constructed and not overly complicated. Questionnaires for young children require picture or graphic response choices, even when the questions are read aloud to the child. Responses may be faces, such as those shown following, to indicate feelings.

How do you feel when it's your turn to read out loud?

Happy   OK   Sad

Responses can also be boxes or circles to indicate how much respondents like something or are interested in something.

How much do you enjoy
reading time in the library?

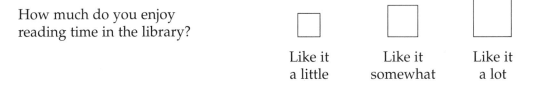

Like it a little   Like it somewhat   Like it a lot

◆ SHOULD YOUR SCALE HAVE A NEUTRAL RESPONSE?

What does a neutral response such as "Undecided/No opinion" in a rating scale mean? It could be any of the following:

- Lack of knowledge: The respondent has no basis for judgment.
- Reading difficulty: The respondent may choose the midpoint to cover up an inability to read.
- Reluctance to answer: The respondent may not wish to share his or her true opinion.
- Inapplicability: The question does not apply to the respondent—and there's no other way to communicate this.

If you choose to omit a neutral response, consider the following:

- Word responses so that a firm stand can be avoided (tend to agree, tend to disagree) if the respondent so desires.
- Include options for explaining inability to respond such as "no basis for judgment" or "prefer not to answer" if the topic is potentially sensitive or requires specific knowledge or experience.
- Provide a "Not applicable" option.

If you do decide to use an "Undecided/No opinion" response choice, put it at the bottom of the list rather than in the middle, and if you are using a Likert-type rating scale, do not include these responses in the person's total score. Rather, report the percentage of respondents who selected this response choice.

◆ DOES THE ORDER OF THE SCALE ANCHORS AND RESPONSE CHOICES MAKE A DIFFERENCE?

The answer to this question is "yes"! Most adult respondents have seen many questionnaires and have certain expectations about the order of response choices and scale anchors. They expect the "positive" scale anchors to come first in the list of scale anchors and that higher numbers have more positive meanings.

- Always present agree-disagree choices in that order. Presenting them in disagree-agree order will seem odd to many respondents.
- Present positive to negative (e.g., Very satisfied/Very dissatisfied) and excellent to poor response choices with "positive" choices or anchors first.
- With numeric rating scales, higher numbers should mean more positive, more agreement, more satisfaction, and so forth.

Response choice order can make individual questions easier or more difficult to answer. Whenever there is a logical or natural order to answer choices, use it. For example, the question on risk behavior presented earlier in the chapter had the response choices in order of degree of risk.

Which of the following best describes the risk behavior used by your manager?
- ☐ Takes action without regard to consequences
- ☐ Weighs risks before proceeding
- ☐ Avoids risks whenever possible
- ☐ Will not take risks

The question would likely be more confusing to respondents if the response choices were ordered as follows:

Which of the following best describes the risk behavior used by your manager?
- ☐ Weighs risks before proceeding
- ☐ Takes action without regard to consequences
- ☐ Will not take risks
- ☐ Avoids risks whenever possible

If you have questions about how to order your response choices, check this out in your pilot test. (See Chapter 6, "Pilot Testing the Questionnaire," for details.)

◆ THE CATEGORY "OTHER"

A rule of thumb: Don't use "Other" as a response choice!

When "other" is placed after a long list of choices, some respondents may not bother to read through the list and just select "other." Other respondents may reject a choice for some trivial reason when that response really fits them—and select "other." Sometimes there's a place to "explain" or "specify" what the respondent means by "other." But often in the analysis of these written-in responses, the data analyst finds that many of these responses can fit into one of the preexisting categories.

If you truly feel that you must use "other," do it after careful consideration, using the results of the focus groups and the pilot test to make the final determination. The downside to not using "other" is that a few respondents may omit an item because no response "fits" them. As with any rule of thumb, there are exceptions—depending on what you want to know.

Consider the following example:
During the past year, my preschool-aged child had the following care arrangements:

___ Attended a preschool that had an academic curriculum

___ Attended a preschool that did NOT have an academic curriculum

___ Stayed at home with parent or other relative

___ Other

In this case, the researchers were interested in finding out whether children in the current kindergarten class had attended an academic preschool, attended some other type of preschool, or stayed at home under the care of a family member. They were not interested in the details of any other child care arrangements.

HINT: Pay particular attention to feedback about the response scales during the pilot test. (See Chapter 6, "Pilot Testing the Questionnaire," for details.)

◆ SCORING LIKERT-TYPE RATING SCALES

Scoring Likert-type rating scales requires that you assign points to each of the scale anchors in a meaningful way. An example of assigning points to scale anchors is presented here for an agreement scale:

Strongly agree	5
Agree	4
Neither agree nor disagree	3
Disagree	2
Strongly disagree	1

To obtain a "score" for one of your objectives, assign a point value to each choice the respondent has made, and sum the points. With the preceding scale, a higher score indicates stronger agreement. Remember that with a Likert-type rating scale, all questions must relate to the same construct so that it makes sense to add the responses together to obtain a total score (e.g., Anastasi, 1982; Nunnally, 1978). However, using scale anchors of agreement, satisfaction, or frequency does not always mean you have a Likert-type rating scale. All items in a Likert-type rating scale must be related to the same construct, and it must make "sense" to add the responses together to obtain a summed score.

As discussed in Chapter 2, you may want to reverse the wording on some questions as a way to avoid response set. A response set may occur when a person selects the positive answer for all or most questions, possibly without reading each question carefully.

Following are some questions from a Likert-type rating scale on negotiation. (The scale was part of a survey project to identify respondents' typical behaviors with various aspects of negotiation. The data-based decision from this survey project was whether to offer training in negotiation.) Scale anchors were as follows:

Almost always like me

Usually like me

Sometimes like me

Rarely like me

Almost never like me

1. I feel it is more important to make my point than to listen to ensure everyone understands me.

2. I try to avoid negotiations because they may become conflict situations.

3. I am confident that I can obtain a "good deal" when I negotiate.

4. I do not consider knowing the other negotiator's personality an important part of the negotiation process.

The respondent used a 5-point response scale to indicate to what degree each behavior was typical of him or her. A higher score was interpreted as meaning the person was more likely to use effective negotiating strategies, while a lower score suggested that the person could benefit from some training in negotiation strategies.

The directions encouraged the respondent to read each statement carefully. But to ensure that they were reading carefully, half the items were worded negatively so that the respondent had to disagree with the negative statement.

In the preceding example, Questions 1 and 3 are positively worded, but Questions 2 and 4 are reversed, or negatively worded.

If you use a combination of negative and positive statements, you'll need to reverse the coding, as follows:

Almost always like me	1
Usually like me	2
Sometimes like me	3
Rarely like me	4
Almost never like me	5

This scoring model is used with the negative items . . . where *agreement* means the respondent must *disagree* with the statement.

When you use reverse-worded questions, focus on respondent feedback in the pilot test to ensure that all items are understood as you intended.

Practice Activity

Score the following Likert-type rating scale, paying particular attention to the questions that require reverse coding. The total score should yield a higher score for agreement about the respondent's feelings most of the time. The letters in the squares denote the respondent's answers to each question.

The Feelings Scale

Please read each of the statements carefully, and then mark how often each statement describes you by circling the letter that matches your choice. There are no right or wrong answers.

Please use the following scale:

> *A = Most of the time*
> *B = Some of the time*
> *C = Not very often*

	A	B	C
1. I am happy with myself at school.	[A]	B	C
2. I get upset when other children tease me.	A	[B]	C
3. I enjoy trying new things in class.	[A]	B	C
4. I get confused easily by some of my schoolwork.	A	B	[C]
5. I can do anything when I try hard.	A	[B]	C
6. I get schoolwork that is too hard for me.	A	[B]	C
7. I don't like to raise my hand during discussions.	A	B	[C]
8. I feel important to my teacher.	[A]	B	C
9. I like recess.	A	[B]	C
10. I dislike school.	A	B	[C]

To have higher scores for agreement, use the following values for positive items (1, 3, 5, 8, and 9): A = 3, B = 2, and C = 1.

The following items will require reverse coding: 2, 4, 6, 7, and 10, and the value for each of the anchors is as follows: A = 1, B = 2, and C = 3.

Did you compute 26 for the total score?

NOTE: This activity is for practice in coding reverse-worded questions; 10 questions are not enough to obtain stable results and a good sample of behavior (Nunnally, 1978). Meaning of this type of scale resides in the total score, not the individual items.

◆ CODING RATING SCALES

Responses to rating scales cannot be summed but, rather, are analyzed using frequencies, percentages, charts, and graphs. In Chapter 8, "Analyzing the Data and Making Data-Based Decisions," there's a detailed example of how to code the responses to a rating scale and how to analyze those responses. That information is not repeated here.

Checklist for Creating Response Scales

Use the following checklist to make sure you've completed all the activities necessary to create your response choices for your rating scales or your scale anchors for your Likert-type rating scales.

- ❑ Do the response choices match the needs of your target audience?
- ❑ Do any of the response choices overlap?
  - ○ If yes, how can the response choices be revised so they don't overlap?
- ❑ Did you use too many choices—so the respondent might have difficulty making the fine distinctions you're asking for?
  - ○ If yes, how can you revise the choices so the respondent will not have difficulty selecting a response choice?
- ❑ Do the response choices lead the respondent to a particular answer?
  - ○ If yes, how can the responses be revised so they don't lead the respondent to a particular choice?
- ❑ Will the respondent need to interpret any of your response choices because not enough information was provided?
  - ○ If yes, what other information should be provided so that no interpretation is necessary?

4

Putting the Questionnaire Together

Aquestionnaire is more than the questions and the responses—although these are key pieces. But your respondents need more . . .

First, they need directions!

Providing clear and concise directions is critical to ensure that respondents understand what you want them to do. You'll need some general instructions at the beginning of the questionnaire, then specific directions for each type of question you have included in your questionnaire.

Second, respondents need a questionnaire formatted so that it appears pleasing, interesting, and easy to follow. First impressions are critical! Formatting, layout, font size—these all affect response rate. Potential respondents look at the overall questionnaire when they decide whether to spend their time answering your questions. This chapter covers formatting issues for both paper-based and Web-based questionnaires.

Third, they need questions in an order that is logical and easy to follow. Another purpose of this chapter is to help you determine the optimum order for your questions to encourage high response rates.

And you need demographic information for your analyses. The chapter also provides some guidelines for gathering the demographic information you need.

 **STEP 8: CREATE THE QUESTIONNAIRE**

In this chapter, you will learn how to complete Step 8, creating a questionnaire that is professional looking, useful, and functional.

◆ DIRECTIONS

Clear directions are a critical success factor! Questionnaire directions accomplish the following:

- Summarize the purpose of the survey project
- Let respondents know exactly what you want them to do . . . check one response, check multiple responses, circle an answer, write in an answer, and so on
- Ensure that the respondent's answers to your questionnaire are valid
- Let the respondent know that participation is voluntary but strongly encouraged

Following is a set of example instructions.

The purpose of this survey project is to understand your views of peer-assisted instruction. Responding to this questionnaire is voluntary; we very much want your response. The School Advisory Council will use your input to improve the program. Read each statement below and decide how much you agree or disagree with that statement. Circle the letter that corresponds to your answer using the following key:
A = Agree strongly
B = Agree somewhat
C = Disagree somewhat
D = Disagree strongly

When creating your questionnaire directions, consider these guidelines:

- Place like types of items together and provide directions for each set of items.
- Do not use the term "most appropriate" when you refer to a response on a rating scale (such as satisfaction or agreement). This suggests to respondents that there are correct or preferred answers.
- Provide a new set of directions each time you change scale anchors or types of item formats. For many types of survey projects, you'll need to use different question formats to meet your objectives—and that's fine. Just remember to let respondents know how they are to answer each type of question.

Suppose the first 10 statements in your questionnaire ask about the extent to which respondents agree with each statement and the next 10 statements ask about the frequency of certain activities. Each set of statements requires different scale anchors, so each requires a set of directions.

Following is another example of directions for a frequency rating scale:

Read each statement and decide how often you feel that way. Circle the letter that corresponds to your answer using the following key:
A = Most of the time
B = About half of the time
C = Once in a while
D = Rarely

On occasion, questionnaires may require several types of response formats, but the type of responses required do not need additional directions other than those at the beginning of the questionnaire. Following is an example.

Bullying at Our School

We want to know how extensive bullying is at our school—and we need your help. Responding to the questionnaire is voluntary, but we really need your responses. Your responses will be private, so please do not put your name on the questionnaire. We'll use the information to lessen the amount of bullying that's happening at our school. Please read each question carefully and provide the information requested.

1. Have you been bullied at school this year?
   a. No (Please go to Question 6)
   b. Yes (Please continue with Question 2)

2. How often are you bullied?
   a. A few times a day
   b. Once a day
   c. Once or twice a week
   d. Once a month

3. How much of a problem is bullying for you?
   a. It bothers me so much I don't like to come to school.
   b. It bothers me a lot, but I still come to school.
   c. It bothers me a little.
   d. It doesn't bother me.

4. Where are you usually bullied?
   a. In the hallways at school
   b. In my classroom
   c. In the cafeteria
   d. On the playground
   e. In the bathrooms

5. What types of bullying have you experienced this year at school? Please select all that apply.
   a. I've been called names.
   b. I've been physically threatened.
   c. I've been shoved.
   d. I've been physically hurt.
   e. Something of mine has been stolen.
   f. Something of mine has been damaged.

6. Have you seen other students being bullied at school?
   a. Yes
   b. No (Please go to Question 10)

7. What is your most common reaction when you see others bullied?
   a. I join in the bullying.
   b. I tell an adult.
   c. I walk away.
   d. I watch.

8. Without naming the bully (or bullies), please describe that person's age:
   a. About the same age as the person being bullied
   b. Younger than the person being bullied
   c. Older than the person being bullied

9. Without naming the bully (or bullies), please indicate who did the bullying:
   a. Boy
   b. Girl
   c. A group of students

Please tell us about you.

10. I am a
    a. boy.
    b. girl.

11. What grade are you in?
    a. Third
    b. Fourth
    c. Fifth

Thank you for answering these questions.

When in doubt about whether to include additional directions, err on the side of too much information. If your respondents don't understand what you want them to do, they may not provide valid information. And you won't know whether they became confused about any aspect of the questionnaire, because they are answering the questionnaire at their location—and all you see are their responses! Pilot testing your directions will help ensure that respondents understand what you want them to do. (See details on how to conduct your pilot test in Chapter 6, "Pilot Testing the Questionnaire.")

 Directions on the Web must be clear and useful just as for a paper-based questionnaire. But to ensure that the respondent remembers the directions, you may need to place them on the top of each page. On a paper-based questionnaire, respondents can easily flip back a page or two to review the directions. Respondents may be less likely to do this on the Web—often because they may not remember which screen contained the directions! On the Web, you can use one color for the directions and another for the questions and responses—so respondents know when they see words in a particular color they need to pay attention to the directions!

◆ DEMOGRAPHIC INFORMATION

An important rule here: Ask only for data that you will use!

Demographic information is collected for three purposes:

- To describe the characteristics of those who respond to the questionnaire
- To provide a way to disaggregate your data into subgroups to make comparisons in your analysis
- To "filter" respondents on the basis of certain experiences

If you are doing a small action research project, it may not be necessary to describe the respondents, because you already know who they are. And you may not want to form any subgroups for analyses. But for most survey projects, you should gather the demographic information. If you plan to publish your results, you will need, at a minimum, age, gender, and race/ethnicity (American Psychological Association [APA], 2001).

What variables will help you disaggregate your data so you can understand it better? Listed next are some demographic variables that have been used in other survey research studies:

- Gender
- Age (in categories)
- Race/ethnicity
- Educational level
- Family income
- Job (e.g., teacher, principal, school counselor, parent)
- Environmental variables related to guiding question (e.g., type of school attended)
- Particular experiences related to guiding question (e.g., participation in a workshop)

Be careful though—certain demographic questions may depress your response rate, especially if some questions are sensitive and the respondent is concerned about the anonymity of his or her responses. Examples include detailed marital status categories such as divorced or single living with significant other.

Describing the Respondents

Who responded to your questionnaire? Demographic questions help you create a profile of the respondents. In that way, people who read your survey project report can determine whether your results might generalize to their school districts and situations.

Disaggregating Your Data for Analyses

You'll need demographic data to disaggregate your data to compare the responses of different subgroups, such as gender, ethnicity, educational level of parents, and so forth. Determine what the reporting requirements are—and then gather the appropriate demographic information. For example, if you are gathering information from parents, do you need to know which parent responded (gender)? What about race/ethnicity? If you're doing a districtwide questionnaire, do you need to examine results by school?

The key for choosing demographic variables is to plan the analyses so you know exactly which subgroups you want to study. And of primary importance is how you will use the results of the questionnaire—for example, the type of decision you want to make, based on the results of your data analyses.

HINT: Use as few demographic questions as possible, and be careful about what you ask. Respondents might think you're prying and not respond to the questionnaire.

Where Do Demographic Questions Go?

In most cases, they go at the end of the questionnaire. If these questions appear earlier, potential respondents might decide not to continue. However, if they reach the last page and find these questions, they might continue because they've already invested so much time answering the questions. Or they might return the questionnaire without these questions completed—which in many cases is better than a total nonresponse.

Demographic questions for our case study were described in Chapter 1 ("Launching Your Survey Project") and are also included in the questionnaire in the Resource section.

◆ FORMAT

The goal of creating a pleasing, user-friendly format is to ensure that the questionnaire is attractive, easy to understand, and easy to complete. The format of your questionnaire communicates important information to respondents. If the layout is pleasing, the directions clear, the typeface readable, and the statements free of spelling and typographical errors, the message is, "I took time and thought to prepare this questionnaire for you. Will you please thoughtfully fill it out for me?"

This section focuses on the following elements of questionnaire design:

- Overall appearance
- Question order
- Question formats

Layout is critically important for all questionnaires, no matter the delivery medium. Following are suggestions for both paper-based and Web-based questionnaires.

Overall Appearance and Design

The first impression that questionnaire respondents should have is awareness of the professionalism, quality, and attractiveness of the questionnaire. It should pique the respondents' interest so that they will begin the questionnaire. Once a person starts there's a good chance he or she will complete the questionnaire—if it's of reasonable length, if the respondent is not confused because of poor directions, or if the respondent is not upset with any of the questions. Your questionnaire should have a title and begin with the overall directions.

Paper-Based Questionnaires

Following are guidelines to help you create a high-quality paper-based questionnaire.

- Arrange the directions and items so that the layout is pleasing, with sufficient white space so the items and response options are not crowded.
- Use double spacing between items but single spacing within the item.
- If Likert-type scales are used, place scale anchors at the top of *each* page.
- Provide separate directions each time you change item types.
- If you use multiple sections—and require multiple sets of directions—use section headings.
- Do not split an item over two pages.
- If possible, use an inkjet or laser computer printer with a scalable font. A scalable font is one that allows you to change sizes and use bold or italics for emphasis. Your questionnaire will look much more professional!
- Include page numbers on each page.
- Plan for data analysis by arranging the responses on the page in such a way that they are easy for the respondent to complete and easy for the data entry person to enter into a database for statistical analysis.

- Avoid cramming too much information on one page. It is better to have a slightly longer questionnaire (page-wise) than one with fonts and spacing that make it hard to read.
- Make sure your page and question layouts are consistent. Do not put answer choices on the right for some questions and on the left for others.

At the end of the questionnaire, remember to thank respondents for answering the questions and remind them how to return the questionnaire.

Web-Based Questionnaires

 Formatting Web-based questionnaires has special challenges, because unlike paper-based questionnaires, what you see is not necessarily what you get. For example, your questionnaire will most likely look different in different browsers. Some of the software designed to format and deliver questionnaires works better with a Netscape browser than with an Internet Explorer browser, and for some, it's the other way around. This is something to check out in your pilot test—and something that your Web consultant can help you with (if you're using one).

A Web-based questionnaire must be easy to navigate. (Navigation means moving from screen to screen, understanding how to provide responses, and so forth.) The more difficult it is for the respondent to navigate, the less likely it is that the person will complete the questionnaire, resulting in a lower response rate. Each page of the questionnaire must load quickly. If there are a lot of graphics in the questionnaire, it will take longer to load each page, and the potential respondent may quit responding.

The first screen the respondent should see is a welcome screen that is motivating, provides information about answering the questions, and emphasizes that responding to the questionnaire will be easy and interesting to the respondents, and gives directions. After the welcome screen, the first question to be answered should be interesting and visible on one screen (no scrolling) and easy to answer in terms of computer skills (such as using a mouse, clicking on a response, or using the scroll bar).

Throughout the questionnaire, there should be specific instructions about how to take each necessary computer action for responding to the question, such as clicking on a drop-down list and selecting a response, selecting more than one response, deselecting a response if the person changes his or her mind, and moving forward and backward in the questionnaire.

A Web-based questionnaire must do the following:

- Adhere to principles of good Web design. (If you are not familiar with these principles, see, e.g., Krug & Black, 2000; Niederst, 2001; Nielsen, 2000; or work with a Web designer.)
- Include an introduction or welcome page. Explain the reason for the questionnaire. Web-based questionnaires don't have cover letters—so all the information in a cover letter must go on the introduction page.
- Put instructions at points where they are needed throughout the questionnaire.
- Avoid using too many colors or fonts—they can be distracting. It's tempting to use all the bells and whistles available for Web page design—but don't!

- Avoid cramming too much information on one page.
- Use bolding, italicizing, and changing the color of words to make your questions easier to understand. For example, use color and font changes to make instructions distinct from question text and make the questionnaire easier to follow. But be consistent in your use of color and font changes!
- Use a light background, such as white or light gray, with dark letters, such as black, navy, or maroon. This has been found to be most readable (Solomon, 2001).
- Use graphics sparingly. Graphics require more bandwidth than text, which means they will take longer to download—and the respondent's browser may crash.
- Make sure respondents don't have to scroll horizontally to view the complete width of the questionnaire page. Most people find horizontal scrolling annoying.
- Make sure your page and question layout are consistent. Do not put answer choices on the right for some questions and on the left for others.
- Number the pages so that respondents know where they are in the questionnaire, using the numbering style 2 of 6, 3 of 6, and so on.
- Consider using a "percentage complete" sliding scale at the bottom of the page to indicate to the respondent how near to the end of the questionnaire he or she is.
- Use drop-down lists when you have several answer choices, but use radio buttons for most responses. Drop-down lists require more bandwidth and so take longer to transmit—but with five or more response choices, a drop-down list makes the page layout look less cluttered.
- Require only minimal computer skills, including the ability to use an Internet browser, enter a specific URL, use a mouse, and follow simple navigation instructions.

Unique Features of Web-Based Questionnaires

A unique feature of a Web-based questionnaire is the ability to require the respondent to answer a question before continuing. Use this feature sparingly and only on key questions because the person may become upset with this question format and quit the questionnaire.

A second unique feature of Web-based questionnaires is the ability to ask a question based on the person's response. For example, if the respondent indicated that he or she was dissatisfied with the program and did not make a comment in the space provided under the rating scale, the next screen could say, "You indicated you were dissatisfied with the program. Will you please indicate the reasons for your dissatisfaction?"

A third unique feature is combining importance ratings and ranking of those items rated as "Very important." (See Chapter 2, "Asking the Right Questions," for more details on this type of question format.) For example, a survey project was designed to determine which workshop topics were most important for a teacher's professional development. There were 15 different topics—too many for a ranking format question. Instead, the respondents used an importance rating scale ("Very important" to "Very unimportant") to rate each of the 15 different topics. When these ratings were completed, a list of all topics the respondent had rated as "Very important" was presented, and the respondent was asked to rank order this shortened list of topics.

Consider the people who will respond to your Web-based questionnaire and their computer abilities as you design your layout. Using answer grids to present answer choices in two columns can look attractive, save space, and help avoid vertical scrolling. But these formats are a bit more difficult for some respondents to understand than is a simple vertical list of response choices. If you think your target population might have some trouble understanding how to respond to the questionnaire, use these formats sparingly—and check the use of these in your pilot test. (An example of a grid-type response format is presented later in this chapter.)

Formatting Guidelines for Both Paper-Based and Web-Based Questionnaires

- Provide a title to the questionnaire.
- Provide section headings, if needed.
- Don't split questions across pages.
- Keep answer spaces in a straight line, either horizontally or vertically.
- Be consistent in your placement of the place for the respondent to provide responses.
- Group together questions on the same topic to make the questionnaire easier to answer.
- Number the pages or screens so that respondents can determine how much of the questionnaire is left for them to answer.
- After respondents push the "submit" button, have a screen that thanks them for participating. Put this same message on the last page of the paper-based questionnaire.

Question Order

The flow of the questions should be logical, often starting with more general questions and then moving to more specific or detailed questions. Think of a questionnaire as an outline of a conversation you would have with someone if you could speak with him or her in person.

There are two broad issues regarding question order and response choice order. One is how the question order can encourage people to complete the questionnaire. The other is how the order of response choices or rating anchors could affect the results of your questionnaire.

Ordering Questions So Respondents Complete the Questionnaire

Ideally, early questions should be easy to answer to encourage respondents to continue responding to the questionnaire. Whenever possible, leave difficult or sensitive questions, including demographic questions, until near the end of your questionnaire. That way, people will have invested time in answering questions to that point and are more likely to continue and complete the questionnaire.

If your questionnaire contains some broad questions and some specific questions, use a funnel ordering that goes from general to more specific. If your questionnaire has different topics, place all of the questions for a topic together.

The content of questions early in the questionnaire might affect a responden answer to later questions. For example, mentioning an idea or issue in one questio can make respondents think of it when they answer a later question, when they might not have thought of it had it not been previously mentioned. As an example, suppose you created a questionnaire about discipline issues in school. One of the questions included a list of concerns, including discipline on the school bus. Later in the questionnaire, you have an open-ended question about areas of concern relating to discipline. Because of the earlier question's mention of potential discipline issues on the school bus, the respondent might also include it here when, without the earlier mention of the school bus, he or she might not have included it.

Respondents tend to think more about questions asked earlier in the series and so give more accurate answers to them. Thus, if you have some questions that require a thoughtful response, place these near the beginning of the questionnaire.

Another way question order can affect results is "habituation" or response set. This problem applies to a series of questions that all have the same response choices, such as Agree–Disagree. Some respondents might start marking the same response without really reading the question carefully. But a way around this is to balance the Agree–Disagree questions in a way that forces respondents to read carefully and think about their responses. Later in this section you'll see an example of balancing Agree–Disagree questions. You'll also find information about positively and negatively worded questions in Chapter 2.

Ordering Response Choices for Each Use

When you order the response choices for a question, consider the following guidelines.

- A respondent confronted with a long list of choices is likely to read the first few carefully and select from those. Limit response choices to a maximum of seven in a list. If you need information about a greater number of choices, consider structuring the information needed into two questions.
- Consistently start the scale anchors for Likert-type rating scales with the positive responses, such as "Strongly agree," "Very satisfied," "Very likely," and so on.

Page Layouts

If you use open-response questions, leave enough space for a response—but not so much that respondents think you want them to write an essay! Three to five lines are usually sufficient. With Web-based questionnaires, the text box usually has a scroll arrow, so respondents see only a small portion of what may be available.

Determine if you want to allow respondents to put in "other comments" at the end of the questionnaire. If you use this, you'll need to plan to analyze the information using the guidelines for analyzing open-ended questions presented in Chapter 2.

Questions with answer grids save paper and computer screen space. (See the example in Table 4.1.) Using this type of format avoids a series of repetitive questions. However, this format is more useful with an educated audience. Consider this in your pilot test.

Some questions require the answers to be listed under each question. See the questionnaire about bullying on page 69 as an example.

Table 4.1   Example of Grid Format Question

Please indicate how often you have participated in the following activities in your child's classroom during the current school year by checking the box that corresponds to your answer for each of the following activities:

Activity	None	1–2 times	3–4 times	5 or more
Helped with a special event such as a field trip				
Served as a computer aide				
Served as a teacher assistant				
Helped with the extended-day program				
Provided individual tutoring to a student during school hours				

You can include the scale anchors with each question as in the following example.

EXAMPLE

Our school produces information for families that is linked to children's success in school.

☐ Extensively

☐ Frequently

☐ Occasionally

☐ Rarely

☐ Not occurring

Our school provides families with information on developing home conditions that support learning.

☐ Extensively

☐ Frequently

☐ Occasionally

☐ Rarely

☐ Not occurring

See Figure 3.1, Chapter 3 ("Creating Response Choices for Rating Scales"), for an example of a layout of a rating scale using the same anchors for each question.

For a Web-based questionnaire using rating scales, be sure the scale anchors appear on the same screen as the questions. For example, if the respondent needs to scroll to answer several questions in a section, you may need to place another set of scale anchors in the middle of the questions. Alternatively, you can design the questionnaire so the respondent goes to the next page (with scale anchors at the top) rather than using scrolling.

Balance Agree–Disagree Items

When all your questions are worded so that endorsement or agreement is at the left side of the page (or screen), some respondents might exhibit response bias, which is a tendency to agree with the statement. This tendency becomes more pronounced as they continue through the questions. One way to overcome this tendency is to balance items to help ensure that respondents are reading the questions and responding thoughtfully. In this way, respondents who tend to agree with all statements must circle *disagree* for some questions in order to consistently endorse a particular point of view. But be sure to include in the directions a statement about reading each question carefully. (See Chapter 2, "Asking the Right Questions," for examples of positively and negatively worded questions and Chapter 3, "Creating Response Choices for Rating Scales," and Chapter 6, "Pilot Testing the Questionnaire," for suggestions.)

Approximately one-third to one-half of the questions should be negatively worded. But watch for convoluted wording as you reverse the meaning of the questions. Do not use double negatives. Pilot test these questions to be sure they are being read carefully and interpreted correctly.

See Chapter 3, page 64 for an example of a Likert-type rating scale with balanced questions.

Filter Questions

Filter questions are used to qualify a respondent and are particularly good for Web-based questionnaires when you are not able to select the people who will have access to your questionnaire. For example, a school district was interested in finding out how well a preschool experience prepared children for kindergarten. The school district regularly hosts Web-based questionnaires on its Web site, and many parents visit the Web site regularly. To ensure that parents with the desired characteristics provided the data, the questionnaire contained the following filter question:

My child attended preschool at least three days a week during the past year.

- ○ Yes
- ○ No

If the person clicked the "Yes" button, he or she will go to the first screen of the questionnaire. If the person clicked the "No" button, he or she would receive a

"Thank you for your interest" message, and the questionnaire would be completed. Filter questions are not useful for paper-based questionnaires. Rather, if there are certain sets of questions that only respondents with certain experiences should answer, a "skip" format is better. The following section provides guidelines and an example of a skip pattern.

Skip Patterns

Skip patterns are used when some items will be answered by only a certain portion of the respondents. For example, you might want only respondents who have had certain experiences to respond to certain items. When this is the case, you'll format your questionnaire so that respondents without these experiences can skip these items. Be sure the directions are clear ... so respondents will know exactly which items they are to answer.

EXAMPLE

1. Do you have Internet access at home?

   (A) No (skip to Question 6)

   (B) Yes (please continue with Question 2)

2. How often do you access the Internet for research purposes?

   _____ Once a week

   _____ Two to three times a week

   _____ Four or more times a week

3. How long is your average Internet session?

   _____ 60 minutes or less

   _____ 61 to 120 minutes

   _____ Over 2 hours

4. How often do you visit chat rooms?

   _____ Once a week

   _____ Two to three times a week

   _____ Four or more times a week

5. How likely would you be to access a chat room for help with your survey project if one were available?

   _____ Very likely

   _____ Somewhat likely

   _____ Not at all likely

6. Do you use the Internet from the library?

   (A) No

   (B) Yes

Skip patterns may be used with both paper-based and Web-based questionnaires. The difference is that for a paper-based questionnaire, the respondent can see all the questions, as in the preceding example. For a Web-based questionnaire, the respondent sees only those questions that result from a skip pattern. As a questionnaire designer, you determine the skip pattern, and then the logic of the skip pattern will need to be programmed into the delivery of the questions for a Web-based questionnaire. In your pilot test, it's very important to test these skip patterns to ensure that they are working as you intended.

Benefits of Using Skip Patterns

Using skip patterns results in fewer questions to answer for some respondents because they respond only to those questions that are relevant to them. This usually results in a higher response rate because respondents do not spend time answering questions that are not appropriate to them. A caveat to using skip patterns is to ensure that respondents follow directions as you intended. To help avoid errors, use a combination of graphics such as arrows, formatting such as indenting, and clear directions. Table 4.2 provides a comparison of filter and skip pattern questions.

Table 4.2   Comparison of Filter and Skip Pattern Questions

Type	*When to Use*	*Example*
Filter	You need to determine eligibility to respond.	Whether a child has attended preschool in the past year.
Skip	You need to route respondents to parts of the questionnaire they are qualified to answer.	Particular experiences or activities, such as attending a workshop, using the Internet, or participating in a community event.

◆ BUILDING RELIABILITY AND VALIDITY INTO YOUR QUESTIONNAIRE

Throughout this book, you've read about building quality into your questionnaire by ensuring that questions are clearly written, following the guidelines of good question writing, and mapping (i.e., linking) to your objectives and guiding question. The reason for doing all this is to ensure that your questionnaire is "good," that the data are accurate and credible so you can be confident in the results of your questionnaire. *Good* in the context of any measurement tool used to gather data refers to validity and reliability.

A valid questionnaire is one that measures what it is intended to measure. There are several types of validity evidence; the one that is appropriate for most questionnaires is content validity, or evidence that the questions relate to the objectives of the survey project. (For more information on validity, see, e.g., Anastasi, 1982; Gall, 2002;

Fraenkel & Wallen, 2002.) Gathering evidence of content validity should be done now, before the pilot test.

Content validity evidence focuses on the judgments of experts about the degree to which each question links to the objectives and, overall, whether the questions linked to an objective sufficiently cover that objective to yield meaningful information. To evaluate the content validity of your questionnaire, identify a small group of subject matter experts and ask them to provide the following information:

- Does the question clearly link to the objective as intended?
- Together, do all the questions linked to an objective provide thorough coverage of the topic?
  - Are there questions that overlap each other and therefore provide essentially the same information?
  - Are there topics that should be included that were not?
- As a whole, to what extent will the questionnaire yield the data required?

If you conduct this type of review now, you can make any needed changes prior to the pilot test.

A reliable questionnaire is one that measures consistently. If you administer your questionnaire to the same people at two different times separated by a week or so, you would expect them to answer the same way both times, assuming nothing has changed in their lives. This is an example of "test-retest reliability" evidence and is appropriate for all types of questionnaires.

If you are using a Likert-type rating scale and plan to sum the responses to yield a score for each respondent, then another type of reliability evidence is appropriate. This is "internal consistency reliability" evidence, which focuses on whether all the items measure the same construct as you intended.

Plan to evaluate the reliability of your questionnaire during the pilot test. In Chapter 6, "Pilot Testing the Questionnaire," you'll find an example of how to evaluate the test-retest reliability of your questionnaire as well as some suggestions on how to evaluate the internal consistency of your Likert-type rating scale.

A valid measure always has some degree of reliability, but a reliable measure may or may not have validity for the purpose for its intended use.

Now, before you go on, complete the following checklist to be sure you have a well-designed questionnaire.

Checklist for Putting the Questionnaire Together

Use the following checklist to ensure that your questionnaire is ready for the pilot test.

- ❑ Is there an overall set of directions for the questionnaire?
- ❑ If you use different question formats, are there separate and clear directions for each response format?
- ❑ For rating scales, are there scale anchors on each page that match the questions on that page?
- ❑ Are the question and its associated responses on one page, not split over two pages?

❑ Are the answer choices in a logical order, such as alphabetical, numerical, or by degree of intensity?

❑ Are there any typographical or spelling errors?

○ If yes, have you corrected these and proofed one more time?

❑ Are there any grammatical or punctuation errors?

○ If yes, have you corrected these and proofed one more time?

❑ For a paper-based questionnaire, are the items numbered sequentially and correctly?

❑ For a paper-based questionnaire, is the overall layout pleasing, with sufficient white space and margins?

❑ For a Web-based questionnaire, is the layout on each screen easy to read, with sufficient space and clear information about navigation?

❑ If you used a Likert-type scale, did you balance positive and negative questions so the respondent does not always choose the positive or negative choice to present a consistent position?

❑ If you used skip patterns, are they correctly formatted?

❑ If you used skip patterns, are the directions clear to the respondent?

❑ Do the demographic questions for a paper-based questionnaire appear at the end of the questionnaire?

❑ Does the questionnaire end with "Thank you for responding"?

5

Identifying and Contacting Respondents

Who has the information you need to make your decision? In Chapter 1, "Launching Your Survey Project," you identified your target audience, but it's likely that you will not want to invite everyone in your target audience to participate. How do you select who will be invited? What methods of selecting participants can be used with paper-based questionnaires? With Web-based questionnaires? This chapter begins with information on different sampling methods you might use to select your sample.

How many respondents do you need to make valid conclusions and sound decisions? How many people will you need to contact to obtain that many respondents? An important component of contacting potential respondents is to remember that they must voluntarily choose to respond to your questionnaire. As a result, not everyone who receives an invitation will respond. In this chapter, you will find some guidelines to help you determine how many people to invite to participate to achieve the number of respondents (the people who complete your questionnaire and return it to you) you need for your analyses.

Identifying the appropriate group of respondents (the target audience) is a part of the initial planning, and determining how many to invite is covered in this chapter. But convincing them to respond is another matter! A cover letter (or invitation for a Web-based questionnaire) is really a marketing vehicle—and you have only one chance to make a good first impression on the potential respondent and convince him or her to respond to your questionnaire. For access to some respondents such as students, you'll need a gatekeeper letter as well. A list of the critical components of successful cover letters is provided in this chapter as well as sample letters.

A *gatekeeper* is a person who gives permission for you to contact members of your target audience to invite them to respond to your questionnaire.

Using Web-based questionnaires brings with it special challenges in contacting potential participants. We'll look at some guidelines and caveats about using this delivery medium.

Let's begin by identifying the processes available to select your sample. Then we'll go over some guidelines for determining how many people to invite.

◆ DETERMINING WHOM TO INVITE: IDENTIFYING THE SAMPLE

 **STEP 9: SELECT THE SAMPLE**

Obtaining the participation of the right people is critically important. No matter how well your questions are worded, how persuasive your cover letter, or how pleasing the format of the questionnaire, if you don't invite the right people to respond to the questionnaire, your results will not be believable or accurate.

Who are the right people? Those who have the information you need. You identified your target audience in Chapter 1. As a reminder of our discussion, here's a table from that chapter (Table 5.1).

Table 5.1 Examples of Guiding Questions and Target Audiences

Guiding Question	Target Audience
What types of sports programs will parents and the community support?	Parents at the school plus a sample of members of the community who are not parents at the school
Which class activities should be kept and which should be changed?	Students and teachers
How do students feel about homework assignments that require Internet-based research?	Students
What kinds of reading-related activities do parents of early-elementary students use with their children?	Parents of early-elementary students

Once you've identified your target audience, you need to determine how many people you should invite. Do you need to send an invitation to everyone in the target audience? The answer is "probably not." (An example of a survey project that includes everyone is one that has a very small target audience, such as parents of all kindergarten children in a small district or all principals and school administrators in a small county or district.) But for purposes of our discussion, let's assume that you need to select a sample from your target audience.

A *sample* is a group selected to represent a larger group, called the *population*.

Representativeness means that what you know from the sample would be essentially the same as if you included the entire population in your survey project.

So ideally you need a sample that is representative of the target audience (population) to which you want to make generalizations. Decisions required here include determining what method of sampling to use (more detail following), how many people you'll need to contact (sample size—more detail following), and how to locate these people so you can send them an invitation.

Let's consider target audiences of parents, teachers, and students. These target audiences have the benefit of being completely specified—that is, lists of these people exist. If you contact everyone on the list, you are using the *population*. A population is the entire target audience. However, you may not want to include everyone in the population, particularly if the population is quite large. In this case, you would use a sample. We'll use the term *sampling frame* to denote the members of the population from which the sample will be selected.

A *sampling frame* is a list of the population (target audience) from which you'll select your sample.

A sample is a group of people from your sampling frame that, ideally, is representative of the population. (We'll talk about sampling error, or the error that the sample is *not* representative of the population, later in this chapter.) To draw valid conclusions from your results, your sample must reflect the characteristics of the population.

How many people should you invite? To answer this question, consider how you will use the results. As noted earlier, it's good to use multiple data sources when the decision to be made is high stakes. In this case, you'll need credible data from a large number of respondents who are representative of your target audience. If your decision is less important, and if you also have other sources of information, then a smaller number of respondents will most likely suffice. (Earlier, a high-stakes decision was defined as one that takes a significant amount of resources to implement, one for which the consequences of making an error in the decision are potentially costly, and one for which a large number of people are interested in the decision.)

How familiar are you with sampling methodology? If you're working with a small target audience, you may want to invite everyone to respond to the questionnaire. In this case, you don't need to worry about sample size or sampling method because you are using the entire population. But if you have a fairly large target audience, and if you are not comfortable with statistics and sampling methodology, you will want to work with a statistician to plan your sampling strategy, including determining the number of people to contact to obtain the number of respondents you need.

Samples are selected using either *probability* or *nonprobability* sampling methods. We'll first consider probability sampling methods and then look at nonprobability sampling methods.

Probability Sampling

In probability sampling, each member of the population has a known probability of being invited to respond to the questionnaire. (You can calculate that probability using a mathematical formula, but that level of detail is beyond the scope of this book.) We'll describe two types of probability sampling: simple random sampling and stratified random sampling. An important advantage of probability sampling is that sampling error (sometimes called the margin of error or level of precision) can be calculated. Sampling error is the degree to which a sample might differ from the population and therefore not be representative of the population. When you make inferences to the population, you report your results with plus or minus some multiple of the sampling error.

A *simple random sample* is one in which each person in the population or sampling frame is equally likely to be chosen. An example of simple random sampling is to put each person's name on a slip of paper, place these in a hat, mix them up, and draw the names out of the hat. But with a population of more than 50 or so people, this method becomes quite cumbersome. A better way to draw a random sample is to use a table of random numbers, which is a list of numbers that fall in a random order. Each person in the population (or sampling frame) must have a unique identification number. Tables of random numbers are found in many research methods books (e.g., Fraenkel & Wallen, 2002) or on the Web using a search engine such as Google. Table 5.2 is from a random number generator program found on the Web.

For purposes of example, let's say that you have a population of 125 school superintendents who participated in a special summer workshop over the past two years. You've determined that you need to send an invitation to 50 of these superintendents to get the number of respondents you need. You get the lists of names of these superintendents from the college where the workshop was held and assign a number to each person, from 1 to 125. Start in cell 1A, and go down column 1, selecting those people whose numbers appear in the table; then continue up column B and down column C. In this example, it's not until column C that we select the first person, 038. In column D, we select another four people, 072, 094, 089, and 055. Continue this process until you have the names of the 50 people to invite to respond to your questionnaire. For purposes of example, the numbers of the people who would be invited to participate in the survey project are in boldface. Since this is only a part of a table of random numbers, we don't have 50 people selected; we would need to use a larger table.

When you use a table of random numbers you can start anyplace, and move up or down or sideways, but once you start you must be consistent.

A *stratified random sample* is one in which the population is divided into groups, or strata, that share a common characteristic such as attending a school in the district that has several different types of schools or a demographic characteristic such as gender or race/ethnicity. Then a simple random sample is selected from each stratum. The number chosen within each stratum is proportional to its frequency in the population for that stratum. Stratified random sampling is used when one or more strata in the population are quite small and might be missed in a simple random

Table 5.2   Random Number Generator

Row #	A	B	C	D	E	F	G	H	I	J
1	227	421	726	866	365	548	537	257	432	587
2	583	492	847	**055**	317	639	825	478	**002**	602
3	639	635	264	208	953	781	777	824	608	611
4	209	981	777	162	498	951	484	861	647	205
5	362	405	633	**089**	617	863	269	**079**	338	890
6	324	158	865	570	195	465	904	836	386	476
7	975	482	**038**	448	315	**043**	837	700	436	650
8	382	659	810	919	870	346	832	613	771	190
9	596	734	579	**094**	**044**	991	301	137	463	**043**
10	770	949	235	**072**	704	174	327	806	**056**	321

sample. This sampling method is particularly useful when you plan to disaggregate your data and you want to be sure you have enough responses from each subgroup.

An example of a survey project where stratified random sampling would be appropriate is in a school district with schools of greatly varying sizes, such as a district with regular schools, charter schools, and magnet schools. If you use simple random sampling with a list of all classes from all schools, it is possible that classes from some types of schools might not be included at all. In this example, suppose there are 31 schools in the district: 3 charter schools, 1 magnet school, and 27 regular schools. If all the classes were numbered and a simple random sample selected, it is possible that no classes from the magnet school would be selected and, possibly, none of the classes from the 3 charter schools. Therefore, even if you had a good response rate, you would not be able to disaggregate the data into subgroups corresponding to these 3 types of schools. Using stratified random sampling, you would select classes from each stratum (type of school). You can select either an equal number of classes from each type of school and weight the responses based on the percentages of classes from the stratum in the population, or you can select classes based on the proportion in the population of that group of 31 schools.

Other examples of strata include years of experience in teaching or demographic variables such as gender, ethnicity, or age. You must have a reason for selecting the strata you use, and it must be a variable that you use in your analyses. (See, e.g., Fraenkel & Wallen, 2002, or Gall, 2002, for more information on random sampling and stratified random sampling.)

Nonprobability Sampling

In nonprobability sampling, participants are selected in some nonrandom manner to be invited to respond to your questionnaire. Types of nonprobability sampling include systematic sampling, convenience sampling, quota sampling, and snowball sampling. A major drawback to using a nonprobability sample is that the degree to which the sample differs from the population is unknown, so the sampling error cannot be calculated. Use nonprobability sampling when you do not have access to a list of all members of the population. The quality of a nonprobability sample depends on the knowledge, judgment, and expertise of the survey project team. When you use a nonprobability sample, it's important to gather demographic information so that you know who has responded to the questionnaire.

In an earlier example, it was noted that we could define a sampling frame for parents, teachers, and students. However, the first survey project on the list in Table 5.1 will also include members of the community who are not parents at the school. It will be both challenging and costly to create an accurate sampling frame for this group because it means having to identify each member of the community. Therefore, for this part of the target audience, a nonprobability sampling procedure may be necessary.

A *systematic sample* is one in which every *n*th name is selected from the population list. The first step is to determine the number of people required (more about that a bit later in this chapter) and then divide the number in the sample by the number in the population. The result is the size of the step you take in the list. Here's an example: Suppose you have 500 people in your population and you've determined that you need a sample of 100; 500 divided by 100 is 5. You select every fifth name from the list. You begin by using a table of random numbers to determine where to start—somewhere between persons 1 and 5 on the list.

A *convenience sample* is one that is selected because the people are convenient to contact. They might be parents who attend a PTO meeting, teachers who attend a particular workshop, or members of the community who were at a mall on the day the data are collected. In none of these cases can we be sure that the results of the questionnaire will provide accurate information for decision making because we don't know how representative this group of respondents is of the population.

A *quota sample* is the nonprobability equivalent to stratified random sampling. As in stratified sampling, the researcher identifies the population subgroups or strata. But rather than selecting people randomly, the researcher uses convenience sampling to identify the number of people needed and fills the "quota" of people needed in each strataum.

A *snowball sample* is a type of nonprobability sample used when there are few people having a certain characteristic. The first few people are identified, and then each is asked to provide referrals. For example, if you wanted to study parents of twins, you might identify one or two parents with twins and then ask each of these parents to identify other parents with twins. A disadvantage of using this technique is that it is unlikely that you will have a representative sample of the population.

What Type of Sampling Method Should You Use?

So what's the bottom line? The type of sampling method used depends on the survey project objectives, the scope of the survey project, the criticality of the decision to be made, sources of other information available to make the decision along with the questionnaire data, and the risk of using results from a sample of respondents that is not representative of the population. If feasible, use a probability sampling method. In many school-based studies, this can be done because you'll be able to specify the sampling frame. It also depends on the overall survey project budget, the method of gathering the information (paper-based or Web-based questionnaires), the subject matter, and the kind of respondent needed.

How Many People Should Be Invited to Respond to Your Questionnaire?

Now that you are aware of the different methods available to *select* people to invite to respond to your questionnaire, you need to consider *how many* you should invite. How many respondents do you need to make valid conclusions? How many people will you need to contact to obtain that many respondents? If you invite too many, you're wasting resources. If you invite too few, you may not have enough data to make good data-based decisions. And remember, it's likely that not everyone will respond to your questionnaire. The discussion here refers to those target audiences for which you can create a sampling frame.

1. *How many people are in your target audience or population?* If it's 200 or fewer, it is best to include the entire group.

2. *How much sampling error is acceptable?* Smaller sampling errors require larger sample sizes. Small random samples may have large sampling errors, resulting in data that do not have the level of accuracy you'll need to make data-based decisions. The level of sampling error that you select is based on several considerations, including resources and the criticality of the decision (see, e.g., Fraenkel & Wallen, 2002).

3. *What response rate do you expect?* The difference between the number of people invited and those who respond is called the *response rate*. Response rates in survey projects related to education and educational issues can range from 10% to over 70%. On average, paper-based questionnaire response rates are in the 30% to 50% range (Baruch, 1999; Dillman, 2000), and responses to Web-based questionnaires are similar. You need to consider the expected response rate as you determine how many people to invite to respond to your questionnaire.

If your response rate is low—for example, 30% or less—then it's particularly important that you validate your results, perhaps with a small number of telephone interviews, observations, or other sources of information. The process of using additional sources of information is called "triangulating your data."

For many survey projects, results are used to inform decisions—and other information is also considered. And some questionnaires are exploratory—with the results being used to do further follow-up questionnaires. In this case, smaller sample sizes are generally acceptable. Table 5.3 includes some suggested sample sizes based on what you plan to do with the results.

Remember, numbers shown in Table 5.3 are the people invited, not those who respond!

Some things to keep in mind:

- A small representative sample is better than a large unrepresentative sample.
- A high response rate in a large nonprobability sample is worse than a high response rate in a small probability sample.

• Questionnaire results based on low response rates may provide inaccurate information because those who responded may not be representative of the entire population—even if you used random sampling methodology.

Table 5.3   Suggested Sample Sizes

Condition	Recommended Sample Size
No existing survey data—exploratory study	200 to 300
Some previous data, want to divide the results into two subgroups	300 to 500
Have some previous data Want to divide responses into sets of up to four groups Want to compare with previous survey data	600 to 1,000

The preceding discussion provides guidance for selecting samples when you can identify the sampling frame for your target audiences. But for some Web-based questionnaires, this may not be possible.

Identifying Respondents for Web-Based Questionnaires

 Earlier, you learned that there are two major ways to contact potential respondents for a Web-based questionnaire: using e-mail invitations directing a person to a Web site or using a variety of methods to get potential respondents to a Web site. If you are using e-mailed invitations and you can create a sampling frame, then the preceding sampling discussion applies to you. However, if you don't have a list of members of your target audience population, read on!

If you don't have a list of e-mail addresses (and hence a sampling frame) you'll need to use a variety of means of publicizing the availability of the questionnaire on a Web site. Be sure the people from whom you need information have access to the Web. If you use publicity to direct potential respondents to your Web site, you will have no control over who responds because all those who choose to respond are volunteers interested enough to go to your Web site. At the present time, people with regular access to the Internet may be systematically different from those without access. Sources of potential bias include skewed demographics and self-selection. With the increasing number of school districts that have Internet access and Web sites, these differences will continue to lessen.

Types of Samples for Web-Based Questionnaires

Note: All these types of samples are nonprobability.

An *unrestricted sample* is one that includes anyone on the Internet who finds the questionnaire. There is usually poor representativeness because of self-selection and a low participation rate. If your questionnaire will be available for a month or longer and if you are trying to get lots of responses, you might want to submit it to a search engine to increase odds that respondents will find it. (You may want to work with a Web consultant if you're using a Web-based questionnaire and are not sure how to do this.)

A *screened sample* is one that uses filter questions early in the questionnaire to screen potential participants and adjusts for unrepresentativeness by imposing quotas based on demographics. Another type of screened sample is one that uses a filter question to qualify potential respondents. If potential respondents do not have the right experience, for example, they get a screen saying "Thank you for your interest" but cannot access the questionnaire.

A *recruited sample* is one in which members of the target audience are recruited via phone, mail, e-mail, or in person. They are provided with instructions including a URL and a password. The survey project team starts with a list of known members of the target audience and then asks these people to identify other members of the target audience so they, too, can be invited to respond to the questionnaire. As a result, only those recruited can access the questionnaire. This technique can be used when there is no database from which to recruit the participants but for which you have some names of the target audience to begin the recruiting process.

It's a good idea to gather demographic information about the respondents in addition to those demographic variables you plan to use for disaggregating the results in the analyses. You'll want to describe respondents in some detail when the respondents to a Web-based questionnaire are volunteers and you cannot create a sampling frame. In this way, those reading the survey project report can evaluate the findings and recommendations in the context of the description of the respondents.

> The sampling frame for our case study includes the parents from the three elementary schools in the district. Because the schools are small and the total population is approximately 1,500 parents, we will invite the entire population. Based on an estimated 40% response rate, we'll need 600 respondents so that we can disaggregate the data based on the demographic questions.

◆ OBTAINING ACCESS TO MEMBERS OF YOUR TARGET AUDIENCE

If your target audience is elementary, middle, or high school students, you'll need permission from the school administration, the teachers involved, and perhaps the district's research unit or Institutional Research Review Board. In these situations, and many similar ones, you'll need a *gatekeeper letter* to request permission to obtain access to members of your target audience. Gatekeepers include people who do not respond to your questionnaire, but who must give permission for you to contact members of your target audience. Gatekeepers include parents, school administrators, and teachers. If your target audience is students, it's also important to obtain parental consent for their child's participation.

Let's look at how to write letters to these people, whom we'll call "gatekeepers."

Why Do You Need a Gatekeeper Letter for Parents?

The newly revised Elementary and Secondary Education Act signed into law in January 2002 requires school districts to formulate policies for notifying parents and for protecting families' privacy when students are asked to respond to questionnaires that contain questions about their sexual activities, political beliefs, religious practices, drug use, and a variety of other sensitive topics. Why might questionnaires be used to collect data on these topics? Schools are the best place to get an understanding of what's going on in the lives of adolescents. Even if your questionnaire does not contain sensitive questions, it's still a good idea to request permission of parents for their child to respond to your questionnaire.

Parents need to provide *informed consent* before their child can participate in a study. Potential adult respondents also need to provide informed consent. Guidelines for participation in a study such as a survey project have been published by the American Educational Research Association (AERA; 2000) and the American Psychological Association (APA; 2003). In addition, the Buckley Amendment, or the Family Education Rights and Privacy Act of 1974, protects an individual's records, such as those maintained by a school district. It states that records maintained for one purpose (such as grades, kept for the purpose of recording student performance) cannot be used for another purpose (such as a research study) without the consent of the student and, in the case of minors, of their parents.

Informed consent involves providing details about the study to the prospective participant, including the purpose of the study, how the study will be conducted, a description of any risks and benefits, an offer to answer questions about the study, and assurance that the person may withdraw from the study (not complete the questionnaire) at any time.

There are two ways of obtaining informed consent from parents for their child to respond to a questionnaire. One is *active permission* and the second is *passive permission.* For active permission, the parent must sign and return to the school (or survey project team) a form indicating that their child may respond to the questionnaire. However, with active consent, approximately 20% to 30% of parents do not return these forms. For passive consent, parents must sign and send back a form indicating their child may *not* participate in the survey project. Only 1% to 2% of parents return these opt-out forms, resulting in a greater number of students who can be invited to respond to questionnaires.

Letters to Parents for Consent

A letter to parents is required if your target group consists of minors (under 18 years of age). Parents need to know the following:

- Why their child is being asked to be in the study
- Why it's important for their child to be part of the study
- What the study is all about
- When and where the child will fill out the questionnaire
- How much time the questionnaire will take
- Who will have access to the information
- What will be done with the results (Will they be used to understand behaviors, create policy, and so on?)
- What benefits are expected from participation in the study
- Who to ask if they have questions
- That their child may choose not to respond to the questionnaire even if they give their permission

There must be a space where the parents can sign, indicating that they give permission for their child to be invited to participate in the study. If you are using the passive permission approach, ask parents to sign and return the letter only if they do *not* want their child to respond to the questionnaire. Even if parents give permission for their child to complete the questionnaire, the child can choose to refuse. Make provisions for students who opt out by suggesting they work on their homework assignments or some other activity while the other students are completing the questionnaire. Sample 5.1 provides a sample letter to parents.

Sample 5.1 Example Permission/Opt-Out Letter to Parents

RiverChase Middle School
123 Oak St.
Nellysford, VA 22978

Dear Parent:

Your child has been selected to participate in a project about study skills. As part of this project, we are asking that your child fill out a questionnaire in which they will describe their study habits and preferred study methods. Each student in the eighth grade will be invited to fill out this questionnaire.

The purpose of the study is to understand how students study—as they do their homework and as they prepare for tests. The results of the study will be used to help the students develop effective study habits that will help them be more successful in school.

The questionnaire should take approximately 10 minutes to complete and will be handed out during an extended homeroom period on March 10. Only the survey project team will have access to the results; in addition, the questionnaires will be anonymous as there will be no identifying information on the questionnaire. Responding to the questionnaire is voluntary.

If you do not want your child to participate in this study, please sign the form below and return it to your child's homeroom teacher by March 4. If you give your permission for your child to participate in the study, you do not need to return the form.

Thank you for your cooperation and participation in the study.

Yours truly,

Suzanne Brooks
RiverChase Guidance Counselor

****

Study Skills Project Opt-Out/Permission Slip

RETURN THIS FORM TO YOUR CHILD'S HOMEROOM TEACHER

I do *not* give my permission for my child to participate in the Study Skills Questionnaire to be administered during the homeroom period on March 10.

/S/ _____   _____
Parent Signature   Date

_____
Child's Name

Obtaining Permission to Conduct the Survey Project

In Chapter 1, you read about gaining needed approvals, including those from an institution's Research Review Board. Each school district or other entity your target audience comes from will have specific procedures for gaining the needed approvals and permissions. Obtain all needed approvals during the planning phase. If you are a student or professor at a college or university, you will also need permission from your institution's Research Review Board before you can contact the school district to request their permission to administer your questionnaire.

Writing Effective Letters to Gatekeepers

The gatekeeper may know you only through your letter and will judge you (and your survey project) accordingly. If your letter is sloppy, the gatekeeper may assume that the rest of your work will be sloppy also and will be unlikely to grant access to the target group.

A good gatekeeper letter should conform to these guidelines:

- Use a business letter format.
- Spell the person's name correctly.
- Have no spelling, grammar, syntax, or typographical errors in the letter.

A gatekeeper letter should provide information to the gatekeeper about the following:

- Why it is important for them to agree to the study
- What's in it for them (benefits of the study)
- How much time it will take for a respondent to complete the questionnaire
- What the logistics are for doing the questionnaire (Will their time and staff be required?)
- Why their school or organization was chosen
- The purpose of the questionnaire
- What you plan to do with the results
- When you will contact them to answer any questions they may have about your survey project

Start out "selling" your project, then request permission, and then provide the details about how you propose to distribute the questionnaires and gather the information.

Include a copy of the questionnaire with the gatekeeper letter so that person will know exactly what you are asking respondents to do. Remember that it's critical that the questionnaire format be professional and free of errors. If you are using a Web-based questionnaire, provide the URL so the gatekeeper can review the questionnaire. If the questionnaire is not yet on the Web, provide a paper copy, and indicate your plans for delivering the questionnaire via the Web.

Sample 5.2 provides an example of a model cover letter for a gatekeeper.

Sample 5.2 Example of Model Cover Letter for a Gatekeeper

National Commission of Child Study
107 E Broad Street, Washington, DC 20003

October 1, 2003

Carla C. Lewis, Principal
Northside High School
1245 Swift Lane
South Beach, NC 27064

Dear Ms. Lewis,

The National Commission of Child Study has commissioned a questionnaire to determine levels of parent involvement in their child's education. Your school was chosen as representative of medium-sized schools in your district. Results from the study will be used to describe patterns of parent involvement and to make recommendations for ways for parents to become more involved with their child's school. A set of results will be provided for your school if you choose to participate. We very much would like for your school to participate in this important study.

The questionnaire will require approximately 15 minutes for the parents to complete. We will provide all the materials required for the study, including an envelope for parents to return the questionnaire directly to the research team. We ask that homeroom teachers distribute the questionnaires to their classes for the child to take home to their parents during the week of October 15. All responses will be kept confidential; results will be reported for the group as a whole.

I will contact you early next week to provide any additional information you may require. A copy of the questionnaire and letter to the parents is enclosed for your review. Thank you in advance for your cooperation.

Yours truly,

Jessica Blake
Senior Research Coordinator

 HINT: Think like a marketing executive: The potential respondent is your customer. What needs does the customer have that responding to your questionnaire could fulfill?

◆ **CREATING COVER LETTERS AND INVITATIONS**

STEP 10: CREATE COVER LETTERS AND INVITATIONS

Let's begin by learning how to create cover letters and invitations that will result in a high response rate.

The adage *You only have one chance to make a good first impression* is particularly true of the invitation and cover letter.

> **You have less than one minute to "sell" your questionnaire and convince the person to become a respondent.**

You usually have less than one minute to grab the potential respondent's attention and convince him or her to read the rest of the invitation or cover letter and respond to your questionnaire. Therefore, your first contact with a potential questionnaire respondent is critical to the overall success of your survey project.

The following terms indicate the distinction between contacting respondents for paper-based questionnaires and Web-based questionnaires:

Cover letter: Used with paper-based questionnaires, whether the questionnaire is sent through the mail or administered in a group setting.

Invitation: Used with e-mail and Web questionnaires—the person is invited to complete an e-mail or Web-based questionnaire. The invitation provides the same type of information as the cover letter.

The cover letter (or invitation) is essentially a marketing piece. You're selling something, and you want to make sure you meet the "customer's" needs. In this case, the customer is the potential questionnaire respondent.

> HINT: In the first paragraph of the cover letter or invitation, preferably in the first sentence, answer the question: "What's in it for me?"

Critical Elements of a Successful Cover Letter or Invitation

Your cover letter or invitation should include the following:

- The reason the person should complete your questionnaire, or what's in it for them
- The purpose of the study

- Why the person was chosen
- Why responding to the questionnaire is important
- About how long it will take to complete the questionnaire
- When the questionnaire should be returned (due date)
- How the respondents should return it (prepaid envelope? give to the teacher?)
- Assurances of confidentiality of data and anonymity of information
- Who the person can contact if he or she has questions about the survey project
- Information about incentives—if you're using them (see discussion of incentives in Chapter 7, "Maximizing Your Response Rate: Collecting the Data")
- How the respondents can obtain a copy of the results (if you want to provide this option)

In addition to these key elements, your invitation or cover letter should be

- *Brief.* Use a maximum of one page. Shorter is better.
- *Informative.* Key points should be covered succinctly: Why was the person chosen? What is the purpose of the survey project?
- *Interesting.* Keep the readers' attention and motivate them to respond to the questionnaire.
- *Persuasive.* What's in it for the respondent? Why is it important for the person to respond?
- *Motivating.* What emotional, altruistic, or other reason is there for the person to complete the questionnaire?

 HINT: Put a distinctive logo on everything you send—the pre-announcement of the questionnaire, the cover letter, the questionnaire, and the follow-up reminders.

Things to Avoid: Learn From Other's Experiences!

- Never start a cover letter with "I"—focus on the recipient, not yourself.
- Don't use "hope" or "hopeful." Stronger words encourage participation.
- Proofread the letter *very* carefully. Grammatical, syntax, or typographical errors show sloppy work; why should the respondent spend time responding to a questionnaire when the survey project team didn't take the time to ensure the quality of the cover letter?
- Use the letterhead of the organization sponsoring the questionnaire.
- Remember to include the survey project's logo (if you have one) so that respondents can connect all communications from the survey project team.

Activity

Following is an activity for you to practice identifying which elements of a good cover letter are missing and to write a revised cover letter that meets the guidelines of good practice.

Using the guidelines presented earlier, identify the challenges in the cover letter in Sample 5.3.

Sample 5.3 Activity: Creating a Winning Cover Letter

TO: School Counselors

FROM: Mary Ann Jeffries, Harding Elementary School

I am a Special Education teacher with the XYZ Township School District and a graduate student at State University. My matriculation is in the field of counseling. I would like to specialize in and concentrate on counseling people with disabilities.

As a graduate student, I was asked to design a questionnaire to collect data for one of my research courses. I have chosen the Metro County area of counselors for narrowing or isolating my data, focusing on Metro County alone; later, I would like to expand to other counties or states.

Your help in filling out this questionnaire would be greatly appreciated and, in the long run, can help other counselors who are interested in helping those people with disabilities, as a lifelong career.

This questionnaire will take only a few minutes of your time to complete. A prepaid envelope is enclosed for the returned questionnaire. If you have questions about the study, I will be happy to answer them. Thank you for your cooperation. Please return it as soon as possible or at your earliest convenience.

Compare your answers with those in Box 5.2 at the end of the chapter.

The cover letter in Sample 5.4 was used in a survey project conducted by a university that was evaluating the effectiveness of its teacher education program. The target audience included the principals and department heads of schools where program graduates were currently employed.

Sample 5.4 Example of Good Cover Letter

State University
3000 Broad Street, Trenton, NJ 08616
October 1, 2003

Dr. Peter Germaine
Social Studies Department
Oceanside High School
South Beach, New Jersey 07191

Dear Dr. Germaine:

The Department of Teacher Education at State University prepares over 100 student teachers every year to teach in the public and private schools of New Jersey. We want our graduates to be well prepared to teach in today's schools. Some of our graduates are currently teaching in the Social Studies Department at Oceanside High School, and we'd like your views on what we can do to improve the quality of our training program. Your responses to the enclosed questionnaire will help us evaluate our current program and plan for revisions in the coming academic year. We will also provide you with a copy of the results of our study.

We realize your schedule is a busy one and that your time is valuable, but we are sure that you want to improve the quality of teacher training as much as we do. Responding to the questionnaire should take less than 15 minutes. Please complete the questionnaire and return it in the enclosed, stamped, pre-addressed envelope by October 15th. Your responses will be kept confidential; we ask for no identifying information on the questionnaire form. The University's Research and Human Subjects Review Committee has approved this study.

Thank you in advance for your cooperation. If you have any questions about this project, please call me at 835-3045.

Yours truly,

Dorothy C. Moore, Ph.D.
Chair of the Department

Sample 5.5 provides an example of a cover letter for in-person administration.

Context: A small group of teachers is working with the school's guidance counselor to understand students' study habits so they can determine what study skills are most effective. The questionnaire is a needs assessment of study skills. A packet consisting of the cover letter (following) and the questionnaire is given to students attending their homeroom class on the day the questionnaire is administered (if they have parental permission to participate in the survey project).

Sample 5.5 Example of Cover Letter for In-Person Administration of a Questionnaire

Dear Student:

Have you ever wondered whether the time you spend studying is used efficiently? We're asking each eighth-grade student to tell us about how he or she studies and what ways of studying he or she finds to be most effective. We've developed a short questionnaire to gather information about your study skills and study habits. We will use this information to create some study skills tips—and if there is sufficient interest, we will also provide some special classes during study halls.

We really need you to answer each of the questions on the short question-naire. It should take you less than 10 minutes to complete the survey. Do not put your name on the questionnaire—all results will be analyzed together for all of the eighth-grade class. If you choose not to complete the questionnaire, please work quietly on your homework.

When you have completed the questionnaire, please place it in the box on your homeroom teacher's desk.

Thank you for your participation!

Suzanne Brooks
RiverChase Guidance Counselor

Sample 5.6 provides a script for a teacher administering a questionnaire in class. A script provides the text of what the person administering the questionnaire should say. When you contact the person who will administer the questionnaire for you, provide details about the purpose of the survey project and answer any questions that person has. Help him or her anticipate questions the participants may have, and provide information necessary to answer these questions. Encourage that person to use the script provided to ensure that all questionnaires are administered in the same way.

Context: Homeroom teachers have agreed to administer the questionnaire for the study skills project during a homeroom period. They were provided with the following script. (Note: This script is in addition to the cover letter, shown in Sample 5.5, provided to the students.)

Sample 5.6 Example of Script for Administering a Questionnaire in Class

About a week ago, each of you were given a letter to give to your parents about the study skills project. If your parents signed a form asking that you *not* complete the questionnaire, you can work on your homework while the other students complete the short questionnaire.

The purpose of the questionnaire is to gather information about how you study. We know that some of you spend many hours on your homework assignments while others of you spend less time. But it's not the amount of time you spend doing your homework—it's how you use that time. We'd like to know how you study—what you do to get your homework done.

The questionnaire is short—it will take you about 10 minutes. Your answers will be anonymous—don't put your name on the questionnaire. A small group of teachers will work with Ms. Brooks to create some study skills tips—and if enough of you are interested, some classes—to help you use your study time wisely. If you choose not to complete the questionnaire, please work quietly on your homework.

Do you have any questions before I give you a copy of the questionnaire? When you complete your questionnaire, please place it in the box on my desk.

Critical Components of a Successful Invitation for a Web-Based Questionnaire

E-mail invitations need the same strong marketing flavor as a letter for a paper-based questionnaire. However, short paragraphs and bulleted lists are more effective than long paragraphs of text. Usually, two paragraphs provide the necessary information, which must include the purpose of the questionnaire and why it's important for the person to respond. You can provide additional detail on the introductory page of the questionnaire on the Web site. The invitation should be informative, interesting, and persuasive.

Following are the required contents of an e-mail invitation:

- *Selection:* With all the spamming going on, let the person know how you selected him or her. Include the name of the survey project sponsor in the subject line of the e-mail, such as "A request from RiverChase Elementary School" or "We need your opinion!"
- *Project contact:* Provide the name and phone number of someone to contact for questions respondents may have about the survey project.
- *Due date:* Clearly state when the respondent must complete and return the questionnaire.
- *Incentives:* Offer information about incentives—if you use them. Refer to the discussion of incentives in Chapter 7, "Maximizing Your Response Rate: Collecting the Data."

For a questionnaire where the respondent must access the Web, the invitation must also include the following:

- A link to the URL—so potential respondents can get to the questionnaire
- Technical support contact—in case the person can't access the URL
- Password—if one is required for access to your questionnaire
- Availability period—the dates that the questionnaire will be available on the Web

Sample 5.7 provides an example of an e-mail invitation.

Sample 5.7 Example of E-mail Invitation

Subject line on email: A request from South Brook School District

Dear Parent,

We need your help! We need 10 minutes of your time! The South Brook School District is developing activities that will permit parents to become more actively involved in their children's education. We'd like your feedback to help us in our planning.

- In what kinds of activities would you like to participate?
- What limitations do you have—time of day, need child care, etc.?

From October 15th though November 1st, the questionnaire will be available on our school's Web site, www.southbrookschools.tn.edu. Please plan time to go to the Web site to respond to the questionnaire. Your input will allow us to create parent programs that are responsive to your needs.

If you have questions about the project, or cannot access the Web site, please call me at 567-1212 or send me an email at jdoyle@southbrookschools.tn.edu. Thank you for your help!

James Doyle,

Project Coordinator
South Brook School District
2210 Brookside Avenue
Monroe, TN 37024

Using Web-Based Questionnaires With No Invitations

 Some Web-based questionnaires do not have invitations because the survey project team is unable to identify and contact members of the target audience. An example is a questionnaire posted on a school district's Web site open to all community members or questionnaires posted on a professional education association's Web site.

When you post your questionnaire to your Web site, you need to plan for two things: letting people know the questionnaire is there and controlling access. These might seem like contradictory goals, but you want the right people to respond to the questionnaire. And you want them to respond only once—especially if there's a valuable incentive!

Publicizing the availability of a Web-based questionnaire can be done with fax "blasts," links from related Web sites with a brief paragraph about the survey project, notices in local newsletters or parent communications, or publicity at conferences. These types of communication depend on audience and timing. For example, some school districts use Web-based questionnaires to gather information from parents, students, educators, and interested community members on a regular basis, so members of these target audiences are likely to expect notification about the availability of these questionnaires.

What if you want to control access to your questionnaire? You can do two things: The first is to set the meta tags for the Web page where the questionnaire begins so it's not picked up by Web search engines. (If you're not familiar with meta tags or search engines, we suggest you work with a Web consultant to help you with your Web-based questionnaire. That person will help with the technical aspects—you'll still need to create the questionnaire, invitation, and so forth.) The second is to use a filter question to determine if the potential respondent has the experience, knowledge, or other demographic characteristic (such as residing in a particular school district—see Chapter 4, "Putting the Questionnaire Together," for details and examples of filter questions) that you require. If someone does not have this necessary characteristic, you can have a note pop up thanking the person for his or her interest but blocking further access to the questionnaire.

Characteristics of Respondents for a Web-Based Questionnaire

When you don't invite specific participants to respond to your questionnaire, you need to know who's responding. You can do this with a short set of demographic questions at the beginning of the questionnaire. The position of the demographic questions on a Web-based questionnaire with no invitation differs from the advice earlier to place the demographic questions at the end of the questionnaire. It's critically important to have this information because you cannot control who is being invited to respond to your questionnaire. You can require that people complete the demographic questions before they access the rest of the questions.

Access Control for Web-Based Questionnaires

When you want to make sure that people don't respond to your questionnaire more than once, you can use "cookies." When a respondent completes the questionnaire and presses the "Submit" button, a cookie is placed on his system. If the person tries to take the questionnaire again, the system sees the cookie and will not allow the person to access the questionnaire. But some people have their browser set to not accept cookies. In this case, you'll need to depend on the information in the demographic questions to determine who is responding to your questionnaire and whether you should include their data in your analyses.

> *Cookies* store user profile information on the user's computer and enable a Web site to access it each time you go to that site. This is how a Web site recognizes users and is able to customize the user's experience.

For our case study, an invitation to participate in the Web-based questionnaire was sent home with the students.

Dear Parents,

We need your help! As you know, one of the goals of our school is to provide many opportunities for parents to participate in the "life of our school." How successful have we been in providing opportunities for you?

During the two-week period of October 1–October 15, we will post a questionnaire on our school's Web site (www.riverchase.va.edu). The purpose of the questionnaire is to determine current levels of parental participation in school activities and your satisfaction with those activities—and for parents who do not participate, to understand barriers to their participation. We'd also like to know how satisfied you are with the opportunities for involvement that are currently available, and what additional opportunities our school can provide that would be interesting to you.

Your response is important! Our goal is to have 100% parent participation to this important questionnaire! Based on the responses to the questionnaire, we will revise and update our participation opportunities for parents.

If you have questions about the project, or cannot access the questionnaire, please call me at 643-1234 or contact me via email at jgilbert@riverchase.edu.

Yours truly,

Jonathan Gilbert
Team Lead, PTO Survey Team

◆ THE RIGHTS OF RESPONDENTS

Earlier in this chapter, you learned about determining how many people to contact and creating winning cover letters and invitations; now let's consider the rights of those you invite to respond to your questionnaire.

Box 5.1 summarizes rights of respondents. Consider these carefully as you conduct your survey project.

Box 5.1   Questionnaire Respondent's Bill of Rights

Each person who chooses to respond to a questionnaire has a right to

- Be assured that his or her responses will be kept confidential
- Quit responding to the questionnaire at any time
- Be treated courteously in the tone of the request to respond to the questionnaire and in the thank-you at the end of the questionnaire
- Respond to a questionnaire that has well-written, interesting questions
- Respond to a questionnaire that is professional looking
- Respond to a questionnaire that is easy to navigate (e.g., clear directions, filter questions, skip patterns)
- Omit responses to very personal questions
- Know who (what group or what individual) will see the results of the questionnaire

Confidentiality and Anonymity

Questionnaire respondents have the right to have their responses kept confidential—that is, the individual responses cannot be attributed to the respondent. You can maintain confidentiality by assigning identification numbers rather than names to the questionnaires as you enter the data into your spreadsheet for analysis. When you report results, these should be at the group or subgroup level if you disaggregate your data (subgroups can be formed based on demographic characteristics). You must provide confidentiality of the data whether you use paper-based or Web-based questionnaires.

Anonymity means that you gather no information that could identify an individual respondent. You can easily do this with a paper-based questionnaire by not asking for the respondent's name or any other personal identification information. (You can still ask demographic questions so that you can form subgroups and describe the respondents.) Anonymity can also be achieved with a Web-based questionnaire by not asking for personal information, although some respondents question the anonymity due to the use of cookies (see earlier for a definition of a cookie). In this case, it's important that you provide assurances about confidentiality.

We've covered a lot in this chapter, and you should now have your plan for selecting the participants as well as the number of participants you should invite to receive the number of completed questionnaires you need. You should also have created the necessary gatekeeper letters, parent permission letters, cover letters, and invitations.

When these important activities are completed, you're ready to pilot test everything. But before you do, complete the following checklist to ensure that you're really ready!

Checklist for Identifying and Contacting Potential Respondents

Use the following checklist to help ensure that you have a good cover letter or invitation, and a solid plan for selecting the number of people required for your survey project.

❑ Has the response rate been estimated?

❑ Has the number of people to be contacted been determined, taking into account the sampling error and estimated response rate (with help from a statistician as needed)?

❑ Have the plans for disaggregating the data for your analyses been taken into account as the sample size was determined?

For a Web-based questionnaire:

❑ Has the method of contacting potential respondents been determined?

❑ Will this method (or methods) yield a sufficient number of respondents?

❑ Will sufficient demographic data be gathered so that you know who is responding to your questionnaire?

❑ If a letter to parents or guardians is needed, does it follow the examples provided in this chapter?

❑ If a gatekeeper letter is necessary, does it follow the examples provided in this chapter?

❑ Is the cover letter or e-mail invitation clear, interesting, and motivating?

E-mail invitation for e-mail or Web-based questionnaire:

❑ Does the invitation clearly state why the person was chosen to participate in the study?

❑ Does the invitation clearly indicate when the questionnaire must be returned (or the availability period if it's on the Web)?

❑ Does the invitation say that responses to the questionnaire are kept confidential?

❑ Does the invitation say how the respondent can learn the results of the study?

❑ If the questionnaire is on the Web, is the URL provided?

❑ Does the invitation indicate who to contact if the respondent experiences technical challenges in responding to the questionnaire?

Sample 5.8   Activity: Creating a Winning Cover Letter: Suggested Answers

As you read the cover letter, did you find it interesting? Would it have persuaded you to respond to the questionnaire?

Let's first look at the specific challenges in this letter and then at a revised version that should yield a better response rate.

There is no letterhead or logo on the cover letter.

TO: School Counselors

FROM: Mary Ann Jeffries, Harding Elementary School

The recipient's name should be included—use the mail-merge function of your word processor to personalize the letters.

I am a Special Education teacher with the XYZ Township School District and a graduate student at State University. My matriculation is in the field of counseling. I would like to specialize in and concentrate on counseling people with disabilities.

The first paragraph started with "I"—and sounds more like a letter of application than a cover letter inviting a person to respond to a questionnaire. This paragraph should be deleted. Never start a cover letter with "I" or include background of the person sending the cover letter. Focus instead on the purpose of the survey project, the reason the person is being invited to respond to the survey, why it's important for him or her to complete the questionnaire, and what's in it for that person.

As a graduate student, I was asked to design a questionnaire to collect data for one of my research courses. I have chosen the Metro County area of counselors for narrowing or isolating my data, focusing on Metro County alone; later, I would like to expand to other counties or states.

That the researcher is a graduate student who plans to expand the project later is not relevant.

Your help in filling out this questionnaire would be greatly appreciated and, in the long run, can help other counselors who are interested in helping those people with disabilities, as a lifelong career.

It's challenging to determine "what's in it for the respondent"; perhaps the results of the questionnaire will provide information to help counselors work with people with disabilities, but that's not completely clear. It appears that the person was chosen because he or she is a school counselor. There needs to be a bit more about why the study is important.

This questionnaire will take only a few minutes of your time to complete. A prepaid envelope is enclosed for the returned questionnaire. If you have questions about the study, I will be happy to answer them. Thank you for your cooperation. Please return it as soon as possible or at your earliest convenience.

Provide a time estimate—10 minutes? 30 minutes? What does "a few minutes" mean? We know how the questionnaire should be returned—in the prepaid envelope provided—but we don't know when it's due. The person is told that he or she will get answers to any questions about the study—but there is no information about how to contact the researcher.

Sample 5.9 Example of Rewritten Cover Letter

This is an example of the rewritten letter from the activity on creating a winning cover letter

Letterhead

Mary Jones
Counselor, Rockville High School
1270 Old School Road
Madison, VA 22983

Dear Ms. Jones,

As a counselor, you are aware of the value of resources about the best practices in counseling. You've been selected to respond to a survey about working with students with disabilities because of your current work at Rockville High School. The purpose of the questionnaire is to identify challenges counselors such as yourself have encountered in working with this student population, as well as best practices that you've successfully used with these students. The Virginia State Guidance Counselors Association is sponsoring this study.

The questionnaire will take about 15 minutes to complete. Please return the completed survey by February 15, using the enclosed prepaid envelope. In return for your time in completing the survey, we will send you a summary of the results.

If you have questions about this project, please contact me at 555-2351 and I will be happy to talk with you.

Yours truly,

Mary Ann Jeffries
Team Lead,
Counseling Survey Project

6

Pilot Testing the Questionnaire

W ould you buy a car without taking a test drive? Would you buy a software program that had not been tested by the manufacturer? You most likely would not, and questionnaire development is no different. This step is so critical that if you don't have the time and resources to conduct a pilot test of all pieces of your survey project, then you probably should not be doing the project!

This chapter provides suggestions for conducting your pilot test, including evaluating all aspects of the questionnaire (questions, response choices, directions) and the cover letter. It also provides suggestions for evaluating the reliability of your questionnaire. (See Chapter 4, "Putting the Questionnaire Together," for more information on evaluating the quality of your questionnaire.) You should also pilot test your coding of the responses and your data analysis—just to make sure that everything works as you intended.

 STEP 11: CONDUCT A THOROUGH PILOT TEST OF ALL ASPECTS OF THE SURVEY PROJECT

Pilot testing provides answers to the following questions:

- Are all the questions clearly worded?
- Might some of them be sensitive—so that respondents might skip them?
- Are some of the questions too difficult to understand—even for a willing respondent?
- Are the directions clear—so that respondents clearly understand what is expected of them?
- Do the skip patterns work as intended?

The bottom line is that a pilot test helps ensure that you'll be getting the data you need to make your decision, assuming that you have a good response rate. And it's the only way to find out if everything works—including the data analysis.

Without proper checking, errors go undetected. With good procedures and planning, most errors can be avoided. Murphy's law: If anything can go wrong, it will—and a corollary, if you didn't check on it, it did.

Benefits of Conducting a Pilot Test

It's rarely possible to foresee all potential misunderstandings or biasing effects of questions and procedures, but conducting a pilot test will mitigate issues and enable you to do the following:

- Determine whether the cover letter or invitation is likely to work—that is, is the "marketing" message clear and persuasive?
- Identify problems with question content
  - Confusion with the overall meaning of a question
  - Misinterpretation or misunderstanding of individual terms or concepts
- Identify skip patterns that don't work as you intended
- Determine whether formatting is "user friendly"
- Find out if everything "works"
- Gather evidence about the reliability of your questionnaire
- Determine whether the coding for the analyses works as intended
- Conduct a dress rehearsal to see that everything connects together as you planned

When you have completed the pilot test and made the necessary revisions to any elements of the questionnaire, then it's time to produce the questionnaire so that it's ready for distribution.

In this chapter, you will find a series of questions to guide your pilot test. You'll also find descriptions of some of the different methods available for conducting a pilot test.

There are several methods of conducting a pilot test, including focus groups, "structured or think-aloud" interviews, respondent debriefings, and analysis of nonresponse rates to the pilot test.

> ## If you can't do a pilot test, don't do the survey project!

Failure to include a pilot test may mean a lower response rate if the potential respondents don't understand what they are to do and questionable data if respondents misinterpret the questions. In spite of its importance, pilot testing is often done in a hurried, nonsystematic manner and is the element most likely to be squeezed out due to cost and time pressures.

Questions to Guide Planning Your Pilot Test

What elements of a survey project should be pilot tested? Every aspect of the survey project, from cover letter to the questionnaire to the data analysis and reporting plans!

- Cover letter/invitation: Will it motivate response to the survey?
- Questionnaire
  - Length
  - Layout
    - Is there enough space for any open-ended questions?
    - Is the sequencing of topics and questions logical?
    - Is the overall look professional and pleasing?
  - Question format: Where does the person enter his or her response? If you use a grid format for a question, will the participant understand how it works? Are you using any fixed-sum format items? Will the participant experience any difficulties with these?
  - Directions: Are there directions for the overall questionnaire, plus directions when there are changes, such as different response scales or different sections? What about directions for the skip patterns—will the respondent end up where you intended for him or her to be?
- Questions: The goal is to determine whether there is a common understanding of the question. If participants are confused about the meaning of any question, gather suggestions for revising the question.
  - Are there any ambiguous or confusing questions?
  - Are there any terms or concepts that the members of the pilot group might not understand? Any potentially unfamiliar terms? Any acronyms that should be defined?
  - Does the person understand the question in the way that you intended?
  - Test questions for clarity and function: Will the answers to these questions provide the information needed to achieve the objectives of the survey project?
- Response choices and scale anchors
  - Do the pilot test participants understand the response choices?
  - Were they able to identify a response choice that matched the way they would answer the question?
  - If you used scale anchors for a rating scale, were these clear and comprehensive?
- Data analysis
  - Do the coding and tabulating work as planned?
  - Do the data analysis procedures work as planned?
  - Will the questionnaire provide the data you need to inform the data-based decisions you need to make?

What method should be used to conduct the pilot test? There are several available, as described later. Determine what best fits your project.

Who should do the pilot testing? The survey team coordinates the pilot testing and identifies participants.

Who should be the subjects in the pilot test? The subjects should be persons representative of your target audience but who are not part of your sample; you should also include people with skills in survey research and measurement.

How large a sample is needed for the pilot test? You'll need 10 to 30 people depending on the complexity of the survey. You may need to conduct a second pilot test if significant changes result from the first pilot test.

Selecting Participants for the Pilot Test

There should be two types of people in the pilot test: (a) those who are representative of the target audience and (b) survey and measurement specialists. One or two questionnaire or measurement specialists should be sufficient to provide feedback. If your target audience consists of several segments, such as teachers, parents, and community members, you'll need participants from each of these segments. In addition, the sponsoring organization should participate in the pilot test to provide detailed feedback.

Personal contact is the best way to solicit participation. You don't need many people—but they need to be able to spend the time to provide thoughtful feedback. The number of participants also depends on the complexity of the questionnaire. Those that are long and complex, such as those with skip patterns or multiple sections, will require more participants to ensure that you have a range of participants who represent the range of participants who will be invited to respond to the questionnaire.

◆ METHODS TO CONDUCT THE PILOT TEST

Focus Groups

A focus group is a form of in-depth interviewing with a small group of persons who are representative of the population or who have detailed knowledge of the population. Focus groups generate data through the give-and-take of group discussion. Listening as people share and compare different points of view provides great information—not just about what they think, but why they think the way they do. A skilled facilitator, preferably someone other than the person who wrote the questions, must conduct a focus group. The quality of the information from a focus group depends on the skills of the facilitator. There should also be a second person to assist and to take notes.

During the focus group, gather information about formatting, questions and response options, and appearance of the questionnaire—all the elements listed earlier in this chapter. The facilitator can probe participants' understanding of the questions and response options. In addition, the focus group participants should review the cover letter or invitation.

A focus group lets you observe a high level of interaction for a limited period of time—usually 60 to 90 minutes. The give-and-take in the group may help you identify insights less accessible with individual reviews of the draft questionnaire.

Structured or "Think-Aloud" Interviews

These are one-on-one structured interviews in which the respondent describes thoughts as he or she responds to the questions. These are also called "think-aloud" interviews. You can find out potential problems with the questions, including the wording, the response choices, and the skip patterns if you use these. You can also determine whether the directions are clear—if the person needs to ask for help in working through the questionnaire, you know the directions are not as clear as they need to be! A small number of these interviews, between 10 and 15, can yield sufficient information so that you have a good sense about whether your questionnaire is ready to be sent to the target audience. You can do probing questions, such as asking how people chose their answers, how they interpreted reference periods, or what they thought a particular term meant.

You can also ask for suggestions to clarify the questions or the directions based on participants' input. If a respondent seems confused by a question, ask him or her to paraphrase the question. If the paraphrase is not what was intended, talk through the best way to phrase the question to achieve the desired understanding of the question. Requesting the participant to paraphrase some of the more complex questions will help ensure that the questions are clear and are being interpreted as intended.

 For a Web-based questionnaire, you can sit beside the person as he or she goes through the questionnaire online to observe reactions to the directions, the questions, and the navigation. You can also observe the respondent's body language as he or she answers the questions and navigates the questionnaire. Are there any points in the questionnaire where the respondent appeared to be confused by the directions or the questions? Are there any places where the respondent appeared to be frustrated by the navigation?

> HINT: Involve people representative of the target audience, questionnaire experts, and sponsors in the pilot test.

Depending on the topic of the questionnaire, you might also consider including two or three people who know nothing about the specific topic. Why, you might ask, include someone in the pilot test who knows nothing about the topic? That person's "naive" perspective can uncover unclear wording that members of the pilot participants from the target audience may miss completely.

Respondent Debriefings

Debriefings are follow-up questions that you ask pilot test participants after they complete the questionnaire. The primary purpose is to determine whether respondents understood concepts and questions in the same way that the survey project sponsors intended. Sometimes results of debriefings identify superfluous questions that can be eliminated.

A critical aspect of successful respondent debriefing is a clear understanding by question designers and survey project team members of potential problems. This enables the development of good debriefing questions. Ideas about potential problems can come from analyses of data from previous questionnaires, a careful review of questionnaires, or from previous experience on other survey projects. Just be sure you follow up with the participants so that you have enough information to revise the questions.

Analysis of Nonresponse Rates

Participants in the pilot test might skip items—they might not understand the question, they might be confused, or they might find the question offensive in some way. These questions should be identified and further probing done to determine the reason for the question's being skipped.

Refusal rates can determine how often respondents find certain questions too sensitive or too confusing to answer. You'll need to do follow-up here to understand how to reword the questions.

If you use "Don't know" as a response choice, the number of times the pilot participants select these choices can help determine how difficult a task is for respondents to do. If there are a lot of "Don't know" responses, the question might be too difficult. For example, if participants are asked to rate the barriers to successful job performance, a lot of "Don't know" responses can indicate that the choices are not appropriate. Explore with the respondents why they selected "Don't know" and make the needed revisions.

Suggested Procedures for Conducting a Pilot Test Using a Focus Group or Structured Interview

Ask the participants to complete the questionnaire as if they were one of the respondents, using the following procedures:

- Read the stem, but cover the choices and write out the answer.
- Uncover the choices and see if the written answer fits or matches one of the choices.
- If the answer does not fit or match one of the choices, ask the respondent what his or her understanding of the item was.
- If an item confuses a respondent, ask that person to explain what was confusing.
- If a respondent had to make an assumption about what was being asked, ask what assumptions he or she made.
- If a respondent has any concerns about the questionnaire, such as the way the questions are asked, what experiences the respondent must have in order to provide valid responses, or the amount of reading or reading level of the questionnaire, ask him or her to discuss these concerns with the survey project team (or interviewer).

◆ PILOT TESTING FOR WEB-BASED QUESTIONNAIRES

Web-based questionnaires need the same careful checking of the wording of the questions, the appropriateness of the response choices and scale anchors, and the clarity of the directions. And there are other things to consider as well.

Web-based questionnaires permit use of multimedia and graphics in the questionnaire. However, some potential respondents may have bandwidth challenges. That is, they may be using a dial-up modem with a very slow line speed, and downloading complex graphics or multimedia may take several minutes—in some cases, perhaps up to 30 minutes. As a result, the potential respondent might quit responding to the questionnaire. Limit graphics to what is required—and pilot test the questionnaire using different access methods, including dial-up modems with slow speeds as well as high-speed connections such as LAN, DSL, or cable modems.

During the pilot test, in addition to the questions, response choices and scale anchors, and directions, ask pilot test participants to check the following:

- *Access:* Do all connections work, or is access limited to one browser (e.g., some things don't work with Netscape if they are created with Internet Explorer and vice versa)?
- *Navigation:* How does the respondent move from page to page?
- *Directions:* Are the directions provided at the top of each screen?
- *Response mode:* If both radio buttons and drop-down response lists are used, are the directions clear about how to respond to each question?
- *Response scales:* Are these always in view as the respondent answers the questions?
- *Review previous responses:* Can the respondent revisit screens of the questionnaire that have been completed using a back button or other mechanism?
- *Required questions:* Are there some questions that require responses before moving forward? Do these work as planned?
- *Fixed-sum questions:* Are the fixed-sum questions working as planned? For example, do some questions require the respondent to estimate percentages, such as the percentage of time spent on various activities? If the percentages do not sum to 100%, a message should display asking the respondent to check his or her numbers—and not let the respondent move forward until the numbers do sum to 100%.
- *Submit button:* Does the submit button work as planned? Does a "Thank-you" note display at the end?
- *Database:* Do the respondent data flow to the database as planned? Do all the connections work?

HINT: During the pilot test, access the Web-based questionnaires from different browsers and line speeds.

◆ TESTING THE DATA ANALYSIS

As you conduct your pilot test, you'll be gathering responses to the questions from the pilot test participants. Use these data to evaluate how well your data analysis plans meet your needs. Will you have the data you need to make your data-based decisions?

◆ EVALUATING THE QUALITY OF YOUR QUESTIONNAIRE: RELIABILITY

In Chapter 4, "Putting the Questionnaire Together," we talked about the information you'll need to evaluate the quality of your questionnaire: evidence of validity and reliability. Chapter 4 provided some suggestions about how to gather evidence of the content validity. This chapter provides some suggestions for gathering evidence of reliability. Note that because this is the pilot test, the evidence is preliminary, so consider it carefully before you make changes to the questions based on the reliability analyses from the pilot test. Evaluate the reliability of your questionnaire when you complete your data collection. Whether you do your reliability analyses during the pilot-testing phase or after the data collection, the procedures for analyses are the same.

As noted in Chapter 4, two kinds of reliability evidence are appropriate for questionnaires: test-retest (appropriate for all types of questionnaires) and internal consistency (appropriate for Likert-type rating scales). To gather evidence for test-retest reliability, you'll need to work with a small group of 10 to 15 participants who will respond to the questionnaire two times, with at least a week between responses. You'll need to keep track of the pairs of questionnaires from each respondent because you'll be comparing the individual responses. You might set up a table such as the one shown in Table 6.1.

Table 6.1   Data for Evaluating the Reliability of a Questionnaire

Question	Respondent 1		Respondent 2		Respondent 3	
	Time 1	Time 2	Time 1	Time 2	Time 1	Time 2
Q1						
Q2						
Q3						
Q4						
Q5						
Q6						

Once you have the data in the format as shown in Table 6.1, determine how many pairs of responses to each item were the same, how many were off by 1 point and how many were off by more than 1 point. Ideally, less than 5% of the pairs should be off by 1 point or more. If several questions are off by more than 1 point, review these questions carefully. You may want to talk with some of the participants to understand why they changed their responses.

A second way to evaluate the reliability evidence is to correlate the responses from all participants for a single item. Correlation coefficients should be in the upper .70s or higher. Items with lower correlations should be evaluated for clarity and appropriateness for the target audience. You can use a spreadsheet program such as Excel to calculate a correlation coefficient, or you can work with a consultant to help you with the statistics.

If you are using a Likert-type rating scale, you should consider evaluating the scale's internal consistency or how well all the items are measuring the same construct. This calculation is more complex; you should use a statistical analysis software package such as SPSS or SAS. These statistical packages have programs that will calculate the reliability coefficient for you. As with the test-retest coefficient, the internal consistency coefficient should be in the upper .70s or higher.

Paper-Based Questionnaires

To pilot test the data analysis portion of the survey project, enter the data from the pilot test respondents into the database you plan to use. For example, you might use a spreadsheet such as Lotus 1–2–3 or Excel. Or you may use a statistical analysis package such as SAS or SPSS. Go through the data coding and data entry steps. Does the layout of the questionnaire make it relatively easy to enter the data? Are all the data entry points consistently on one side of the questionnaire? Are there any places for potential confusion about how to enter the data? It's better to tweak the questionnaire layout now than risk data entry errors when you get the questionnaire responses back later.

Web-Based Questionnaires

 Web-based questionnaires are usually linked with a database so that results from the questionnaire flow directly into the database. To ensure that the data flow is correct, complete a few questionnaires, keeping track of the responses, then check the database to ensure that the responses in the database correspond to what was input.

When you have a small set of data in the database, perform whatever export function is required to move the data into the tool you'll use for analysis. As with the paper-based questionnaire, you can use either a spreadsheet or a statistical analysis software package. Make sure the export function is working properly.

STEP 12: USE THE INFORMATION FROM THE PILOT TEST TO MAKE NECESSARY REVISIONS AND PRODUCE THE QUESTIONNAIRE

You've worked hard to plan and conduct the pilot test. It's important that you carefully evaluate the results and make any needed changes. If the wording changes are minor, the survey project team can review these changes. However, if there are major changes and you've substantially revised several of the questions, used different scale anchors, revised the skip patterns, or rewritten the directions, then you should conduct a second pilot test. In this case, it's fine to go back to those who participated in the pilot test and ask them to review the revisions to ensure that their concerns have been addressed.

◆ PRODUCING THE QUESTIONNAIRE

After all the work you've put in so far, you're nearing the finish line! It's time to make copies of the questionnaire (for mail or face-to-face distribution) or prepare the computer file for use on a Web site or in an e-mail if you are collecting the responses electronically. Making copies of your questionnaire and cover letter and preparing the packages for distribution to potential respondents signals that you're ready for data collection! There are still some things to do, such as planning for maximizing your response rate by using prenotification and follow-ups (discussed in the next chapter). But you've already determined how many people to contact, so for paper-based questionnaires you know how many copies to make.

Making Paper Copies

Following are some suggestions to help make this part of your survey project go smoothly:

- Use good-quality paper, preferably white or ivory.
- Plan ahead for copying. Do you have requisitions, purchase orders, or what-ever you may need to get the copying done? If you're using a copy center, have you checked their requirements for turnaround time? Is the question-naire in the format the copy center needs?
- Plan how you will address the letters and envelops. Will you create individu-ally addressed cover letters, perhaps using mail merge software?
- Assemble the mailing list. What plans do you have for addressing the envelopes and preparing the return envelopes, if that's what you plan to use?
- Make plans for stuffing the envelopes, including the cover letter, question-naire, return envelope, and incentive (if used).
- Address one complete package of materials to yourself so that you can check on the amount of time mail delivery is taking.

The final step is to mail the questionnaires!

Launching a Web-Based Questionnaire

If you are using either e-mail or a Web-based mode of delivery, you should have made the arrangements to get the questionnaire into an e-mail or Web-ready format during the pilot test. At this point in the survey project, you'll need to be sure you've incorporated recom-mended changes, based on the results of the pilot test.

If you are using an e-mail invitation, do you have the e-mail addresses of the persons who will receive the questionnaire?

Depending on the number of people you'll be inviting to respond, you might want to stagger the delivery of the e-mail invitations so that you won't get too many people trying to access the server at the same time.

If you are using a Web-based questionnaire, you should have detailed plans in place for contacting potential respondents.

Now that you've completed your pilot testing and have made all needed changes to the questionnaire and cover letter, you're ready to distribute the questionnaire to the participants. But before you do that, take a moment to review the following checklist to ensure that you're really ready to continue.

Checklist for Pilot Testing

Use the following checklist to help ensure that you have completed all the elements of pilot testing, made the needed revisions, and produced the questionnaire so it's ready for distribution.

- ❑ Have you planned time for the pilot testing in the overall project schedule?
- ❑ Have you carefully planned to test all elements of the survey project?
- ❑ Have you identified participants who are representative of your target audience?
- ❑ Have you identified one or two questionnaire or measurement specialists to review the questionnaire and data analysis plan?
- ❑ Have you determined the best way to conduct the pilot test (e.g., focus group, structured interviews)?
- ❑ Have you checked all the components of the questionnaire?
  - ○ Cover letter and invitation
  - ○ Questions and responses
  - ○ Format, including skip patterns
  - ○ Directions
  - ○ Data analysis
- ❑ Did you gather evidence of the reliability of your questionnaire—and make changes to the questions as necessary?
- ❑ Did you gather evidence of the validity of your questionnaire?
- ❑ If you're using e-mail or a Web-based delivery, do you have the infrastructure in place to make this happen?
- ❑ If you are using paper copies, have you made arrangements with a copy center?
- ❑ For a paper-based questionnaire, have you included yourself on the list to receive the questionnaire so you can check mailing times?

7

Maximizing Your Response Rate

Collecting the Data

Congratulations! When you reach this point, you've already completed 75% of the steps required for a successful survey project! You've done your planning, written the questions, the directions, and the cover letter or invitation. You've formatted your questionnaire and conducted a pilot test. You've created a method to contact potential respondents by creating a mailing list or a process to contact potential respondents for a Web-based questionnaire. You've also determined how many people to invite to respond to your questionnaire. You're now ready to distribute your questionnaire and gather your data!

 ## STEP 13: DISTRIBUTE THE QUESTIONNAIRE AND GATHER THE DATA

This chapter provides suggestions for increasing your response rate by using prenotification and follow-up letters. It also offers some guidelines for handling the responses as they come in. But before you send out the questionnaire, let's look at ways that you can maximize your response rate.

◆ WHY DO PEOPLE NOT RESPOND TO QUESTIONNAIRES?

Think of questionnaires that you've received—whether a paper-based questionnaire or an invitation to respond to a Web-based questionnaire. Why did you decide not to respond? People whom you invite to respond to your questionnaire probably have some of the same reactions.

- The recipients are not interested. So if only those who are interested respond, what kind of bias might be present in your data? Results may overestimate degree of interest.
- Too much time is required to respond. It's not worth it to potential respondents to invest their time in responding to your questionnaire.
- The recipients are not convinced they need to or should respond. They don't see what's in it for them.
- The directions are confusing.
- The questionnaire came at a bad time, such as a busy time at work, the end of the semester, or just before a holiday break.
- The questionnaire had too many open-ended questions that would take too much effort to respond.

So now that we know some of the reasons people don't respond to questionnaires, let's focus on what you can do to encourage those who are invited to respond to your questionnaire—and maximize your response rate. You've already done several things to encourage a good response rate:

- Created a compelling cover letter or invitation
- Provided clear directions for all aspects of the questionnaire
- Limited the questionnaire to the essential questions so that the questionnaire is not so long that the respondent gets tired and quits partway through
- Created a pleasing format resulting in a professional-looking document
- Created a Web-based questionnaire with good design and easy navigation

◆ WAYS OF INCREASING RESPONSE RATES

But there are other things you can do, including the following:

- Send a prenotification for paper-based, e-mail, or Web-based questionnaires with invitations.
- Send out the questionnaire at the "right time" in participants' lives.
- Use incentives (if appropriate).
- Provide follow-ups to remind recipients of receiving your cover letter or invitation and encourage them to rearrange their priorities to respond to your questionnaire. This reminder is not intended to overcome resistance to responding to the questionnaire, because those who really don't want to respond will ignore follow-ups.

We'll consider each of these elements in this chapter.

 HINT: Plan in success factors to ensure you'll have a good response rate.

Send a Prenotification

Send a postcard alerting potential respondents that they will be receiving a questionnaire in the mail within the next week. Indicate why it's important for them to respond to the questionnaire when they receive it.

For a Web-based questionnaire for which you are sending e-mail invitations, send an e-mail with the same information as the postcard prenotification.

For Web-based questionnaires without a means of contacting members of your target group, there is no way to issue a prenotification. You'll need to rely on publicity to encourage people to go to the Web site and respond to the questionnaire.

For our case study, we will send a prenotification in a note home with each student; we will also send an e-mail to each parent for whom we have an e-mail address, and we will publicize the survey project at Back to School Night held the third week of September.

Following is the prenotification note that will be used.

Dear Parent:

We need your help! We are asking you to complete a questionnaire that will take about 15 minutes of your time. It will be time well spent.

From October 1 though October 15, the PTOs of the three elementary schools in Madison County will conduct a survey project. The questionnaire is anonymous and will ask for your opinions about activities our school provides for you to become involved in your child's education. Your feedback is critical as we continually strive to provide ways to work with you and your child to provide the best education possible.

Your input will enable us to provide more effective programs—ones that will best meet your needs. After the survey project concludes, we will communicate back to you our findings and action plans.

The invitation to participate and instructions will be sent on October 1. Please take time to complete this questionnaire as soon as you can, but no later than October 15.

Your opinions are essential and your participation will be greatly appreciated. Thank you.

The PTO Survey Project Team

Send Out the Questionnaire at the "Right Time" in the Participants' Lives

What's going on in the lives of the potential respondents that might influence their decision or availability to respond to your questionnaire? Respondents may include the following:

- Teachers
- Parents
- Students
- School administrators
- Workshop participants

For teachers, consider what's happening during the school year. Don't ask them to respond to a questionnaire at the beginning or near the end of a semester, or when there are districtwide activities going on such as statewide assessment or at the end of the school year. They are too busy doing their jobs to have the time to respond to a questionnaire.

For parents, avoid the end of a semester and the end of the school year when they might be helping their son or daughter with homework or major projects. Also avoid sending out your questionnaire just prior to a school vacation.

For students, avoid the end of a semester and the end of the school year when there might be examinations and major projects due. This is less true for younger children, but generally, there are few survey projects with questionnaires that focus solely on children in the lower elementary grades.

School administrators are busy most of the year but especially so prior to the beginning of the school year and at the end of the school year. Also be aware of what's happening in the community that will affect the workload of this target audience, such as a school bond issue or reporting results of a statewide assessment.

Questionnaires that follow up on some event should be administered at the conclusion of the event. If that's not possible, then send the questionnaires out the last day of the event so that participants have the questionnaires when they return home.

 HINT: Be sensitive to the lives of members of your target audience.

For a Web-based questionnaire, in addition to considering time of the year, you must also consider day of the week. The best response rates come when the invitations are e-mailed on Monday night to be in the recipients' readers on Tuesday morning. For reminders, also send these on a Monday. For most Web-based questionnaires, the optimum amount of time for the questionnaire to be available is 10 business days, starting on a Monday or Tuesday.

 We'll send our Web-based questionnaire out the first Monday of October—a month after school has started.

Use Incentives

Should you use incentives? Is it really necessary? As with so many other things, the answer is, "It depends." For paper-based questionnaires, enclosing a token such as a pen, a small amount of money, or a refrigerator magnet has been shown to increase response rates. Enclosing the incentive with the questionnaire yields higher response rates than promising to send an incentive when the questionnaire is returned. Entry into a raffle generally does not yield the response rates that other types of incentives do.

Using incentives with Web-based questionnaires is a bit trickier. How will you get the incentive to the respondent? If the Web-based questionnaire is not anonymous, then you can send the incentive to each person who returns the questionnaire. Another idea is to provide a coupon of some sort that appears after the person has hit the "submit" button. The respondent prints the coupon and uses it. But it appears that incentives for Web-based questionnaires are not necessary unless the questionnaire is very long or requires quite a bit of work and thought on the part of the respondent.

Whether to use an incentive depends in part on the existing motivation of the potential respondents. If the topic is interesting and meaningful, an incentive is probably not necessary. If your appeal is based on altruism, you probably don't need an incentive. Sometimes an offer of sharing the results serves as an adequate incentive.

Provide Follow-Ups

A key to success is follow up, which can include the following:

- A reminder postcard or e-mail
- A second copy of the questionnaire for a paper-based or e-mail questionnaire
- A follow-up note outlining value to the recipient of completing the questionnaire

> HINT: Follow up on nonrespondents. A low response rate does more damage to the credibility of survey project results than does a small sample with a high response rate.

For a Web-based questionnaire, 50% of the responses come within the first 24 hours, with the majority coming within four days. Sending a reminder a week after you've sent the e-mail invitation will result in another, smaller spike in responses.

For a paper-based questionnaire, send the reminder notices approximately 10 days after you've sent the initial questionnaire. If you are not tracking respondents, as with an anonymous questionnaire, you'll need to send the follow-up letter and a second copy of the questionnaire to everyone on your list, with a thank-you to those who have already returned the completed questionnaire.

How many completed questionnaires are enough? The answer is, "It depends"! What is the size of the target audience? If it's fairly small, fewer than 100, then you should try the highest possible response rate. A 100% response rate is ideal, but try for at least 75%. You may require more than one follow-up reminder to attain this response rate.

Table 7.1 later in this chapter summarizes the many factors that can affect your response rate.

◆ WHY IS RESPONSE RATE IMPORTANT?

With a higher response rate, you are more likely (but not guaranteed!) to have respondents who more closely match the demographic characteristics of the target audience.

One important reason is that nonrespondents may differ in some systematic way from respondents. When this occurs, your results may be biased. If you don't know the characteristics of the nonrespondents, it will be difficult to infer the characteristics of the population represented by the nonrespondents. One of the things you can do is to monitor the response rate and conduct additional follow-up activities if it is low.

With a larger target audience, representativeness is often more important than total response rate. If you are gathering demographic information so that you can summarize responses from different subgroups, you'll need to be sure you have enough respondents in these subgroups to have meaningful information. Many statistics books can provide you with formulas for computing the number of questionnaires to send out to obtain a good response rate. A "good" response rate is one that will provide enough information to support an informed decision.

◆ WHAT IS A GOOD RESPONSE RATE?

The answer to this question is as high as possible. You want to be confident that you'll have the information you need to make a decision. So in addition to doing all that you can to encourage a high response rate, you also need to plan for working with a lower-than-desired response rate. When you do have a small response rate—for example, under 40%—then you should compare the demographics of your respondents with those of the target audience. In this case, it's particularly important to use other sources of data, combined with the responses to your questionnaire, to make your decision.

In Chapter 1, "Launching Your Survey Project," it was suggested that you check journal articles for reports of completed survey projects to help you find out what's been done as well as provide ideas for specific questions you might want to include in your questionnaire. When you did that, you probably found that published studies tended to have good response rates. Many scholarly journals do not publish results of survey research with low response rates or responses that are not representative of the target audience. Dillman (2000) indicates that many paper-based questionnaires with careful attention to design have response rates as high as 70% for general public populations. Baruch (1999) found that response rates for paper-based questionnaires were typically in the 55% range. But depending on the topic of the questionnaire, your response rate might be higher. A study comparing mail and Web-based questionnaires found a response rate of 43% for the paper questionnaire compared with 33% for the Web-based questionnaire (Matz, 1999). For Web-based questionnaires using e-mail invitations, Cook, Heath, and Thompson (2000) conducted a meta-analysis of 49 studies with 68 questionnaires and found an average response rate of 39.6%, which is somewhat lower than paper-based mail questionnaires. Factors they identified as increasing response rates included number of contacts, personalized contacts, and prenotification.

 One challenge in using a Web-based questionnaire without an invitation is that you don't know the population or sampling frame. You don't know how many people learned about your questionnaire and decided not to respond. Thus, there's no way to calculate a response rate for a Web-based questionnaire that doesn't use invitations.

Response rates are often lower for fancy Web-based questionnaires—those with many graphics and with intense colors. The reason for this is that these questionnaires take more time to download, and for some people, their browser may not be able to handle the features used in the questionnaire. In addition, their browser may crash and the person may decide not to try to access the questionnaire again.

Another potential factor in lowering response rates for an e-mail questionnaire is that people might not realize they must use the "Reply" function to respond. They may read the questionnaire when they open the e-mail and attempt to respond. But unless they are using the "Reply" function, they will not be able to enter their answers. To avoid this potential challenge, be sure to include in the invitation that the person must use the "Reply With History" function to respond to the questionnaire. (E-mail programs may vary, and some may require that respondents use a tools function to include the message in their reply.)

Tracking the Questionnaire Responses

You'll need some method of tracking the questionnaire responses and monitoring your response rate. With a paper-based questionnaire, you can begin entering the data into your spreadsheet and conduct preliminary analyses of the demographic characteristics to determine how representative the respondents are of the target audience. You may want to do additional follow-ups if your respondents are not representative. For a Web-based questionnaire, the responses flow into a database or spreadsheet, so you can also conduct preliminary analysis. However, if you're not using invitations, it will be challenging to conduct much follow-up.

Suggestions for Increasing the Response Rates for Web-Based Questionnaires

- Send the questionnaire invitations on a Monday or a Tuesday.
- Clearly specify the time period the questionnaire will be available.
- Keep the look simple so the questionnaire loads quickly. Questionnaires with graphics that require high bandwidth are likely to have lower response rates with many audiences.
- Use the appropriate response icons and directions so the respondent can navigate the questionnaire easily. Use radio buttons for single choice options (select one of the following), drop-down lists for questions with more than six responses, and check boxes for questions with multiple selections.
- Be aware of messages that color can provide. Also be aware of visual limitations (e.g., color blindness) as you select the page layout and color.
- Ensure confidentiality of the data. Most Web users know that with cookies and other tracking their responses usually can be tracked.
- Send an e-mail follow-up one week after the initial launch.
- Determine how you will send any incentive that you provide to the respondent. A good guideline is to provide an incentive only for a very long questionnaire—one that takes more than 30 minutes to complete.
- Contact the respondents in advance. As with mail questionnaires, advance contact appears to increase response rates for Web-based questionnaires.

Even with all your careful planning, there are some factors you can't control. One of these is Web congestion—a lot of people trying to access the Web site at the same time. If people experience slow response time as they navigate your questionnaire, they might quit partway through. In addition, factors such as speed to download the questionnaire, ease of access to the server, and ease of navigation are likely to affect response rate.

◆ SUMMARY OF FACTORS RELATED TO INCREASED RESPONSE RATES

Table 7.1 provides a summary of factors found to affect response rates. Information in this table is based on the author's experiences as well as on several sources, including the following: Cook et al. (2000), Dillman (2000), Green and Hutchinson (1996), Kittleson (1997), and Thomas (1999).

For paper-based questionnaires, the factors that most influence response rates include postage class, enclosed or promised incentives, prenotification and follow-up, high-quality format and appearance, and credible sponsorship.

For Web-based questionnaires, questionnaires that load fast (i.e., contain few graphics) and use features that are accessible by most potential respondents tend to have higher response rates. As for paper-based questionnaires, prenotification and follow-up are important. Prenotification when you are using e-mail invitations also helps to increase the response rate.

Table 7.1 Summary of Factors Related to Increased Response Rates

Note: The following suggestions are based on research studies of response rates to mail and electronic questionnaires. At the present time, however, there is only limited research on electronic questionnaires.

Factor	Paper-Based	Electronic
Anonymity	Appears not to affect response rates, but confidentiality of data is important	With cookies and other tracking, most respondents believe it is impossible to have an anonymous electronic questionnaire. Confidentiality of the results is critically important.
Color	White or ivory is best	Light background with dark (black or navy) letters
Prenotification	Sending a postcard or letter, or telephoning the respondents to let them know an important questionnaire is coming increases the response rates. Start using your logo here.	Sending a prenotification e-mail seems to work—and shows you care about getting a good response rate.

Factor	Paper-Based	Electronic
Sponsorship	A trustworthy sponsor is important no matter what the medium of delivery of the questionnaire. Institutions the respondents are familiar with, organizations with which they are affiliated, and universities have the most credibility as sponsors.	
Salience	Salience is very important for all delivery media. A salient topic is one that is interesting and important to the respondent.	
Cover letter/ invitation	In cover letter appeals, emphasize how the good of society would be served by responding to the questionnaire (a social utility, science, or altruistic appeal), how the survey project sponsor would be aided by the return of the questionnaire (help the sponsor, sponsor appeal), or how the respondent may benefit by returning the questionnaire (egotistical appeal). The most effective of these is the "egotistical" appeal. Good cover letters increase response rates; poor ones, or none at all, decrease response rates.	
Deadlines	Deadlines influence speed of response but not response rate.	
Follow-up reminders	Phone calls, letters, postcards, or second copies of the questionnaire sent to nonrespondents to the original mailing increase the response rate. With an anonymous questionnaire, you'll need to send it to everyone again. Follow-up increases response rates and is more likely to do so in homogeneous target audiences than in the general population. Use your logo on all follow-ups so the person sees the connection with all of your communications.	Some studies show response rates increase significantly with a follow-up e-mail.
Incentives	Include enclosed tokens (e.g., tea bags, pens, money, or checks) or promised incentives (e.g., money, gifts). The use of any incentive increases the response rate, whether the incentive is enclosed or promised. Enclosed incentives produce higher response rates than do promised incentives. The offer of study results as an incentive is not effective at all.	There doesn't seem to be a need for an incentive for short Web-based questionnaires, but longer questionnaires might need one. The need for an in incentive also depends on the topic; an incentive might be required for long or tedious questionnaires. There is a challenge in delivering the incentive. One method is a coupon the respondent can print from the Web site when the questionnaire is submitted.

(Continued)

Table 7.1 (Continued)

Factor	Paper-Based	Electronic
Postage class	First class, special delivery, or certified mail yields higher response rates than does bulk rate mail. Bulk rate may take up to three weeks to receive. A stamped envelope produces a slightly higher response rate than a business reply envelope for return of the questionnaire. Using a noncontroversial commemorative stamp often causes recipients to open the envelope, whereas they would not have with franked or bulk mail.	Not applicable
Personalization	Using the person's name on the cover letter, personally signing the cover letter, and using stamps for postage rather than a postage meter increases response rates.	Not applicable for Web-based questionnaires. The e-mail should come from the project sponsor and, if possible, should be personalized with the recipient's name.
Questionnaire length—number of questions and number of pages	For most questionnaires, shorter is better for higher response rates. The exceptions are for specialized questionnaire topics to targeted, very interested audiences. A slight reduction in type size and printing on both sides of the page on good-quality paper might reduce a carelessly arranged five-page single-sided questionnaire to one 11 × 17 sheet of paper, using both sides.	Length—within reason—and the use of a password don't seem to make a difference in the response rate.
Format and appearance	Professional-looking questionnaires with pleasing formats yield higher response rates than do questionnaires that are poorly copied, hard to read, or confusing to the recipient.	Use a pleasing, easy-to-follow format that requires little or no horizontal scrolling. Color and design should follow principles of good Web design.

Factor	Paper-Based	Electronic
Use of a password	Not applicable	Requiring the use of a password does not appear to affect response rates.
Technical issues	Not applicable	Clear directions on how to navigate through the questionnaire and respond to questions (e.g., radio buttons, drop-down menus) along with access to technical support increases response rates.

◆ HANDLING THE DATA: CONFIDENTIALITY AND ANONYMITY

As you gather information from your questionnaire, respect the privacy of the individuals participating in your study. The best ways to accomplish this are as follows:

• Give paper-based questionnaires anonymously. Instruct the respondents *not* to put their names on the questionnaire. Provide this information at the top of the questionnaire. Do not write the person's name on the questionnaire yourself or add any code that might appear to be tracking individual responses.

• Store the completed questionnaires in a secure location so that no one other than the project team is able to obtain these surveys. Only by breaking and entering should anyone gain access to the completed questionnaires.

• For Web-based questionnaires, ensure that the database where the results are stored is secure and that only authorized members of the team have access to the data.

Following is a checklist to help you ensure that you've done all you can to achieve a high response rate and that you've made plans to ensure the confidentiality of the responses.

Checklist for Maximizing Your Response Rate

Use the following checklist to ensure that you've done all you can to achieve a high response rate and that you have made plans for handling the returned questionnaires appropriately.

❑ Have you planned to notify participants that a questionnaire is coming?

❑ Have you planned to distribute the questionnaire at a time in the lives of respondents when they are likely to have the time to respond?

❑ If you're using incentives, have you planned how to distribute them?

❑ Have you planned follow-up procedures?

❑ Have you planned activities for achieving a great response rate?

❑ Have you made plans to keep the returned questionnaire responses confidential and secure?

Analyzing the Data and Making Data-Based Decisions

A s responses to your questionnaires begin to come back, it's time to do something with those responses. This chapter contains suggestions for organizing and coding the data. We'll use partial results from two short survey projects as well as our case study to provide examples. Information in this chapter lays the foundation for reporting the results, potentially to various audiences, which is covered in the next chapter. Although analyses of questionnaire data may use complex statistical techniques, these techniques are beyond the scope of this book. If you need these types of analyses, you should work with a statistical consultant.

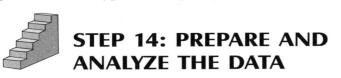

STEP 14: PREPARE AND ANALYZE THE DATA

The responses to your questionnaires are called *raw data* and you must turn these raw numbers into something that's understandable and usable. Then you're ready to implement the plan for data analysis that you created during your planning and tried out during your pilot test.

◆ WHEN SHOULD YOU CONDUCT YOUR STATISTICAL ANALYSES?

Your cover letter (or invitation) provided a date by which you wanted all the questionnaires returned. But the mail is sometimes slow. How long should you wait for potential additional responses? When can you start coding and processing your data?

For paper-based questionnaires, start entering the data into the database as soon as the questionnaires start coming back. For a mailed questionnaire, it's probably safe to close out data entry about a week after the due date of the questionnaires. After the data are entered into the database, the next task is cleaning the data and then completing descriptive analyses. Adding more questionnaire responses during these activities will not slow down your work. Depending on your timeline for completing the analyses and your recommendations, you might need to cut off the input of additional responses.

For a Web-based questionnaire, you will not get "stragglers"—that is, questionnaires coming in several days after the closing date. That's because you can shut down access to the questionnaire at the deadline so that no additional people can respond.

If you used an e-mail questionnaire, respondents can return the questionnaire weeks after the due date. If you've already completed much of your data analysis, you might want to put these late returns in a separate data file and consider them separately. At a minimum, you should analyze the demographic information.

◆ PREPARING THE DATA FOR ANALYSIS

Guidelines for preparing the data include a discussion of coding the data in preparation for analyses using spreadsheets such as Excel or Lotus 1–2–3 or statistical software packages such as SPSS or SAS. Topics such as editing the data and quality control checks such as checking your data set for reasonableness must also be considered. Following are the steps for preparing your data for analysis:

- Preparing coding documentation
- Coding the data
- Data editing and quality control checks

Preparing Coding Documentation

Prior to beginning the coding, you'll need to create a coding plan. Creating a table such as the example provided in Table 8.1 later in this chapter will provide clear directions to the people doing the coding, as well as documentation about how the coding was done.

Coding the Data

Responses to your questionnaire must be reduced to numbers so that they can be analyzed. The one exception to this is open-ended responses. You'll find guidelines and an example in Chapter 2, "Asking the Right Questions," of how to analyze responses from open-ended questions.

Consider the following set of scale anchors:	Each scale anchor must be assigned a number:
Very important	4 = Very important
Moderately important	3 = Moderately important
Of low importance	2 = Of low importance
Not important	1 = Not important

Generally, the most intense alternative is given the highest number in the coding. When responses are not degrees of intensity, they still need numbers for coding, as in the following example:

How did you learn about Gilchrist Elementary School's homework policies? (Select all that apply.)

a. Parent handbook
b. Parent orientation meeting
c. Monthly newsletter to parents
d. My child's homework calendar
e. My child's assignment notebook
f. The school's homework hotline
g. Special information sheet
h. Teacher conference
i. Gilchrist's Web site
j. Other (specify) _____

For this question, we'll need to provide nine columns for these data—one column for each response choice. The reason for this is that we've invited the respondent to "check all that apply." Coding will be 0 = no and 1 = yes. Because Option j is a write-in choice, we'll also need to summarize those responses. Again, see Chapter 2 to find guidelines for analyzing responses to open-ended questions. Note that the numbers corresponding to the response choices don't have meaning as numbers; they are really names for these responses and are examples of nominal-level data. Scales of measurement are discussed later in this chapter.

Now let's look at how to code two different types of questionnaire responses. In the first example questionnaire, "Bullying at Our School," there are skip patterns, and on one question, respondents could select more than one answer. For all these questions, these numbers were really names for the variables. In the second example questionnaire, "How I Read," the respondent uses a Likert-type scale to respond, with the exception of the demographic questions. In this case, the numbers for the Likert-type rating scale have meaning in that they indicate intensity—in this case, degree to which the respondent typically uses the reading strategies. We'll also look at how the data from our case study was coded.

Coding the Data for the Questionnaire on Bullying

Following is an example of a brief questionnaire on bullying that was included in Chapter 4, "Putting the Questionnaire Together." This questionnaire was created by a team of counselors in response to concerns of parents and teachers about some bullying incidents that had happened at the school. Details about how the questionnaire was administered are included in the sample report in Chapter 9, "Communicating the Results."

Responses to all these questions are categories rather than degrees of intensity. For each question with the exception of Question 5, we'll assign 1 to a, 2 to b, and so on. Coding for Question 5 is somewhat different because it's a question in which a respondent can select multiple answers. We'll code these responses using 0 and 1 for each response choice; 0 means they did not experience that type of bullying, and 1 means they have experienced it. With this type of coding, we can track the incidence of each of the types of bullying.

Table 8.1 presents the questionnaire as well as the coding. This is an example of the documentation we suggest you create to guide the coding process.

Table 8.2 presents a short data set from the responses to this questionnaire.

An identification (ID) number has been assigned to each of the respondents; it's a way of linking the paper questionnaire to the data. Put this ID number on the paper questionnaire so you can keep track. This is for quality control so that if a response seems wrong or doesn't make sense, you can go back to the original questionnaire and verify that the response was coded correctly. Some computer programs require a unique identification number for each data record. A data record is a line of data and represents the responses from one person. Because there are two skip patterns in this questionnaire, some answers will be blank if the person did not have those experiences. In the example data set in Table 8.2, cells are shaded to indicate skipped questions. Shading empty cells is not necessary, but it can help you keep track—and know that there is a meaningful blank cell. Note that the shading will not affect your data analysis.

Note that for Question 5, we have spaces for six responses. For this question, the respondent is asked to select all choices that apply; it is possible for someone to select all six responses if he or she has been the victim of several types of bullying. That's why each possible response for Question 5 is coded as 0 (absence) or 1 (presence).

Table 8.1   Questionnaire on Bullying at Our School: Coding Documentation

Question	Coding

1. Have you been bullied at school this year?
   a. No (Please go to Question 6)
   b. Yes (Please continue with Question 2)
	a = 1
	b = 2

2. How often are you bullied?
   a. A few times a day
   b. Once a day
   c. Once or twice a week
   d. Once a month
	a = 1
	b = 2
	c = 3
	d = 4

3. How much of a problem is bullying for you?
   a. It bothers me so much I don't like to come to school.
   b. It bothers me a lot but I still come to school.
   c. It bothers me a little.
   d. It doesn't bother me.
	a = 1
	b = 2
	c = 3
	d = 4

Table 8.1 (Continued)

Question	Coding

4. Where are you usually bullied?
   a. In the hallways at school
   b. In my classroom
   c. In the cafeteria
   d. On the playground
   e. In the bathrooms
	a = 1
	b = 2
	c = 3
	d = 4
	e = 5

5. What types of bullying have you experienced this year at school? Please select all that apply.
   a. I've been called names.
   b. I've been physically threatened.
   c. I've been shoved.
   d. I've been physically hurt.
   e. Something of mine has been stolen.
   f. Something of mine has been damaged.
	We'll use 6 columns for these responses. Response choices selected are coded 1; if the choice was not selected, it's coded 0.

6. Have you seen other students being bullied at school?
   a. Yes
   b. No (Please go to Question 10)
	a = 1
	b = 2

7. What is your most common reaction when you see others bullied?
   a. I join in the bullying.
   b. I tell an adult.
   c. I walk away.
   d. I watch.
	a = 1
	b = 2
	c = 3
	d = 4

8. Without naming the bully (or bullies), please describe that person's age:
   a. About the same age as the person being bullied
   b. Younger than the person being bullied
   c. Older than the person being bullied
	a = 1
	b = 2
	c = 3

9. Without naming the bully (or bullies), please indicate who did the bullying:
   a. Boy
   b. Girl
   c. A group of students
	a = 1
	b = 2
	c = 3

10. I am a
   a. Boy
   b. Girl
	a = 1
	b = 2

11. What grade are you in?
   a. Third
   b. Fourth
   c. Fifth
	a = 3
	b = 4
	c = 5

Table 8.2 Short Data Set Example for Questionnaire on Bullying

ID	Q1	Q2	Q3	Q4	5a	5b	5c	5d	5e	5f	Q6	Q7	Q8	Q9	Q10	Q11
1	1										1	3	1	1	2	5
2	1										2				1	4
3	2	2	3	1	0	0	0	1	1	1	1	2	3	1	2	3
4	1										1	2	1	3	2	5
5	2	3	3	4	1	1	1	0	0	1	2				1	3
6	1										1	4	1	2	1	4
7	2	4	3	4	0	1	1	0	0	0	1	3	3	1	2	3
8	1										2				1	5
9	1										1	1	1	3	2	4
10	1										1	4	3	1	1	4

Coding the "How I Read" Questionnaire

A team of researchers created some reading activities designed to help students use reading strategies to become better readers. These activities were first taught to teachers in a workshop setting, and then the researchers worked with the students and the teachers to practice these activities. Presented next is a portion of a questionnaire titled "How I Read," about reading strategies students may use as they read stories for pleasure. (All statements relate to the concept of reading strategies and are thus considered to comprise a Likert-type rating scale.) The questionnaire was administered to a group of third- and fifth-grade students. Students indicated how often they used each of the behaviors by responding whether a particular behavior was like them most of the time, sometimes, rarely, or almost never. Following is a portion of the questionnaire, and a portion of the data, presented here for illustrative purposes.

A Likert-type rating scale was used, as follows:

> A = Most of the time
> B = Sometimes
> C = Rarely
> D = Almost never

1. Before I begin reading a new book, I look at the pictures and title and try to guess what it is going to be about.

2. When I don't understand a part of the story, I just keep reading.

3. When I find a word in a story that I don't know, I read the sentences around it.

4. As I read, I can see pictures in my mind about what is happening in the story.

5. As I read a story, I ask myself questions about what will happen next.

6. I am confused by what I read.

7. When I get confused about a part of the story, I skip that part of the story.

8. I ask the teacher to tell me the words I don't know.

9. I think about what will happen next in the story.

10. I skip over words I do not know.

The "How I Read" questionnaire has a Likert-type rating scale. As noted in Chapter 3, "Creating Response Choices for Rating Scales," responses to Likert-type rating scales can be summed provided the questions relate to a single construct (Anastasi, 1982; Nunnally, 1978). You can verify that all your items relate to a single concept by having subject matter experts review your items. You can also use factor analysis, a statistical technique that searches for clusters of variables (see, e.g., Kline, 1994; Lackey, Sullivan, & Pett, 2003, for details).

The questions on this questionnaire have been "balanced" to help ensure that respondents read each question carefully rather than skimming through and selecting "Most of the time." To score these questions, you'll need to use a reversed scale for five of the questions. Following are the scoring details.

Scoring: Items 1, 3, 4, 5, and 9 are good reading strategies; the scale anchors are assigned the following values:

> A = Most of the time 4
>
> B = Sometimes 3
>
> C = Rarely 2
>
> D = Almost never 1

Items 2, 6, 7, 8, and 10 are examples of poor reading strategies; the scale anchors are assigned the following values:

> A = Most of the time 1
>
> B = Sometimes 2
>
> C = Rarely 3
>
> D = Almost never 4

The following demographic data were collected:

Gender (girl or boy): Boys are coded "1," and girls are coded "2." These numbers are labels for categories to provide an example of nominal data.

Grade level (third or fifth grade): Third grade is coded "3," and fifth grade is coded "5." Again, these numbers are labels for the categories of grade level.

Partial results of the survey on reading strategies are provided in Table 8.3.

Note that the table includes the score for the reading questionnaire in addition to the individual responses. A data set will contain only the responses until you do some computation. The score for each person has been computed because this information will be used in later examples.

Table 8.3 Table of Partial Results for the "How I Read" Questionnaire

ID	Q1	Q2	Q3	Q4	Q5	Q6	Q7	Q8	Q9	Q10	Reading Score	Gender	Grade Level
01	2	2	1	2	2	2	2	2	2	1	18	1	3
02	2	3	2	3	2	3	2	2	1	2	22	2	3
03	2	3	2	2	3	2	2	3	3	3	25	2	3
04	4	3	4	4	3	3	3	3	3	3	33	2	3
05	2	1	3	2	1	3	2	3	2	2	21	1	3
06	2	2	1	2	2	2	2	2	2	1	18	1	3
07	2	1	2	2	1	2	2	2	2	1	17	1	3
08	1	2	2	1	1	1	2	2	2	2	16	1	3
09	2	2	2	3	2	3	3	2	3	2	24	2	3
10	3	2	3	3	2	2	3	3	2	3	26	2	3
11	2	3	1	2	3	1	1	2	3	1	19	1	3
12	1	1	1	1	2	2	2	1	2	1	14	1	3
13	3	3	2	2	3	4	2	2	3	2	26	2	3
14	3	2	3	3	2	3	3	3	3	3	28	2	3
15	2	3	3	2	3	3	2	2	3	3	26	2	3
16	2	3	2	2	3	3	3	2	2	3	25	2	3
17	3	2	3	3	2	2	3	3	3	3	27	2	3
18	2	3	3	2	2	3	3	2	2	2	24	2	3
19	2	2	3	2	2	2	2	2	2	2	21	2	3
20	4	3	3	4	3	3	3	2	3	3	31	2	5
21	3	2	3	3	4	3	3	3	2	3	29	1	5
22	3	3	4	3	3	3	4	3	3	3	32	1	5
23	3	4	4	4	3	3	3	4	3	3	34	1	5
24	4	4	4	3	3	4	4	3	4	3	36	1	5
25	3	4	3	3	4	4	4	4	3	4	36	2	5
26	2	3	3	2	3	3	3	3	3	3	28	2	5
27	3	2	3	3	2	2	3	3	3	3	27	2	5
28	4	3	4	3	3	3	2	3	3	3	31	1	5
29	2	3	2	2	3	3	3	3	2	2	25	1	5
30	2	3	2	2	2	3	2	2	2	2	22	1	5
31	3	3	3	2	3	3	3	2	3	3	28	1	5
32	3	2	2	2	3	3	3	2	3	3	26	2	5
33	4	3	3	3	3	3	3	3	3	3	31	1	5
34	4	3	4	4	4	3	3	3	4	3	35	1	5
35	4	4	4	3	4	4	3	3	3	4	36	2	5

And finally, let's look at the coding for the questionnaire from our case study.

Following is the detail on how we coded the responses to the parent involvement questionnaire we developed for our case study.

Please refer to the Resource section for the entire questionnaire. Coding for the data is described here, but because of the size of the data set, it is not included in this book.

Question 1 is a table of activities currently provided by the schools. There are 15 activities listed; each activity has the possibility of two responses: awareness and participation. Letter the activities sequentially 1a through 1o, as follows:

ID	1a1	1a2	1b1	1b2	1c1	1c2	1d1	1d2	1e1	1e2	1f1	1f2

The coding continues through 1o1 and 1o2 but is not included here.

There are two parts to Question 1: awareness (1a), coded 1 for yes and 0 for no, and participation (1b), coded 0 for none, 1 for 1 to 2 times, and 2 for 3 or more times.

Question 2 asks how satisfied respondents are with each of the activities in which they have participated. Because this is a Web-based questionnaire, only those activities in which respondents participated will be included for this question. However, we need to set up the coding to include all 15 activities. The satisfaction scale has 4 points. The format of the coding will be the same as for Question 1—we'll need 15 columns.

Question 3 presents a list of those activities that respondents rated as "Very dissatisfied." (A feature of a Web-based questionnaire is that a question can be custom created based on a person's response to a previous question.) In this questionnaire, all activities that the respondent rated as "Very dissatisfied" are listed, and respondents are asked to provide details about their reasons for being so dissatisfied. This is an open response question and is not summarized here.

Question 4 is a list of barriers. We'll need to provide coding in such a way that a parent can select several barriers as appropriate. We'll label these as 2a through 2i; we'll use a code of 1 if that barrier is checked and 0 if that barrier is not checked.

Question 5 is an open-response question that asks about other barriers. Results to the open-response questions are not included here.

Question 6 is an open response question that asks respondents to list other activities for parents they would like to see offered. This open-response question is not summarized here.

Question 7 presents the same list of activities as in Question 1, and respondents are asked how likely they would be to participate in these activities during the current school year, if the barriers they indicated were removed. A 4-point scale is used: Very likely, Somewhat likely, Somewhat unlikely, and Not at all likely.

Questions 8 through 12 are the demographic data. These variables are coded as we did the questionnaire on bullying, and details are not included here.

Data Editing and Quality Control Checks

After you have your data in a spreadsheet, look it over for reasonableness. Look for numbers that are out of range, missing data, and patterns of responses. For example, Question 1 in the bullying questionnaire has possible values of 1 and 2. If you see any other number in that column, then it's likely there has been a data entry error. When you find a data entry error, you should do more extensive checking to verify that the rest of the data have been entered correctly. This process is called "cleaning the data."

If you note that several respondents have skipped a lot of the questions, look over the hard copies of the questionnaires to be sure that's really the case. The questionnaire about bullies used a skip pattern. If respondents have not been bullied, they will respond only to Questions 1 and 6 through 11. However, if they have not seen other students being bullied, then they would respond only to Questions 1, 6, 10, and 11. In this case, having questions without responses would be expected.

Look for patterns of responses. Sometimes this indicates that the respondent has marked an answer without reading the question. For example, if a respondent chose Option A for all questions in the bullying questionnaire, it's likely he or she did not read the question. In this case, it's best to delete responses from that respondent from your data set.

In the reading strategies questionnaire, it's especially important to check for patterns of responses because it used a flip (reverse) pattern of questions. In this questionnaire, half the questions were worded such that the respondent who uses good reading strategies will choose Option D, "Almost never," and half were worded such that someone with good reading habits will choose Option A, "Most of the time." For example, for Question 2, "When I don't understand a part of the story, I just keep reading," a person who uses good reading strategies would select option D, "Almost never." However, for Question 3, "When I find a word in a story that I don't know, I read the sentences around it," the good reader would select Option A, "Most of the time." If you find that a respondent has selected all As or all Ds when a flip pattern is used, consider deleting these responses from your data set.

◆ DESCRIBING THE RESPONSES

The first step in analyzing the responses to your questionnaire is to describe the results by doing the following:

- Use demographic information to describe the questionnaire respondents
- Summarize the questionnaire results for the total group
- Disaggregate the results for subgroups based on demographic or experiential data

The suggestions presented here focus on describing the information using descriptive statistics such as percentages, averages, and measures of variability as well as charts and graphs to depict these results. Some readers may wish to use more advanced statistical techniques to analyze your questionnaire responses, providing your data meet the required assumptions (see, e.g., Abrami, Cholmsky, & Gordon, 2000; Glass & Hopkins, 1996; Hays, 1994; Sprinthall, 2003). No matter what techniques you use to summarize your data, two concepts are important: variables and scales of measurement. These are described next.

Variables

A variable is something that can vary (have different values) along a dimension. A variable is anything, that when measured, can produce two or more different numbers. Examples of variables include age, attitudes, how hard you work, or degree of interest in participating in different classroom activities.

There are two important characteristics of variables:

- Continuous versus discrete
- Measurement scale

Continuous Versus Discrete Variables

A continuous variable is one that can take a variety of values, including decimals and fractions. An example is the score on the "How I Read" questionnaire.

A discrete variable is one that has only whole numbers, numbers that may be ranking or classification. Classification variables use numbers as labels, such as when we assign a number to a demographic characteristic. The questionnaire on bullying has discrete variables.

Scales of Measurement

Data from questionnaires can be categorized in terms of the type of information communicated by the numbers. These categories are called *scales of measurement*. Knowing the scale of measurement of your data is important because it helps determine the appropriate statistical techniques to use. There are four scales of measurement:

Nominal. Numbers are used to identify groups with something in common. For example, you can code your demographic data with numbers. Suppose students who respond to your questionnaire come from three different schools, and you want to disaggregate the data by school. You'll need a code or label for purposes of analysis, so you assign numbers as follows: RiverChase = 1, Gilbert = 2, and Madison = 3. These numbers are simply labels and have no intrinsic meaning. Another example of nominal data is represented by the responses to the questionnaire on bullying.

Ordinal. Numbers are used to indicate an implied order or ranking. The ranking format items described in Chapter 2 provide rank order information about whatever items are ranked. In the example provided in Chapter 2, participants were asked to rank their perceptions of the effectiveness of several activities in making their school safer.

Interval. Numbers provide order information as in the ordinal scale and also have the additional characteristic of equal-appearing distances or equal-appearing intervals between adjacent numbers. Data from Likert-type rating scales are considered interval-level data. The scores from the "How I Read" questionnaire provide an example of interval-level data.

Ratio. Numbers have all the characteristics of the preceding scales of measurement as well as an absolute zero. Zero represents the absence of the characteristic being measured. Ratio-level scales are rarely used in education because of the need for a meaningful zero. For example, a score of zero on a measure of learning strategies or self-concept does not mean the absence of that characteristic. An example of ratio data that might be used in a questionnaire is amount of time on task or number of years of experience. It is meaningful to say that a person spent no time on task or had no experience in a particular area. We can also meaningfully say that a person who spent 10 minutes on a task spent twice as long as a person who spent 5 minutes on the task.

Table 8.4 summarizes these scales of measurement and indicates some analyses that are appropriate for each kind of data.

Table 8.4   Scales of Measurement and Statistical Tests

Scale of Measurement	Appropriate Statistical Analyses
Nominal	Percentages, charts and graphs, chi-square test (for differences and relationships)
Ordinal	Nonparametric tests such as Mann-Whitney U or Kruskal-Wallis analysis of variance (see Gibbons, 1976)
Interval	t test, correlations, analysis of variance, and many others
Ratio	Same as for interval-level data

Descriptive Statistics

Following are some ways of describing your data. This discussion is not intended to replace a statistics book, but it will briefly summarize some commonly used descriptive statistics.

Frequency Distribution. A way to organize your raw data initially is with a frequency distribution. A frequency distribution shows the number of times each score (or number) appears.

Mean. The mean is the mathematical average of a set of scores. It is computed by summing all the scores and dividing by the number of scores. The mean is appropriate when you have interval-level data, as in scores from the reading strategies questionnaire.

Median. The median is the 50th percentile, or the point that cuts the distribution in half. The median is appropriate with ordinal data or with distributions of interval-level data that are highly skewed.

Mode. This is the most frequently occurring score. Arrange the scores in order (as in a frequency distribution) and identify which score or element occurs most often. A mode can be used with any of the scales of measurement.

Standard Deviation. The standard deviation is a way to describe the variability of your data. It can be thought of as indicating the average amount by which scores deviate from the mean. Together, the mean and standard deviation provide a good description of the distribution of your interval- and ratio-level data.

Range. The range is the distance between the two extreme scores in your distribution. It is useful with interval- and ratio-level data.

Inferential Statistical Tests

You might decide to use inferential statistics in your analyses if your data meet the required assumptions. For example, we can use a *t* test to compare the mean of the reading strategy scores from our questionnaire from the third and fifth graders. Or you might use a chi-square test to compare the types of bullying over grade levels. Using inferential statistics (compared with descriptive statistics) permits inferences or generalizations to the population from which the sample was drawn. Inferential statistics are appropriate when you have used probability sampling to select participants in your survey project. When you disaggregate your data, you may use these types of statistical tests to determine whether observed differences between the groups are likely to be stable and repeatable (e.g., Fraenkel & Wallen, 2002; Johnson & Christensen, 2000).

A discussion of inferential statistics is beyond the scope of this book. However, it should be mentioned that depending on the number of responses you have and the method you used to select participants, inferential statistics may be appropriate to analyze your results. Even if you do use inferential statistical tests, you'll also need to use descriptive statistics such as those described earlier in this chapter to provide information about the respondents.

◆ WHAT METHOD OF STATISTICAL ANALYSIS SHOULD YOU USE?

The answer depends on several factors, including the purpose of the survey project and your guiding questions and objectives; the kinds of data you have, based on the kinds of questions you created; the number of responses you have; and whether you are planning to disaggregate your responses in your analyses. Let's look at each of these factors.

Purpose of the Survey Project, Guiding Questions, and Objectives

As you developed the project plan for your survey project, you created a plan for data analysis, such as comparing subgroups, examining the relationship or association between variables, or looking for changes over time. If you are interested in comparing groups, then you might use a *t* test, an analysis of variance, or a chi-square test, depending on the kinds of data you have and how you selected your sample. If you are interested in looking at the relationship between variables, you would use a correlation coefficient. There are several types of correlation coefficients, again depending on the kinds of data you have. If you are interested in looking for changes over time and have administered your questionnaire more than once, you can use graphs or charts to plot trends, or if your data warrant it, you may use statistical analyses.

Number of Responses

One reason for so much emphasis on response rate is that you want as many responses as you can get. The higher the response rate from a random sample, the more likely that these responses will be representative of the target audience. In addition, the more responses you have, the more kinds of analyses are available to you. For example, for the case study on parent involvement, we had 756 responses for a 50.5% response rate. With this large a number of responses, we can use many different types of statistical analyses and can disaggregate the data in several ways.

For the questionnaire on bullying, although there was a good response rate (83%), the target audience was small, so only percentages, charts, and graphs can be used. So what's the bottom line? If you have 30 or fewer responses, you should use percentages, charts, and graphs. With a larger number, there are a greater variety of statistical analyses available to you. See a statistics book (e.g., Abrami, Cholmsky, & Gordon, 2000; Glass & Hopkins, 1996; Sprinthall, 2003) for additional information on sample size and statistical tests, or work with a statistical consultant.

Disaggregating the Results to Explore Subgroup Differences

It is likely that you will want to disaggregate your results. Most survey projects relating to the No Child Left Behind (NCLB) Act will include analyses by race/ethnicity and gender. Other survey projects may include disaggregating the data by years of teaching experience, participation in certain activities, and school attended, among others. If you plan to disaggregate you data, your need to have at least 30 responses per subgroup, preferably more (e.g., Fraenkel & Wallen, 2002; Johnson & Christensen, 2000).

◆ ANALYSES OF THE RESULTS OF THE QUESTIONNAIRE ON READING STRATEGIES

Let's work with the results of the reading strategies questionnaire first. The first thing to do is create a frequency distribution, shown next.

Score	Frequency
14	1
16	1
17	1
18	2
19	1
21	2
22	2
24	2
25	3
26	4
27	2
28	3
29	1
31	3
32	1
33	1
34	1
35	1
36	3

The range of possible scores on the reading strategies questionnaire was 10 to 40. (We knew this range because there were 10 questions. If a respondent indicated they almost never used any of the reading strategies, their score would be 10. If a respondent indicated they used each of the reading strategies most of the time, their score would be 40.) There were more scores toward the high end of the scale, which is good since these students had participated in some training in reading strategies activities and the intended outcome was for students to use these reading strategies.

Next let's look at the demographic information—gender and grade level.

Gender-by-Grade-Level Cross-Tabulation

	Grade Level		
	Third	Fifth	Total
Boy	7	9	16
Girls	12	7	19
Total	19	16	35

Figure 8.1   Demographic Data for the Reading Strategies Questionnaire

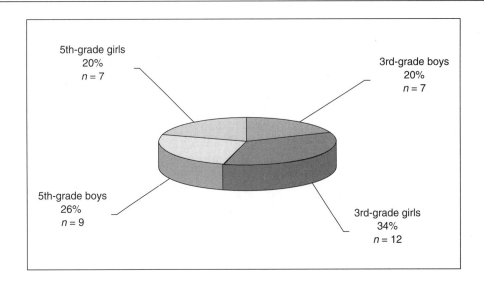

It's more interesting and informative to look at this same information in chart form as shown in Figure 8.1.

Because the questionnaire was given after students had participated in a series of activities to learn the different reading strategies, a frequency distribution for the individual questions should be created to determine which strategies students are using either most of the time or some of the time. This type of analysis can also be done by grade level or grade level by gender.

Question	Most of the Time	Sometimes	Rarely	Almost Never
1. Before I begin reading a new book, I look at the pictures and title and try to guess what it is going to be about.	7	11	15	2
2. When I don't understand a part of the story, I just keep reading.	3	11	17	4
3. When I find a word in a story that I don't know, I read the sentences around it.	7	14	10	4
4. As I read, I can see pictures in my mind about what is happening in the story.	4	13	16	2
5. As I read a story, I ask myself questions about what will happen next.	4	16	12	3
6. I am confused by what I read.	2	9	20	4

Question	Most of the Time	Sometimes	Rarely	Almost Never
7. When I get confused about a part of the story, I skip that part of the story.	1	13	18	3
8. I ask the teacher to tell me the words I don't know.	1	16	10	2
9. I think about what will happen next in the story.	2	19	13	1
10. I skip over words I do not know.	5	9	19	2

The next step is to describe the reading strategy scores using a mean and standard deviation. The mean is computed by adding all the scores together and dividing by the number of scores—in this case, 35. The mean for the total group is 26.2.

Compute the standard deviation, using the following formula:

$$\sqrt{\frac{\sum X^2 - \frac{(\sum X)^2}{N}}{N}}$$

where:

X represents the scores on the reading questionnaire.

N is the number of respondents.

The standard deviation for the reading strategy scores for the total group is 5.99.

For disaggregating the data, you should have a minimum of 30 respondents per subgroup, and preferably more, to provide meaningful comparisons. But for purposes of illustration, we will compute the means and standard deviations for the subgroups. We'll disaggregate the data by grade level, then by gender, and finally gender by grade level.

	Boys		Girls		Total	
	Mean	SD	Mean	SD	Mean	SD
Third grade	17.57	2.22	25.58	3.06	22.63	4.81
Fifth grade	30.22	4.68	30.71	4.57	30.44	4.21
Total	24.69	7.46	27.47	4.21		

The results of these analyses will be used in Chapter 9, "Communicating the Results," to create reports for various audiences.

◆ ANALYSES OF THE RESULTS OF THE QUESTIONNAIRE ON BULLYING

Earlier in this chapter, you learned how to code the responses for the questionnaire on bullying and looked at a short data set consisting of 10 responses. All told, there were 84 responses, including 31 responses from third graders, 24 responses from fourth graders, and 29 responses from fifth graders. The entire data set is not included here; instead, you'll see the analyses and how the data were handled.

Let's begin by looking at the demographic data. This is done by creating a cross-tabulation table, the same as for the reading strategies data. This is an example of disaggregating the data.

Gender-by-Grade-Level Cross-Tabulation

| | | Grade Level | | |
	Third	Fourth	Fifth	Total
Boys	14	15	11	40
Girls	17	10	17	44
Total	31	25	28	84

As for the reading strategies data, we'll create a chart with the demographic information. You can create separate charts for grade level and gender. Here, you see the chart for gender by grade level. The format of the pie chart shown in Figure 8.2 is slightly different than for the reading strategies data. Excel and other software packages provide several options for how the chart looks.

Figure 8.2 shows the chart with a summary of the respondents by subgroup of gender by grade level. This is an example of disaggregating the data.

Unlike the reading strategies questionnaire responses where the responses were summed and a score was created for each respondent, the results of the questionnaire on bullying must be analyzed differently because all the data are at the nominal level of the scales of measurement.

First, the data set is disaggregated on the basis of Question 1, which asked whether the respondent has been bullied at school this year. Of the respondents, 22 reported having been bullied at school this year, and 82 reported they had not been bullied. Note that the sample size is now quite small—only 22 respondents. However, only three classrooms participated in this study, and the response rate

Figure 8.2 Gender-by-Grade Level of Questionnaire Respondents

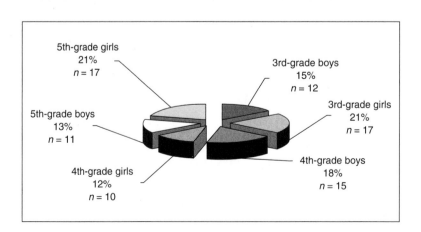

was 83%. Thus, even with a small number of respondents, some decisions can be made about how to address the challenges of bullying in the school. Because of the small number of responses, other sources of information should be used to validate the questionnaire responses (a process sometimes called "triangulating the data").

Next the data is disaggregated to look at the responses of those who report having been bullied. Frequency distributions for their responses to Questions 2 through 5, which describe their experiences, are shown next.

Question 2: How often are you bullied?

Response	Frequency	Percentage
A few times a day	2	9.1
Once a day	8	36.4
Once or twice a week	9	40.9
Once a month	3	13.6
Total	22	100.0

Question 3: How much of a problem is bullying for you?

Response	Frequency	Percentage
It bothers me so much I don't like to come to school.	3	13.6
It bothers me a lot but I still come to school.	9	40.9
It bothers me a little.	8	36.4
It doesn't bother me.	2	9.1
Total	22	100.0

Question 4: Where are you usually bullied?

Response	Frequency	Percentage
In the hallways at school	2	9.1
In my classroom	2	9.1
In the cafeteria	7	31.8
On the playground	9	40.9
In the bathrooms	2	9.1
Total	22	100.0

Question 5: What types of bullying have you experienced this year at school?

Response	Frequency	Percentage[a]
I've been called names.	19	86.4
I've been physically threatened.	7	31.8
I've been shoved.	15	68.2
I've been physically hurt.	2	9.1
Something of mine has been stolen.	6	27.3
Something of mine has been damaged.	6	27.3
Total	55	

[a]Percentages are based on the total number of students reporting bullying, $n = 22$.

Next let's find out how many children experienced multiple types of bullying. We'll sum the responses to Question 5 (5a through 5f) for each response and create a frequency distribution.

Number of Types of Bullying Experienced

Number of Types of Bullying	Frequency	Percentage
1	2	9.1
2	12	54.5
3	5	22.7
4	2	9.1
5	0	0.0
6	1	4.5
Total	22	99.9[a]

[a]Percentages total 99.9 due to rounding.

Continuing the analysis, look at Question 6: How many respondents of the total group of respondents reported seeing other students bullied at school? These responses were counted, and it turned out that 40 students had observed bullying at school, whereas 44 had not observed any other student being bullied at school this year.

The next analyses are based on those 40 students who reported having seen another student being bullied at school.

Question 7: What is your most common reaction when you see others bullied?

Responses	Frequency	Percentage
I join in the bullying.	9	22.5
I tell an adult.	12	30.0
I walk away.	8	20.0
I watch.	11	27.5
Total	40	100.0

Question 8: Without naming the bully (or bullies), please describe that person's age.

Responses	Frequency	Percentage
About the same age as the person bullied	23	57.5
Younger than the person bullied	2	5.0
Older than the person bullied	15	37.5
Total	40	100.0

Question 9: Without naming the bully (or bullies), please indicate who did the bullying.

Responses	Frequency	Percentage
Boy	15	37.5
Girl	10	25.0
A group of students	15	37.5
Total	40	100.0

So far, we've disaggregated the data on the basis of Question 1, whether the respondent had been bullied. We then created frequency distributions for Questions 2, 3, 4, and 5 for this subgroup of respondents.

Next, let's disaggregated the data in a different way, on the basis of Question 6, whether the respondent had observed other students being bullied. For the subgroup of respondents who had observed someone being bullied, we created frequency distributions for Questions 7, 8, and 9.

Now let's look at the data in a different way. We'd like to know who is being bullied: boys or girls? Younger or older students? So we go back to the subgroup of the 22 students who reported they had been bullied at school this year and create a cross-tabulation of gender by grade level.

Gender-by-Grade-Level Cross-Tabulation

| | Grade Level | | | |
	Third	Fourth	Fifth	Total
Boys	6	5	3	14
Girls	4	2	2	8
Total	10	7	5	22

Next, for these students, let's look at whether they had seen other students being bullied, and if so, what their most common reaction was. Of these 22 students, 11 reported having observed other students being bullied. The responses from these 11 students to Questions 7, 8, and 9 are reported next.

Question 7: What is your most common reaction when you see others bullied?

Responses	Frequency	Percentage
I join in the bullying.	3	27.3
I tell an adult.	3	27.3
I walk away.	3	27.3
I watch.	2	18.1
Total	11	100.0

Question 8: Without naming the bully (or bullies), please describe that person's age.

Responses	Frequency	Percentage
About the same age as person bullied	5	45.5
Younger than the person being bullied	1	9.0
Older than the person bullied	5	45.5
Total	11	100.0

Question 9: Without naming the bully (or bullies), please indicate who did the bullying.

Responses	Frequency	Percentage
Boy	6	54.6
Girl	2	18.1
A group of students	3	27.3
Total	11	100.0

◆ ANALYSES OF THE RESULTS OF THE QUESTIONNAIRE ON PARENT INVOLVEMENT

Following is part of the data analysis of our case study presented for illustrative purposes. See the Resource section for the complete questionnaire.

Many of the questions will yield nominal-level data. The exceptions are Questions 2 (satisfaction) and 7 (likelihood of participating in activities if barriers were removed). We will create tables that show percentage of responses for Questions 1 and 4 and the demographic information, and compute means for each response choice for Questions 2 and 7. Note that we did not include the analyses of the open-response questions here.

Question 1: Awareness and participation in activities in the past year

		Percentage Participation		
Activity	*Percentage Aware*	*None*	*1–2 times*	*3+ times*
Parent-teacher conference	100	2	78	20
Homework hotline for parents	87	56	31	13
Field trip with my child's class	95	89	8	3
Library aide	47	52	30	18
Computer aide	31	39	43	18
Teacher assistant	49	52	25	21
Fundraising activities	84	35	53	12
Back-to-school night	99	36	64	0
PTO meetings	100	27	59	14
Small-group coffee hour discussions	15	73	21	6
Monthly birthday party organizer	5	10	60	30
Monthly family night	78	42	39	19
Parent Advisory Committee	31	30	25	45
Parent Resource Center	52	68	22	10
School board meetings	89	82	10	8

Question 2 asked about the respondents' satisfaction with the activities in which they had participated. Respondents rated satisfaction on a 4-point scale, with 4 indicating they were "Very satisfied."

Activity	Average Satisfaction
Parent-teacher conference	3.2
Homework hotline for parents	2.7
Field trip with my child's class	3.4
Library aide	2.1
Computer aide	2.5
Teacher assistant	2.3
Fundraising activities	3.3
Back-to-school night	2.4
PTO meetings	2.5
Small-group coffee hour discussions	1.4
Monthly birthday party organizer	2.1
Monthly family night	3.6
Parent Advisory Committee	3.1
Parent Resource Center	3.6
School board meetings	2.1

Question 3 appeared only if respondents indicated they were "Very dissatisfied" with an activity. Responses were open-ended and are not summarized here.

Question 4: Barriers to participation

Barrier	Percentage Identifying Barrier
I often don't have child care.	28
I didn't know many of these events were happening.	68
I don't know who to contact to volunteer.	48
I don't feel I have the skills necessary.	21
I've had negative experiences in the past.	7
My work schedule won't allow me to participate.	69
I have some feeling of alienation toward school-teachers or administrators.	2
I don't have transportation.	8
I'm not sure how to participate.	27

Question 5 asked the respondent to list any barriers not included in the list in Question 4. These open-ended responses are not analyzed here.

Question 6 was an open-ended question, asking respondents to indicate what other activities they would like to see offered by the school.

Question 7 listed the activities, the same as for Question 1, and asked respondents how likely they were to participate in each of the activities if the barriers they identified in Questions 4 and 5 were removed.

Activity	Average Likelihood
Parent-teacher conference	3.5
Homework hotline for parents	1.3
Field trip with my child's class	0.3
Library aide	0.5
Computer aide	0.3
Teacher assistant	1.2
Fundraising activities	2.3
Back-to-school night	3.2
PTO meetings	2.8
Small-group coffee hour discussions	1.3
Monthly birthday party organizer	0.5
Monthly family night	2.5
Parent Advisory Committee	1.7
Parent Resource Center	2.3
School board meetings	0.3

Demographic information:

School Attended	Percentage
RiverChase Elementary	31
Gilchrist Elementary	39
Madison Elementary	30

Percentage of children in each grade level:

Kindergarten	First Grade	Second Grade	Third Grade	Fourth Grade
21	27	22	18	12

Working status of parents by gender, in percentages:

	Male Respondents			Female Respondents		
	Full-Time	Part-Time	Not At All	Full-Time	Part-Time	Not At All
Self	94	2	4	56	29	15
Spouse	45	36	19	90	6	4

Gender of respondents, in percentages:

Male	Female
24	76

Ethnicity of respondents, in percentages:

White, Not Hispanic	Hispanic	African American	Asian/Pacific Islander	Other
57	13	4	26	0

(Note: There are many other ways to describe the responses by disaggregating the data in different ways, but for purposes of illustration, we'll limit our examples to those shown here.)

The results of these analyses will be used to create a report and recommendations in Chapter 9 and to report the decisions made on the basis of the results of these questionnaires. The survey project team also interviewed some parents and teachers and used this information in addition to the results of the questionnaire.

◆ SUMMARIZING RESPONSES FROM A QUESTIONNAIRE THAT USED THE SEMANTIC DIFFERENTIAL FORMAT

Responses to a questionnaire that used a semantic differential format are treated in the same way as those for the Likert-type rating scale described earlier. Presented next is the example of a semantic differential item. As with the reading strategies questionnaire example, each respondent receives a score; data should be organized much as in the example provided earlier.

Assign values of 1 through 7 to the pairs of adjectives with the positive adjective on the right, and the values of 7 through 1 to the pairs of adjectives with the negative adjective on the right. Sum the total number of points to obtain an individual's score.

In the example that follows, the person's response is marked with an X. After the completed questionnaire was received, the point value that corresponds to that response was added. Both pieces of information are provided in this example.

How would you rate the use of a computer-based chat room to work on your survey project? *Check the appropriate space on each scale.*

Interesting	____:____:____:X(4):____:____:____	Uninteresting
Confusing	____:____:____:____:____:X(6):____	Clear
Useful	____:X(6):____:____:____:____:____	Useless
Efficient	____:____:____:____:____:X(2):____	Time-consuming
Boring	____:____:____:X(4):____:____:____	Fun
Worthwhile	____:X(6):____:____:____:____:____	Worthless
Inappropriate	____:____:____:____:____:____:X(7)	Appropriate
Clear	____:X(6):____:____:____:____:____	Muddled

The score for this respondent is 41; this number is then entered into the data set.

◆ SUMMARIZING RESPONSES FROM A QUESTIONNAIRE THAT USED A RANKING FORMAT

Presented next is an example of a ranking item, with responses from one of the respondents.

Please rank your perception of the effectiveness of the following activities in making your school safer. Use "1" to indicate the activity you believe will be the most effective, "2" to indicate the activity you believe will be second most effective, etc.

Activity	*Ranking*
Having a police presence in the school	5
Enforcing the school's discipline code	1
Providing counseling to students identified as "bullies"	3
Implementing a peer mediation program	2
Providing positive parenting classes	4

Unlike the process used to summarize responses from Likert-type rating scales and the semantic differential format in which scores for each respondent are computed, responses to the ranking format are summarized by group. If you use subgroups based on demographic information, median rankings are reported for each of the subgroups as well as for the total group. Because ranks are considered ordinal-level data, the appropriate measure of central tendency is the median. There are also several nonparametric statistical tests available for ordinal-level data to perform statistical analyses (see, e.g., Conover, 1998; Gibbons, 1976).

The following format is useful for organizing the responses and includes data from the preceding example:

ID	Item 1	Item 2	Item 3	Item 4	Item 5	Demographic 1	Demographic 2
01	5	1	3	2	4		
02							
03							
04							

Data in the cells are the ranks provided by each of the respondents.

◆ ANALYSES OF WEB-BASED QUESTIONNAIRE RESPONSES

 The processes for coding questionnaire responses are the same for Web-based as for paper-based questionnaires. But with a Web-based questionnaire, rather than entering the data into a spreadsheet, the respondents' data will automatically flow to a database. You'll still need to make decisions, however, about how to code the variables during the planning phase and review the data for reasonableness. After this is done, analyses of Web-based questionnaire data are no different from those for a paper-based questionnaire.

For some Web-based questionnaires, analysis can take on a new meaning with dynamic data aggregation and reporting. What this means is that tables, such as those we created for the responses from the questionnaire on bullying, are posted on the Web site and updated automatically when a person submits his or her response. For example, immediately after the "submit" screen, there is a note to the respondent asking whether he or she would like to see the data gathered to date. If so, the respondent clicks on a link and views the aggregated responses.

At this point there has been no "cleaning" or quality checking of the data, so a note to that effect needs to be posted with the data. When the questionnaire closes and it's time to conduct the analyses, it's very important to check the data before using them as they have been entered into the database. You may want to delete respondents who did not provide demographic information or who skipped many of the questions.

◆ DATA BACKUP AND SECURITY

It's critically important to make copies of your data! If you have a system crash during your analysis, the data set you are working on may become corrupted. Always make a backup copy of your data set; it's preferable to keep this backup copy on an external storage device such as a floppy disk, CD, or ZIP drive or on a server. In any case, make sure you have either encrypted or password-protected this backup copy so no unauthorized people can access your data.

◆ DESCRIBING NONRESPONDENTS

It's a good idea to describe people who were invited to respond to your questionnaire but did not. That way you can determine how representative these people are of the target audience. The big question is, Do you have the information to do this? In many cases, you won't have this information, so you'll need to be sure you carefully describe those who do respond so that those reading your results and recommendations can place that information in the context of those who responded.

Now that you have your data coded and analyzed, it's time to use that information to make your decisions and report the results.

STEP 15: USE THE DATA TO MAKE DATA-BASED DECISIONS

You've completed much of the hard work in a survey project, and now it's time to make some decisions. What did you learn from the data? What kinds of decisions can the data support? This section provides some suggestions for using your data to make data-based decisions, using examples from the survey project on bullying and the survey project on reading strategies. Detail on the case study is not provided here because similar processes were used.

For many survey projects, the questionnaire data are one of several sources of information used to make decisions. The additional sources of information validate the questionnaire information, but do not duplicate it. Rather, the information is from other sources, such as research reports, interviews, or observations. For the questionnaires on bullying and reading strategies, other sources of information were used in addition to the questionnaire results.

Making Decisions Based on the Data From the Questionnaire on Bullying in the School

The analyses of these results are presented earlier in this chapter. The response rate was very good—83%. But the interest was in the students who reported that they had been bullied as well as those who reported that they had observed other students being bullied. Twenty-two students reported having been bullied, with more students in lower grades reporting being bullied. Although 22 is a small number, the seriousness of the consequences of ignoring the results because of small numbers are great. Other sources of data will be used to validate the results of the questionnaire.

The data indicated that the majority of bullying took place in the cafeteria and on the playground, places where there tends to be lots of noise and movement with many students around. The most frequent type of bullying reported was name-calling and shoving. But some students reported being physically threatened or physically hurt. Three of the children reported being bullied to such an extent that they did not like to come to school.

Forty students reported having observed another child being bullied. Of these, only 12 (30%) reported that they told an adult. Nine of these students reported they joined in the bullying. The rest of the 40 students either watched or walked away. These results suggest that students need to be made aware of the hurt that bullying can cause to the target child and to learn appropriate responses when they observe bullying at school.

The survey project team provided the results to the counselors, who used the information to make decisions and create an action plan. They want to ensure that each child is completely safe at school, that no child is threatened by another child, and that all students clearly understand the message that the school will not tolerate any type of bullying behavior. In addition to the results from the questionnaire, they also talked with teachers and made observations on the playground and in the cafeteria.

Decisions made on the basis of the results of the questionnaire as well as the additional information were as follows:

- Increase the awareness of bullying by holding a poster contest to create posters about bullying and what to do when a student sees someone else being bullied. Place these posters in the hallway and the cafeteria.
- Create a bully-free zone on the playground and in the cafeteria where much of the bullying was reported to have occurred. Provide special training to teachers, teacher aides, and parents who volunteer for cafeteria and playground duty about what to do when they see bullying occurring.
- Implement a peer mediation program in which peer mediators work with bullies and their targets.
- Involve parents by providing information about the warning signs that their child might be the target of bullying at school.
- Provide a means whereby students can provide information about bullying without fearing reprisal.
- Create an intervention plan in conjunction with the peer mediation program to work with children who seem to be the most frequent targets of bullying.

A task force consisting of teachers, parents, counselors, and school administrators will be created to implement these recommendations.

Making Decisions Based on the Data From the Questionnaire on Reading Strategies

The purpose of this survey project was to determine to what extent students who learned new reading strategies were using them. The results were evaluated in two ways: One was to examine the scores for students, disaggregating them by grade level and gender to look for overall patterns of usage of reading strategies. The second way was to look at the prevalence of use of particular reading strategies to determine where the training program could be strengthened. The survey project team also had information from a prior study that showed a strong positive relationship between reading achievement scores and the extent of usage of the reading strategies. Thus, they wanted to determine whether there were differences between boys and girls in using reading strategies and whether there were differences between third and fifth graders in the use of reading strategies.

As indicated in the analyses presented earlier in this chapter, third graders were not using as many reading strategies as were the fifth grade students; they also found that some third-grade students were using negative reading strategies—that is, using strategies that would hinder the development of their reading skills.

The results showed that third-grade boys had the lowest scores on the reading strategies scale, indicating they used the fewest number of reading strategies on a regular basis. None of these boys used any strategy most of the time, and five of the seven third-grade boys reported that most of the time they skipped over words they did not know. Although this is a small number (remember, this is only a part of the data set for the project), the results held for the larger set of data.

The decision made was to study more closely what reading strategies the third-grade boys were using and to work to create ways of helping them use more positive reading strategies and thus improve their reading skills.

The survey project team who created the questionnaire on bullying and the survey project team who created the questionnaire on reading strategies used the results somewhat differently. The results from the questionnaire on bullying were used to proactively focus on actions to increase the awareness of bullying and to communicate the messages that bullying is not acceptable and that all must work together to create a school that is safe for all students.

The decision made by the survey project team for the reading strategies questionnaire results was that additional study was required of one of the subgroups, the third-grade boys. It may be that a different approach to reading strategies will be needed for these students.

Following is a checklist. Review it to ensure that you are ready to create the reports for the various audiences.

Checklist for Analyzing the Data

Use the following checklist to ensure that you have analyzed all your data; that you have used that information to make appropriate, data-based decisions; and that you are ready to create the reports for various audiences.

- ❑ Have you created a coding scheme for each of your variables, including your demographic data?
- ❑ Have you performed quality control and reasonableness checks on your data set?
- ❑ Do you plan to disaggregate the data for performing subgroup analyses? If so, have you formed these subgroups accurately?
- ❑ Will you need some charts and graphs to depict your data—and perhaps tell the "story" more clearly?
- ❑ Have you had someone else work with you to review all your analyses to check for possible errors?
- ❑ Have you created a backup copy of your data set and stored it in a secure location?
- ❑ Have you considered other sources of data as you review the results of the analyses and make the decisions?
- ❑ Do you have all the information you'll need to start writing your reports and creating your recommendations?

9

Communicating the Results

The final step in a survey project is to communicate the message clearly. Unless you are preparing a formal research (technical) report, it's likely that results can be summarized with charts, graphs, and short reports and that the story can be told with presentation software such as PowerPoint or Freelance.

 STEP 16: CREATE THE REPORTS OF THE RESULTS AND RECOMMENDATIONS

As noted earlier in this book, survey projects are conducted for many different purposes. Throughout, this book has focused on using the results of a questionnaire to gather data to make a decision and to develop a strategy to meet the objectives of the project. If no action will result from the questionnaire, you've wasted your time and that of the respondents. That's one important reason to have the total support of stakeholders and sponsors during the entire project. Implementing the recommendations can require helping people understand the need for action and the consequences of inaction. So you'll need to communicate these results to key audiences!

Consider the audiences who will be receiving the information. Tailor the presentation to meet their knowledge requirements and concerns. Identify your key findings and recommendations with sufficient detail to back up those recommendations. A high-level overview with details available for those interested often provides the required level of information for most audiences. If you present your results to a group, have the complete package, including the questionnaire and cover letter, available to show interested audience members. In addition, be sure to proofread your report. You want it to be correct as well as professional looking. Prior to releasing any version of the report to the different audiences, provide a draft copy of the materials to the sponsors for their review and approval.

Let's begin by considering audiences that might be interested in the results of your questionnaire. Later in this chapter, you'll find examples of reports of the questionnaire on bullying and the questionnaire on reading strategies based on the analyses completed in Chapter 8. There's also a brief report of the results of the case study survey project.

◆ WHO IS THE AUDIENCE?

The first question is, Who is the audience for the report of the results of the questionnaire? There can be several audiences, and their information needs differ, usually in the level of detail required. The goal of each report is to persuasively present the results in the right way—that is, in a way in which the recipients can understand them and take action as necessary.

The types of audiences that you might have for your questionnaire results include the following:

- Stakeholders and decision makers
- Administrators and other executives
- Implementers such as teachers, parents, counselors, and school administrators
- Researchers (a report designed to communicate with other researchers)
- Persons affected by the decisions made based on the results of the questionnaire
- Questionnaire respondents
- Gatekeepers

This is by no means an exhaustive list, but rather one to help you think about who will be interested in your results.

Stakeholders and Decision Makers

The members of this audience are interested in the bottom line: the results. But they also want to know the details that support these results and recommendations so they can feel comfortable implementing the action plan that was created based on the decisions.

Administrators and Other Executives

These people are interested in the high-level recommendations based on the results of the analyses. They know you've just completed a survey project, and they want to know what you've found—but with little detail. A 5- to 10-page presentation provides the level of detail appropriate for this audience. There should be both charts and text—but keep it at the "big-picture" level. You can also put backup charts containing additional details in an appendix.

Implementers

These are the people who will put into practice the recommendations from the survey project team. They need to know very little about how the survey project was conducted, but they do need to know about response rates and sampling frames so they can tailor their implementation accordingly. This audience requires detail in the recommendations section.

Researchers

Researchers are interested in the "how" as well as the "what," so here's where all the detail about methodology goes. They want information about the lessons learned during the project. These include what worked well as you conducted your survey project and suggestions for further research. They also want to know how the results of your questionnaire support or contradict the results of similar survey projects.

Researchers want to know the details of the questionnaire methodology: What were the objectives of the survey project? How did you define the sampling frame? How did you select the participants? How did you decide the method of data collection? How did you do the pilot test? What did you do for follow-up of non-respondents? What was the response rate? How did you analyze the data? What were the results? What decisions and recommendations were made based on the results of the questionnaire?

Persons Affected by the Results

For some survey projects, implementing the results might affect people who were not part of the survey project but who are interested in understanding the reasons for implementing certain programs or making changes in the way things are done. This audience can best be served by a three- to five-page overview, focusing on the decisions and recommendations and the reasons for these recommendations.

Questionnaire Respondents and Gatekeepers

A one- to two-page overview, perhaps with a simple table or chart, will provide the level of detail that most questionnaire respondents require. If they want more information, they will contact you. Provide information about the overall goal of the survey project, the number of respondents, a high-level overview of the results, and how the results will be used. Include a thank-you note as part of the cover letter of the report, thanking them for their participation.

For Web-based questionnaires, you can also provide a URL to the questionnaire respondents and indicate that after a certain date they can visit that site to review the results of the study.

You might decide *not* to offer respondents a copy of the results, and that's fine. But you must provide a copy of the results to the gatekeeper. The gatekeeper will want to know the high-level results, including the recommendations and decisions made based on the questionnaire data. Again a one- or two-page summary will probably be sufficient with an offer of further information if the person is interested. You might want to arrange a visit to discuss the results and answer any questions the person may have.

◆ TAILORING THE REPORT TO AUDIENCE NEEDS

To illustrate reporting questionnaire results, let's begin by considering audiences for the two questionnaires used as examples in Chapter 8. For the questionnaire on reading strategies, the audiences include the researchers who created the reading strategies activities and the teachers whose students participated in these activities. As a reminder, the purpose of this survey project was to determine whether students who had learned about various reading strategies were actually using them. The decisions to be made on the basis of these questionnaire results included determining whether the activities might need to be revised or if additional suggestions for teachers might be needed to ensure that the reading strategies were used.

For the survey project on bullying, there are also multiple audiences: counselors who will design and implement programs designed to reduce the occurrence of bullying, teachers and school staff members who are concerned about the bullying taking place at the school, and parents who gave permission for their child to respond to the questionnaire. As a reminder, the purpose of this survey project was to identify incidences and types of bullying taking place in the school so that decisions could be made about how to make the school a safer place for all students.

We will have several audiences for our results: the sponsors (the PTO), parents, and teachers. And we will create two versions of the report for the PTO: A presentation highlighting the results and recommendations, and a more detailed report that provides backup for the presentation to provide answers to questions that might arise from the presentation. Only the shorter version is included in this chapter.

◆ WHAT ARE THE CONTENTS OF THE REPORT?

- Begin with an introduction and discussion of why the survey project was conducted:
  - What was the guiding question?
  - How will the results be used?
- Clearly state the results, and if you use inferential statistics, discuss statistical versus practical importance.
  - Include charts and graphs as appropriate.
  - Include more sophisticated analyses as appropriate, such as predictive models or multivariate analyses. Consult a statistics text or statistical consultant for help here.
  - Don't assume that association is causation. What other factors could explain the results?
  - If you used open-ended questions, you might want to include some representative responses.
- Include a discussion of methods involved in planning and conducting the survey project, and if you made trade-offs, describe them.

- Disaggregate the data to provide comparisons across subgroups, as appropriate.
- Include response rate and characteristics of the respondents, using descriptive statistics to provide information about the respondents.
- Provide conclusions, recommendations, and possible next steps and perhaps recommended action plans.

Depending on your audience, the six sections listed here can be in a different order and contain differing levels of detail. In most cases, the reader wants to know results first, followed by the supporting details. For a standard research report (i.e., the ones in which researchers talk to other researchers), there is a relatively standard order of contents that starts with the research question or purpose of the study, describes the methodology, and then presents the results and a discussion of the results. Typically, these reports include references to similar research and discuss how the results of the present study support or contradict results of studies in the research literature. Researchers expect this order so they can evaluate the results in the context of the methodology.

Some of your audiences appreciate receiving graphs or charts in their report. Graphs show results at a glance, but graphs can be misinterpreted. When people look at a graph, they make assumptions. Lines that go up are good; lines that go down are bad. Graphs include charts and tables such as cross-tabulations, pie charts, bar graphs, and line graphs. Pie charts use percentages. Bar graphs sometimes show raw data but can also show percentages. If your sample size is quite small, perhaps resulting from a low response rate (or a small target audience such as in our study of bullying), pie charts and other graphs can be misleading unless both the number and percentage are included. When a reader looks at a pie chart with percentages, he or she often does not think about the possibly small numbers that went into those percentages. Be sure your graphs tell the story you want to tell!

◆ REPORTING THE RESULTS OF THE READING STRATEGIES QUESTIONNAIRE

The following sections provide examples of reports for two audiences: researchers and teachers. As noted earlier, the researchers want detail, and the teachers want information they can use to help their students become better readers.

Audience 1: Researchers

The purpose of the survey project on reading strategies was to determine whether students in the third and fifth grades who had participated in special activities designed to help them become better readers were in fact using these strategies. Previous research indicated that students who used particular reading strategies were better readers as demonstrated by their scores on reading achievement tests as well as by teacher reports of student level of comprehension of what they read. The present study was designed to determine whether the third- and fifth-grade students who had participated in some special activities in which they learned about reading strategies actually were using these strategies.

The questionnaire consisted of 10 questions, each of which described a reading strategy that had been taught to the students. There were also two demographic questions: grade level and gender. Five questions were reverse worded—that is, students must indicate they did *not* use that reading strategy if they were a good reader. A sample of each type of question is presented in Figure 1.

Figure 1 Examples of Questions

Positive: I think about what will happen next in the story.

Negative: When I get confused about a part of the story, I skip that part of the story.

The 4-point response scale allowed the respondents to indicate whether they used that particular strategy most of the time, sometimes, rarely, or almost never.

Procedures

A note to parents describing the study was sent home with the students to inform them about the study. An opt-out permission note was used; that is, parents who did *not* want their child to complete the questionnaire returned the signed note. No parent withheld permission for his or her child to complete the questionnaire.

The classroom teacher administered the questionnaire during the reading class by reading a script provided by the research team. Students were told that completing the questionnaire was voluntary; all students agreed to complete the questionnaire. All students present on the day the questionnaire was administered participated in the study.

Results

A total of 35 students participated: 19 from the third-grade class and 16 from the fifth-grade class. Table 1 describes the participants.

Table 1   Respondents

	Grade Level		
	Third	Fifth	Total
Boys	7	9	16
Girls	12	7	19
Total	19	16	35

Data were disaggregated by grade level and by gender to understand possible differences between these subgroups. Means and standard deviations were computed for the third-grade and fifth-grade respondents and then for boys and girls within each grade level. Table 2 summarizes these results. An independent sample *t* test was computed, comparing the means for third and fifth graders (*t* = 5.02, *p* < .00). Sample sizes for the gender-by-grade comparison were considered too small to be tested statistically.

Table 2   Means and Standard Deviations for Grade by Gender

	Boys		Girls		Total	
	Mean	SD	Mean	SD	Mean	SD
Third grade	17.57	2.22	25.58	3.06	22.63	4.81
Fifth grade	30.22	4.68	30.71	4.57	30.44	4.21
Total	24.69	7.46	27.47	4.21		

Next, we examined possible differences in the strategies used most of the time by third and fifth graders. Table 3 summarizes these results.

Table 3   Reading Strategies Used "Most of the Time"

	Most of the Time	
Question	Third Grade	Fifth Grade
1. Before I begin reading a new book, I look at the pictures and title and try to guess what it is going to be about.	1	6
2. When I don't understand a part of the story, I just keep reading.	3	0
3. When I find a word in a story that I don't know, I read the sentences around it.	1	4
4. As I read, I can see pictures in my mind about what is happening in the story.	1	3
5. As I read a story, I ask myself questions about what will happen next.	0	4
6. I am confused by what I read.	2	0
7. When I get confused about a part of the story, I skip that part of the story.	1	0
8. I ask the teacher to tell me the words I don't know.	1	0
9. I think about what will happen next in the story.	0	2
10. I skip over words I do not know.	5	0

Discussion

As had been expected, fifth graders used the reading strategies more often than did the third graders. Although the sample sizes are very small for any grade-by-gender comparison, it is interesting to note that the means for the third- and fifth-grade girls were more similar than were the means for the third- and fifth-grade boys. In particular, the means were lowest for the third-grade boys.

As shown in Table 3, fifth graders tended to use more of the appropriate reading strategies than did the third graders. Interestingly, none of the fifth graders reported using the poor reading strategies (i.e., Questions 2, 6, 7, 8, and 10) most of the time, whereas several of the third graders reported using these strategies most of the time. It should also be noted that relatively few students reported using any of these strategies, whether these strategies were good or poor, most of the time. Rather they tended to report using these strategies "sometimes" and "rarely."

Recommendations

Because it appears that third-grade boys are not using many of the reading strategies on a regular basis, the activities might need to be modified to make them more effective with the third-grade boys. Results of the survey indicated that some third graders are reporting the use of poor reading strategies, so it is important for teachers to focus on identifying when students use these behaviors and help students change these behaviors. It is also important for teachers to reinforce the positive reading strategies that many third-grade girls as well as fifth graders are using.

Additional data should be gathered, including teacher observations of student reading habits and scores on reading achievement tests to determine if students who use these strategies do in fact read better, a finding that has been documented in the research literature previously. Think-aloud protocols, where students explain what they are doing as they read, might be one way to better understand how children are implementing these reading strategies and provide insight into ways to help third-grade boys become more proficient in the use of these reading strategies.

Audience 2: Teachers

The following boxes illustrate the level of detail appropriate for those affected by the results of the survey, the teachers. You'll note that the headings for each of the boxes provide a "storyboard": The audience can understand the essence of the results of reading just these headings. The information contained in the boxes should be made into a presentation format, using presentation software such as PowerPoint or Freelance. You might consider some of the special features of the presentation software, such as special transitions or building the points through successive slides. You might also consider adding graphics and color to emphasize your key messages.

The "How I Read" Questionnaire was given to third- and fifth-grade students.

- The purpose of the questionnaire was to determine whether students were using the reading strategies they had learned.
- Participants included all the students present on the day the questionnaire was given.
  - 19 students from the 3rd-grade class
  - 16 students from the 5th-grade class

The results showed that 5th graders were using more of the strategies than the 3rd graders.

- 3rd graders tended to use negative strategies, such as continuing to read when they did not understand a part of the story, more often than did 5th graders.
- No 5th grader reported using negative strategies "Most of the time."
- 3rd- and 5th-grade girls tended to use a similar number of positive strategies, whereas 3rd-grade boys used fewer positive strategies than did 5th-grade boys

Recommendations include several steps to improve reading skills.

- Revise the activities for 3rd-grade boys.
  - It is possible that the activities were not as effective for 3rd graders, particularly for boys.
- Help 3rd graders understand that some of the strategies they are using will hinder them in becoming good readers.
  - Several 3rd graders are using "negative" reading strategies.
- Reinforce the use of positive reading strategies in 5th graders

More data will help us better understand how children read.

- Gather information from teacher observation.
  - Use think-aloud protocols to probe student use of these strategies while they are reading rather than relying on self-report.
- Gather scores on reading achievement tests to determine whether students who are using the positive reading strategies are also earning high scores on reading achievement tests.
- Together we can help children become more effective readers!

◆ REPORTING THE RESULTS OF THE QUESTIONNAIRE ON BULLYING

For this survey project, there are three primary audiences: (a) counselors who will use the information to design and implement programs to reduce the occurrence of bullying, (b) teachers and school staff members who are concerned about the bullying taking place at the school and want to understand what the school can do, and (c) parents, because they gave permission for their child to respond to the questionnaire and want to know that their child has a safe environment at school.

The survey project team provided a draft report of the results to the counselors, who used this information to create recommendations and an action plan. Teachers and school staff members received a presentation with some details, including the specific plans for working with both targets and bullies, and parents received a short summary, with a focus on what actions the school plans to take to ameliorate the problem.

Audience 1: Counselors

Report on Bullying at Our School

Going to school should be a positive experience. But for the children who are the targets of bullies, that experience can be filled with fear, intimidation, and for some, physical harm. The purpose of the project was to determine the type and extent of bullying occurring at our school. The impetus for the project was the concern expressed by both teachers and parents over some recent bullying incidents. As a result of this concern, a short questionnaire was created to gather this information. A letter was sent to parents of all students in the third-, fourth-, and fifth-grade classes, notifying them of the project and asking permission for their child to respond to the questionnaire. A copy of the questionnaire was provided to parents along with the permission note. A total of 84 parents returned the permission note by the due date, with 17 parents either not returning the note by the deadline or asking that their child not respond to the questionnaire.

Procedures

The questionnaire was administered to 84 students during the first class period on March 10. Teachers read the script provided by the survey project team and answered questions that students had. Teachers reminded students that their participation was voluntary and that they were not to put their names on the questionnaire. All students completed the questionnaire, for a response rate of 83% of the total 101 students in these classes. Figure 1 shows the composition of the respondents.

Results

Of the 84 students who responded to the questionnaire, 22 (26.2%) reported they had been bullied in some way during the current school year. Of these students, 19 reported they had been bullied at least once a week, with 2 reporting being bullied a few times a day. For 3 of these students, the bullying bothers them so much that they don't like to come to school. Only 2 students reported that the bullying did not bother them.

Younger students tended to be bullied more than older students. Table 1 summarizes the grade and gender of the 22 students who reported having been bullied.

Figure 1 Gender-by-Grade Level of Questionnaire Respondents

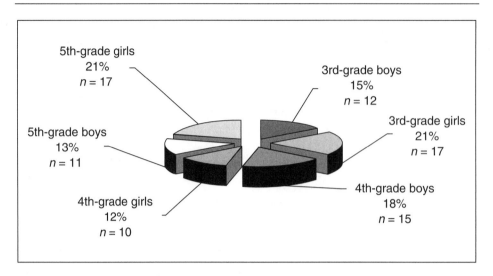

Table 1 Gender and Grade Level of Students Reporting Being Bullied

Third Grade		Fourth Grade		Fifth Grade	
Boys	Girls	Boys	Girls	Boys	Girls
6	4	5	2	3	2

The majority of the bullying took place in the cafeteria and on the playground, places where there tended to be noise and lots of movement with many students in these areas. Two students reported that bullying usually occurred in the hallways, and two others reported that bullying more frequently happened to them in the bathrooms.

The most frequent type of bullying was name-calling (86.4%), followed by shoving (68.2%). Both actions could take place in the cafeteria or on the playground in the context of all the movement and activities of the students in these venues. Seven students reported they had been physically threatened, two reported they had been physically hurt, six students reported something of theirs had been stolen, and six students reported something of theirs had been damaged.

Few students reported they had been the targets of only one type of bullying; the majority (54.5%) indicated they had been the targets of two types of bullying: name-calling and shoving. Table 2 shows the incidence of each type of bullying.

Students were also asked whether they had observed their classmates being bullied. Forty students, nearly half (47.6%) of the respondents, reported having seen another student being bullied. When asked what they did when they observed someone being bullied, 9 reported they joined in

Table 2   Types of Bullying Reported

	Frequency	*Percentage*[a]
I've been called names.	19	86.4
I've been physically threatened.	7	31.8
I've been shoved.	15	68.2
I've been physically hurt.	2	9.1
Something of mine has been stolen.	6	27.3
Something of mine has been damaged.	6	27.3
Total	55	

[a]Percentages are based on the total number of students reporting bullying, $n = 22$.

the bullying, and 12 reported that they told an adult. The remaining 19 either watched or walked away.

The majority (57.5%) of the students doing the bullying were the same age as the target child, with approximately another third (37.5%) being older than the target child. Only two children reported observing bullies who were younger than the target child. Fifteen students reported seeing a boy bully another student, 10 reported seeing a girl bully another student, and 15 students reported seeing a group of students bullying another student.

Responses of the 22 students who reported being bullied were disaggregated and analyzed separately to determine whether they had observed bullying, and if they had, what they most often did. Half of the students who reported being bullied also reported observing another student being bullied. Interestingly, three of these students reported they joined in the bullying, three told an adult, and the remaining five students either walked away or watched.

Recommendations and Next Steps

Based on the results of the questionnaire, plus observations on the playground and in the cafeteria as well as interviews with some teachers, we are making plans to make our school a safer place and one that students will enjoy attending. Here are the things we are planning:

- Hold a poster contest in which students will create posters about bullying with slogans such as the following:
  - "Friends aren't friends if you call them names"
  - "If you see someone being bullied and don't do anything, then your silence is your approval"
- Create a bully-free zone on the playground and in the cafeteria
- Train peer mediators to work with bullies and their targets

- Provide parents with the warning signs of bullying, because their child might not talk with them about what's happening at school
- Provide a box where students can put information about bullies and bullying anonymously
- Implement an intervention plan where the target and bully child will work with a counselor to understand the issues on why the bullying occurred

A task force consisting of teachers, parents, counselors, and school administrators will be created to begin work on implementing these recommendations.

Audience 2: Teachers and School Staff

The following presentation illustrates the level of detail appropriate for the teachers and school staff who will be implementing the new activities. Note the "storyboard" format, with the essence of the message conveyed in the headings of the boxes, which would be headings of slides in a slide presentation format.

The survey project on bullying at our school has helped us identify the incidence of bullying.

- We want our school to be safe for all children.
  - We conducted a questionnaire, based on teacher and parent concerns, to learn more about bullying at our school.
- 84 students responded to the questionnaire; of these, 22 reported they had been bullied during the current school year.
- The most common kinds of bullying included name-calling (86.4%) and shoving (68.2%).
- Some students reported having things stolen (27.3%) or having something of theirs damaged (27.3%).
- Only 2 students reported having been physically hurt.

The incidence of bullying is too much, too often for many students.

- Over half (54.5%) of the students reported they had experienced more than one type of bullying, most commonly being called names and being shoved.
- Younger children were more often the targets of bullying, with most bullying taking place on the playground or in the cafeteria.
- 19 students reported being bullied at least once a week, with 10 students reporting being bullied once a day or more.
- 3 students reported being very bothered by being bullied—so much so that they don't like to come to school.

Almost half the students reported seeing another student bullied.

- Although the most frequent response was to tell an adult (12 or 30%), 9 (22.5%) reported they joined in the bullying.
- Nearly half (47.5%) reported they either watched or walked away.
- Some students (3) who had been bullied reported that when they saw another student being bullied, they joined in.
- Only 3 of these students reported the bullying to an adult, and the remaining 5 students either watched or walked away.

We have identified several ways to make our school safer:

- Hold a poster contest to create posters about bullying
- Create a bully-free zone on the playground and in the cafeteria
- Train peer mediators to work with bullies and their targets
- Provide parents with warning signs indicating their child may be a target
- Provide a box where students can submit information about bullying anonymously
- Create an intervention plan for bully and target students to work with a school counselor

We plan to create a task force to implement these recommendations.

- The task force will include teachers, counselors, parents, and school staff members.
- If you are interested in participating, please contact Jeanne Brooks in the counseling office.
- Thanks for your interest!

Audience 3: Parents

The following shows the level of detail and kinds of information appropriate for parents.

Recently, we gathered information about the incidence of bullying at our school. Some of you expressed concerns about the safety of the school for your child, and we want to be responsive to your concerns.

We gathered information using the short questionnaire that we provided to you recently when we asked permission for your child to participate in this study. As you know, your child responded to the questionnaire with his or her classmates on March 10. What we found was that about one fourth of our students have experienced bullying this school year, with more children in the lower grades being the targets of a bully.

We found that name-calling and shoving were the most frequent kinds of bullying and that over half the children experienced more than one kind of bullying. But more seriously, we found that some children had something of theirs stolen or damaged and that two children reported having been physically hurt.

We learned that much of the bullying takes place in the cafeteria or on the playground, with a few incidents of bullying taking place in hallways, classrooms, and bathrooms. We also learned that for three of the students, the bullying bothered them so much that they don't like to come to school.

When we asked students whether they had seen other students being bullied, nearly half (47.6%) reported that they had. Of these students, 9 reported that they joined in the bullying, 12 said they told an adult, and the remaining 19 students either watched the bullying happen or walked away.

After we reviewed these results, we made observations on the playground and in the school cafeteria. We also talked with several teachers. These observations and the interviews with the teachers corroborated the results of the questionnaire.

Here's what we're going to do to make our school a safer place:

- Hold a poster contest in which students will create posters about bullying with slogans such as the following:
  - "Friends aren't friends if you call them names"
  - "If you see someone being bullied and don't do anything, then your silence is your approval"
- Create a bully-free zone on the playground and in the cafeteria
- Train peer mediators to work with bullies and their targets
- Provide parents with the warning signs of bullying, because their child might not talk with them about what's happening at school
- Provide a box where students can put information about bullies and bullying anonymously
- Implement an intervention plan where the target and bully child will work with a counselor to understand the issues on why the bullying occurred

We plan to create a task force to begin implementing these recommendations. If you are interested in working with us, please contact Jeanne Brooks at the school counseling office at 325-9129.

You can also help by looking for clues that your child may be a target (or a victim) of bullying. Here are some signs to look for:

- Makes excuses for not wanting to go to school
- Has difficulty sleeping or eating
- Shows anxiety about school, such as refusing to go out for recess, eat lunch in the cafeteria, or use the bathrooms
- Tells you he or she has lost personal items or needs money for extra school supplies (more than what would seem normal based on past requests)
- Comes home with a bruise or torn clothing

If you note any of these signs, talk with your child, and talk with your child's teacher or the school counselor. We want your child to feel safe and welcome at our school.

◆ REPORTING THE RESULTS OF THE PARENT INVOLVEMENT SURVEY

Audience: Persons Attending the PTO Meeting

The following presentation illustrates the level of detail appropriate for the teachers and parents who attend a PTO meeting and need the high-level overview, the results, and the recommendations. None of the disaggregated results are included in this presentation.

The questionnaire on parent involvement helped us identify ways to increase current levels of participation.

- All parents from our three elementary schools were invited to respond to the questionnaire.
- 756 parents responded to the questionnaire for a 50.5% response rate.
- Of the 756 parents, 522 (69%) were mothers.
  - 31% were from RiverChase.
  - 39% were from Gilchrist.
  - 30% were from Madison.
  - Of the 15 different types of opportunities available for parents, the majority of parents were aware of only 9.

There was not a direct relationship between knowing about an activity and participating.

- Parent-teacher conferences, back-to-school night, PTO meetings, and fundraising activities had the highest awareness and participation rates.
- Many parents were aware of other activities, including the homework hot-line, the monthly family night, and school board meetings but seldom attended.
- The majority of parents indicated that they were not aware of opportunities to serve as a computer aide, library aide, or teacher's assistant.

Parents were somewhat satisfied with most of the activities.

- Respondents were most satisfied with the monthly family night, the Parent Resource Center, and parent-teacher conferences.
- They were least satisfied with the small group coffee hour discussions.
- There was a strong positive relationship between participating in an activity and degree of satisfaction.

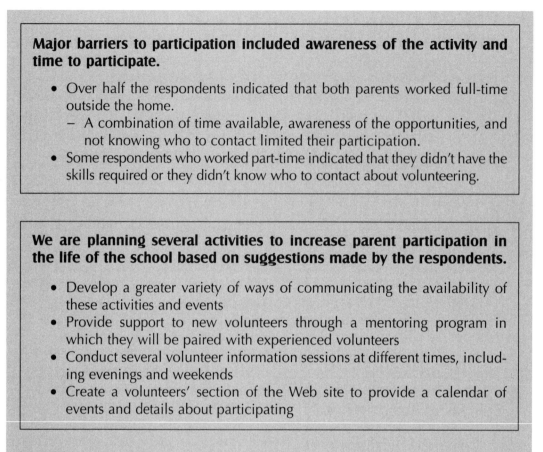

Major barriers to participation included awareness of the activity and time to participate.

- Over half the respondents indicated that both parents worked full-time outside the home.
  - A combination of time available, awareness of the opportunities, and not knowing who to contact limited their participation.
- Some respondents who worked part-time indicated that they didn't have the skills required or they didn't know who to contact about volunteering.

We are planning several activities to increase parent participation in the life of the school based on suggestions made by the respondents.

- Develop a greater variety of ways of communicating the availability of these activities and events
- Provide support to new volunteers through a mentoring program in which they will be paired with experienced volunteers
- Conduct several volunteer information sessions at different times, including evenings and weekends
- Create a volunteers' section of the Web site to provide a calendar of events and details about participating

Note: Examples of detailed written reports were provided earlier in this chapter; one is not included here for the parent involvement study.

Checklist for Communicating the Results

Use the following checklist to ensure that you've created reports for the various audiences. Be sure to consider the level of detail each audience requires.

- ❑ Did you identify the various audiences for your report and identify their information needs?
- ❑ Does each version of your report clearly provide the decisions made (the recommendations) and the plans for implementing these recommendations?
- ❑ Have you planned to create both written reports and presentations, depending on the information needs of your audience?
- ❑ Have you offered to provide an in-person report if any of your audiences would benefit from your presentation?
- ❑ Have you proofread your report carefully to ensure that it's correct as well as professional looking?
- ❑ Have you included a review process to ensure that the reports communicate the message you intended?
- ❑ Have you shared the reports with the project sponsor prior to disseminating them?

Resource: Questionnaire for the Case Study

◆ PARENT INVOLVEMENT QUESTIONNAIRE

(A Web-Based Questionnaire)

This questionnaire is designed to evaluate how well our school is reaching out to involve parents in the life of the school. We'll use the information you provide to create ways to fit the schedules and interests of our parents or to make other adjustments to our activities based on your responses. All responses will be confidential, and there is no identifying information on this questionnaire.

1. For each of the following activities, please indicate whether you're familiar with the activity and, if so, your participation in that activity during the last school year. Please mark your responses by clicking on the circle that matches your choices for each activity.

(Note: If your child is in kindergarten, and you have no other children in the elementary school, please indicate only whether you're aware of each activity.)

Activity	I Am Aware of This Activity		Participation in This Activity in the Past School Year		
			None	1–2 times	3 or more times
Parent-teacher conference	Yes ○	No ○	○	○	○
Homework hotline for parents	Yes ○	No ○	○	○	○

(Continued)

179

(Continued)

Field trip with my child's class	Yes ○	No ○	○	○	○
Library aide	Yes ○	No ○	○	○	○
Computer aide	Yes ○	No ○	○	○	○
Teacher assistant	Yes ○	No ○	○	○	○
Fundraising activities	Yes ○	No ○	○	○	○
Back-to-school night	Yes ○	No ○	○	○	○
PTO meetings	Yes ○	No ○	○	○	○
Small-group coffee hour discussions	Yes ○	No ○	○	○	○
Monthly birthday party organizer	Yes ○	No ○	○	○	○
Monthly family night	Yes ○	No ○	○	○	○
Parent Advisory Committee	Yes ○	No ○	○	○	○
Parent Resource Center	Yes ○	No ○	○	○	○
Attend school board meetings	Yes ○	No ○	○	○	○

2. Following is a list of those activities in which you indicated you participated last year. For each activity, indicate how satisfied you are using the following ratings:

Very satisfied

Somewhat satisfied

Somewhat dissatisfied

Very dissatisfied

(Note: The activities listed here will depend on the responses to Question 1. An advantage of using a Web-based questionnaire is that respondents will be asked to rate only those

activities in which they have participated during the previous school year. If a respondent has not participated in any of the activities, this question will not appear.)

3. You indicated you were "Very dissatisfied" with the following activities. In the space provided, please tell us the nature of your dissatisfaction and what we can do to provide a more positive experience.

(Note: The activities listed here will depend on the responses to Question 2. An advantage of using a Web-based questionnaire is that respondents will be asked to comment on only those activities for which they gave a rating of "Very dissatisfied." If a respondent did not mark any activity as "Very dissatisfied," this question will not appear.)

4. We know that for some parents it may be challenging to participate in school activities as much as they would like. Please indicate whether any of the following are barriers to your participation in the parent involvement activities listed above.

Please respond by clicking the circle next to the item listed if this is a barrier for you.

Barrier	*This Is a Barrier for Me*
I often don't have child care.	O
I didn't know many of these events were happening.	O
I don't know who to contact to volunteer.	O
I don't feel I have the skills necessary.	O
I've had negative experiences in the past.	O
My work schedule won't allow me to participate.	O
I have some feelings of alienation toward school, teachers, or administrators.	O
I don't have transportation.	O
I'm not sure how to participate.	O

5. In the box below, please list anything else that is a barrier to your participation in school activities.

6. Please use the space below to list other activities for parents you'd like to see our school offer for parents and families.

7. For each of the activities below, please indicate how likely you are to participate in that activity this school year. Assume that the barriers listed above (with the exception of not having time) could be addressed.

Activity	Very Likely	Somewhat Likely	Somewhat Unlikely	Very Unlikely
Parent-teacher conference	○	○	○	○
Homework hotline for parents	○	○	○	○
Field trip with my child's class	○	○	○	○
Library aide	○	○	○	○
Computer aide	○	○	○	○
Teacher assistant	○	○	○	○
Fundraising activities	○	○	○	○
Back-to-school night	○	○	○	○
PTO meetings	○	○	○	○
Small-group coffee hour discussions	○	○	○	○
Monthly birthday party organizer	○	○	○	○
Monthly family night	○	○	○	○
Parent Advisory Committee	○	○	○	○
Parent Resource Center	○	○	○	○
Attend school board meetings	○	○	○	○

Please tell us about you.

8. My child/children attend the
   - ○ RiverChase Elementary School
   - ○ Gilchrist Elementary School
   - ○ Madison Elementary School

9. What grade or grades are your children in this school year?
Please click on the circle for each child you have in elementary school this year.

Kindergarten	First Grade	Second Grade	Third Grade	Fourth Grade
○	○	○	○	○

10. Please tell us about your employment.

	Full-Time	Part-Time	Not At All
I am employed outside my home	○	○	○
My spouse is employed outside the home	○	○	○

11. Please indicate your race/ethnicity. This information will be used for analysis of the results.

White, not Hispanic	Hispanic	African American	Asian/Pacific Islander	Other
○	○	○	○	○

12. Please indicate your gender.

Male	Female
○	○

Thank you for responding to our questionnaire. We will use your information to provide interesting activities for you so that together we can provide an even better quality education for your child!

Results will be presented at the PTO meeting in November. We encourage you to attend and to provide input as we plan parent involvement activities that are responsive to your needs and interests.

Bibliography

These are some additional resources that may be useful.

Bachman, D., Elfrink, J., & Vazzana, G. (1996). Tracking the progress of e-mail vs. snail mail. *Marketing Research, 8*(2), 31–35.

Best, S. J., Krueger, B., Hubbard, C., & Smith, A. (2001). An assessment of the generalizability of Internet surveys. *Social Science Computer Review, 19,* 1311–1345.

Blalock, H. M. (1972). *Social statistics.* New York: McGraw-Hill.

Cox, K. (1996). *Your opinion please!* Thousand Oaks, CA: Corwin.

Crawford, S. D., Couper, M. P., & Lamias, M. J. (2001). Web surveys: Perception of burden. *Social Science Computer Review, 19,* 146–162.

Dickson, J. P., & Maclachan, D. (1996). Fax surveys: Return patterns and comparisons with mail surveys. *Journal of Marketing Research, 33,* 103–115.

Dillman, D. (1999). Mail and other self-administered surveys in the 21st century: The beginning of a new era. *Gallup Research Journal, 2*(1), 121–140.

Dillman, D. A., & Bowker, D. K. (2001). *The web questionnaire: Challenge to survey methodologists.* Working paper available from http://survey.sesrc.wsu.edu/dillman/papers.htm

Dillman, D. A., Phelps, G., Tortora, R., Swift, K., Kohrell, J., & Berck, J. (2001, May). *How choice of survey mode influences answers to customer satisfaction surveys.* Paper presented to the American Association for Public Opinion Research Annual Conference, Montreal.

Dillman, D. A., Tortora, R. D., & Bowker, D. (1998). *Principles for constructing web surveys.* Working paper available from http://survey.sesrc.wsu.edu/dillman/papers.htm

Dillman, D. A., Tortora, R. D., Conrad, J., & Bowker, D. (1998). *Influence of plain vs. fancy design on response rates of Web surveys.* Working paper available from http://survey.sesrc.wsu.edu/dillman/papers.htm

Fink, A., & Kosecoff, J. (1998). *How to conduct surveys: A step-by-step guide* (2nd ed.). Thousand Oaks, CA: Sage.

Frary, R. (2000). *A brief guide to questionnaire development.* Retrieved November 30, 2003, from http://www.testscoring.vt.edu/fraryquest.html

Kish, L. (1965). *Survey sampling.* New York: John Wiley.

Morrel-Samuels, P. (2002, February). Getting the truth into workplace surveys. *Harvard Business Review,* pp. 111–118.

Opperman, M. (1995). E-mail surveys—potential and pitfalls. *Marketing Research, 7*(3), 29–33.

Parker, L. (1992). Collecting data the e-mail way. *Training & Development, 46*(7), 52–54.

Redline, C., & Dillman, D. (2002). The influence of alternative visual designs on respondents' performance with branching instructions in self-administered questionnaires. In R. Groves, D. Dillman, J. Eltinge, & R. Little (Eds.), *Survey nonresponse.* New York: Wiley.

Sanchez, M. E. (1992). Effects of questionnaire design on the quality of survey data. *Public Opinion Quarterly, 56*(2), 206–217.

Sudman, S. (1976). *Applied sampling.* New York: Academic Press.

Tourangeau, R. L., Rips, J., & Rasinskui, K. (2000). *The psychology of survey response.* Cambridge, UK: Cambridge University Press.

Listed below are some Web survey packages. I do not endorse any of these but offer them as examples. In addition to formatting the questionnaires for Web delivery, most feature the following activities: (a) managing the distribution of e-mail invitations, (b) built-in statistical analysis and reporting capabilities, and (c) automatic tracking of people who have responded so follow-ups can be sent.

Perseus's Survey Solutions for the Web

Create Research System's The Survey System

Training Technologies' Survey Tracker.

Check also a search engine such as Google, using search terms such as "Web-based survey" or "electronic surveys."

References

Abrami, P. C., Cholmsky, P., & Gordon, R. (2000). *Statistical analysis for the social sciences: An interactive approach.* Boston: Allyn & Bacon.

American Educational Research Association. (2000). *The ethical standards of the American Educational Research Association.* Retrieved November 7, 2003, from www.aera.net/about/policy/ethics.htm

American Psychological Association. (2001). *Publication manual of the American Psychological Association* (5th ed.). Washington, DC: Author.

American Psychological Association. (2003). APA ethics code. *American Psychologist, 57*(12). Retrieved November 7, 2003, from www.apa.org/ethics

Anastasi, A. (1982). *Psychological testing* (5th ed.). New York: Macmillan.

Arhar, J. M., Holly, M. L., & Kasten, W. C. (2000). *Action research for teachers.* New York: Prentice Hall.

Baruch, Y. (1999). Response rates in academic studies: A comparative analysis. *Human Relations, 52,* 421–434.

Conover, J. (1998). *Practical nonparametric statistics* (3rd ed.). New York: John Wiley.

Cook, C., Heath, F., & Thompson, R. (2000). A meta-analysis of response rates in Web or Internet-based surveys. *Educational and Psychological Measurement, 60,* 821–836.

Dillman, D. A. (2000). *Mail and Internet surveys: The tailored design method.* New York: John Wiley.

Fraenkel, J. R., & Wallen, N. E. (2002). *How to design and evaluate research in education* (5th ed.). New York: McGraw-Hill.

Gall, M. D. (2002). *Educational research: An introduction* (7th ed.). Boston: Allyn & Bacon.

Gibbons, J. D. (1976). *Nonparametric methods for quantitative analysis.* New York: Holt, Rinehart & Winston.

Glass, G. V., & Hopkins, K. D. (1996). *Statistical methods.* Boston: Allyn & Bacon.

Green, K. E., & Hutchinson, S. R. (1996, April). *Reviewing the research on mail survey response rates: Meta-analysis.* Paper presented at the annual meeting of the American Educational Research Association, New York.

Hays, W. L. (1994). *Statistics.* New York: Holt, Rinehart & Winston.

Jayanthi, M., & Nelson, J. S. (2001). *Savvy decision making: An administrator's guide to focus groups in schools.* Thousand Oaks, CA: Corwin.

Johnson, B., & Christensen, L. (2000). *Educational research: Quantitative and qual approaches.* Boston: Allyn & Bacon.

Kittleson, M. (1997). Determining effective follow-up of e-mail surveys. *American Journal of Health Behavior, 21*, 193–196.

Kline, P. (1994). *An easy guide to factor analysis.* New York: Routledge.

Krueger, R. A., & Casey, M. A. (2000). *Focus groups* (3rd ed.). Thousand Oaks, CA: Sage.

Krug, S., & Black, R. (2000). *Don't make me think: A common sense approach to Web usability.* Indianapolis, IN: Que.

Lackey, N. R., Sullivan, J. J., & Pett, M. A. (2003). *Making sense of factor analysis: The use of factor analysis for instrument development in health care research.* Thousand Oaks, CA: Sage.

Likert, R. (1932). A technique for the measurement of attitudes. *Archives of Psychology, 140,* 5–53.

Matz, C. M. (1999). *Administration of Web versus paper surveys: Mode effects and response rates.* Master's thesis, University of North Carolina. (ERIC Document Reproduction Services No. ED439694)

McLean, J. E. (1995). *Improving education through action research: A guide for teachers and administrators.* Thousand Oaks, CA: Corwin.

Mertler, C. A., & Charles, C. M. (2001). *Introduction to educational research* (4th ed.). Boston: Allyn & Bacon.

Mills, G. E. (1999). *Action research: A guide for the teacher researcher.* New York: Prentice Hall.

Niederst, J. (2001). *Web design in a nutshell.* Sebastopol, CA: O'Reilly.

Nielsen, J. (2000). *Designing Web usability: The practice of simplicity.* Indianapolis, IN: New Riders.

Nunnally, J. C. (1978). *Psychometric theory* (2nd ed.). New York: McGraw-Hill.

Osgood, C. E., Suci, G. J., & Tannenbaum, P. H. (1957). *The measurement of meaning.* Urbana: University of Illinois Press.

Shaw, M. E., & Wright, J. M. (1967). *Scales of measurement for attitudes.* New York: McGraw-Hill.

Solomon, D. J. (2001). Conducting Web-based surveys. *Practical Assessment, Research, & Evaluation, 7*(19). Retrieved November 30, 2003, from http://ericae.net/pare/getvn.asp?v=7&n=19

Sprinthall, R. C. (2003). *Basic statistical analysis* (7th ed.). Boston: Allyn & Bacon.

Thomas, S. J. (1999). *Designing surveys that work! A step-by-step guide.* Thousand Oaks, CA: Corwin.

Index

CORWIN PRESS

The Corwin Press logo—a raven striding across an open book—represents the union of courage and learning. Corwin Press is committed to improving education for all learners by publishing books and other professional development resources for those serving the field of K–12 education. By providing practical, hands-on materials, Corwin Press continues to carry out the promise of its motto: **"Helping Educators Do Their Work Better."**

CONTENTS

KT-376-599

THE DISAPPEARED

This book describes some of the most baffling and mysterious disappearances of all time. Many of them have remained unsolved for centuries.

ASKING QUESTIONS

When people or things suddenly vanish, it is natural to ask questions – and often there is a simple explanation. Maybe a crime has been committed, or an accident of some kind has taken place.

Since the 1950s many mysterious disappearances have taken place in the stretch of ocean known as the Bermuda Triangle in the western North Atlantic.

But sometimes people vanish in **bizarre** circumstances, and there are no clues to what happened – or the clues that are left behind just add to the mystery. Occasionally, an entire ship will vanish without trace, or an aircraft will take off and never be seen again.

The British explorer Percy Fawcett disappeared in the 1920s while searching for a lost city in the jungles of Brazil.

UNEⓍPLAINED

...RANCES

Warwickshire County Council

BEDWORTH		
9m		
5/10/11		
KRL 4/16		
28 JAN		

This item is to be returned or renewed before the
latest date above. It may be borrowed for a further
period if not in demand. **To renew your books:**

- **Phone the 24/7 Renewal Line 01926 499273 or**
- **Visit www.warwickshire.gov.uk/libraries**

Discover • Imagine • Learn • *with libraries*

**Warwickshire
County Council**

Working for
Warwickshire

DISCARDED

013251349X

Project Editor: Paul Manning/White-Thomson Publishing
Designer: Tim Mayer/White-Thomson Publishing
Picture Researcher: Maria Joannou

Copyright © QED Publishing, 2010

First published in the UK in 2010 by
QED Publishing
A Quarto Group Company
226 City Road
London EC1V 2TT

www.qed-publishing.co.uk

All rights reserved. No part of this publication may
be reproduced, stored in a retrieval system, or
transmitted in any form or by any means, electronic,
mechanical, photocopying, recording, or otherwise,
without the prior permission of the publisher, nor be
otherwise circulated in any form of binding or cover
other than that in which it is published and without a
similar condition being imposed on the subsequent
purchaser.

ISBN 978-1-84835-441-8

Printed and bound in China

Picture credits
Key: t=top, b=bottom, r=right, l=left, c=centre

Alamy Images Mary Evans Picture Library 18l, Paul Williams 20;
Corbis Bettmann 8, Richard T. Nowitz 12, Theo Allofs 25, Wolfgang
Kaehler 29; Getty Images Time & Life Pictures 6, National
Geographic/Sarah Leen 11b, National Geographic 13, AFP/Stringer
22t, Mallory and Irvine Expedition/Jim Fagiolo 23, 31b, De Agostini
Picture Library 26; Photoshot UPPA 14; Shutterstock Steve Collender
2, Eky Chan 3, Christophe Rouziou 5b, Rovenko Design 21, Igor
Plotnikov 22b, Dmitry Rukhlenko 27, Vitor Costa 28-29b; Stefan
Chabluk 4t, 11t, 24r; Topham Picturepoint 16, The Granger Collection
4b, 24l; U.S. Navy National Museum of Naval Aviation 7t, 31t, U.S.
Naval Historical Center Photograph 9; Wikimedia Commons 10, 17,
3bylunch 5t, Zaian 15b, Marie-Lan Nguyen 18r, ©Argenberg/http://
www.argenberg.com/album/ 19; Wikipedia 28t

The words in **bold** are explained in
the Glossary on page 30.

You can find the answers
to the questions asked on
these notebooks on page 31.

DISTRESS SIGNALS

Usually ships or aircrafts that get into difficulties send out distress signals – but not always. When a DC4 airliner disappeared over Lake Michigan during a routine flight from New York to Seattle on 23 June 1950, no call for help was ever received. Debris was later found floating in the water, but the wreckage of the plane itself has never been found.

Just as baffling is the case of the three lighthouse keepers who disappeared on the remote Scottish island of Eilean Mohr. Inside the lighthouse, everything had been left in perfect order. The **logbook** had been kept up to date and there was no sign of anything wrong. Yet the men vanished without trace and were never seen again.

Lake Michigan in North America has been the scene of several unexplained incidents involving ships and planes.

How many answers to famous unsolved mysteries lie at the bottom of the sea?

THE LOST PATROL

Over the last 60 years, the area of ocean known as the Bermuda Triangle has been the scene of many strange disappearances. One of the most mysterious was the case of Flight 19.

 The legendary 'lost squadron', Flight 19, believed lost in the Bermuda Triangle shortly after the end of the Second World War.

DISAPPEARANCE FILE

Subject Flight 19
Date 5 December 1945
Place Coast of Florida, USA
Status UNEXPLAINED

LOST AT SEA

On 5 December 1945, a flight of five US Avenger torpedo bombers took off from Fort Lauderdale Air Force base in Florida, USA. The pilots were due to carry out a routine practice bombing attack at sea.

After the planes had completed the practice, the flight commander, Lieutenant Charles Carroll Taylor, exchanged several routine radio messages with base. But then his messages became stranger. Shortly afterwards, all contact was lost. The planes were never seen again.

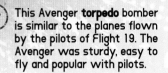

This Avenger **torpedo** bomber is similar to the planes flown by the pilots of Flight 19. The Avenger was sturdy, easy to fly and popular with pilots.

WHAT REALLY HAPPENED?

The truth about Flight 19 will probably never be known. The official story was that the planes simply got lost and ditched in the sea. One theory is that unusual 'magnetic forces' in the Bermuda Triangle may have interfered with compasses and other equipment on board the planes.

NO SURVIVORS

As soon as the aircraft were reported missing, a search was mounted. Aircraft and ships in the area were asked to watch out for wreckage and survivors. Nothing was ever found.

WHAT HAPPENED NEXT?

The US Navy launched an investigation. It was found that after the bombing practice, the planes had headed northeast to the Bahamas, but that for some reason, the flight commander had thought they were heading south west to the Florida Keys. Instead of returning to Florida, in fact he led the planes further out to sea. The report could not explain how he made such a basic mistake. It concluded with the words 'Cause Unknown'.

Who commanded Flight 19?

What type of plane were the pilots flying?

What were the final words of the Navy's report?

When a big ship goes down, investigators can often piece together the story of what happened by studying the wreckage. But if a vessel vanishes without trace, the mystery can remain unsolved forever.

DISAPPEARANCE FILE

Subject	USS Cyclops
Date	March 1918
Place	North Atlantic Ocean
Status	UNEXPLAINED

Some believe that the USS Cyclops' huge cargo of ore made her **unstable** and that she sank in a heavy storm.

One such case was the USS *Cyclops*, a 17,000-tonne **cargo** ship owned by the US Navy. Sometime after 4 March 1918, the ship vanished while carrying a cargo of **ore** from Rio de Janeiro in Brazil to Baltimore, Maryland, on the east coast of the USA.

All 306 of the ship's passengers and crew disappeared without trace. The Navy had lost warships in battle before, but it was very unusual for so many lives to be lost so mysteriously.

DISTURBING

At the time the *Cyclops* vanished, the USA was at war with Germany. Some believed the ship could have been 'stolen' by its German-born captain and handed over to the enemy.

After the search for the missing ship began, the US Navy received a disturbing **telegram** from a US official in Barbados, sent before the *Cyclops* went missing. According to the official, the ship's captain had taken on a lot of extra coal and food, as if he was preparing for a long voyage. The official also said that many of the passengers had German names. His message ended: "I fear a fate worse than sinking."

This crew member was one of 236 officers and men who are believed to have lost their lives when the USS *Cyclops* disappeared.

How many people were on board the USS *Cyclops* when it vanished?

What nationality was the ship's captain?

What was the ship carrying when it vanished?

WHAT REALLY HAPPENED?

One theory, supported by the Barbados telegram, is that German passengers took over the Cyclops, killed the crew and sailed to Germany. But after the war ended, the Germans denied all knowledge of the ship. Many other theories have been suggested, but none that really solves the mystery.

FLIGHT INTO MYSTERY

In 1937, American pilot Amelia Earhart set off to become the first woman to fly around the world. It was a journey from which she never returned.

Aged 40, Amelia Earhart was an outstanding pilot who broke many flying records. Before her disappearance, both she and her navigator Fred Noonan had successfully completed many long flights.

EMPTY OCEAN

Just after midnight on 2 July, Earhart took off from Lae in New Guinea on one of the final stages of her journey. She was bound for Howland Island, a tiny strip of land in the middle of the Pacific, where a US coastguard ship, the *Itasca*, was waiting to guide her in.

Early that morning, the *Itasca* picked up a radio message from Earhart saying that she could not find Howland Island. After this, the signals from Earhart's Electra 10E plane became fainter and fainter. Then there was silence.

DISAPPEARANCE FILE

Subject   Amelia Earhart
Date   2 July 1937
Place   Pacific Ocean
Status   UNEXPLAINED

OUT OF FUEL

At first, people thought that Earhart had run out of fuel and crashed into the sea. Then the radio signals were **analyzed**. One seemed to come from Gardner Island, about 500 kilometres south of Howland. Later, the island was searched, and a skeleton, a woman's shoe and a piece of **aluminium**, possibly from an aircraft, were found.

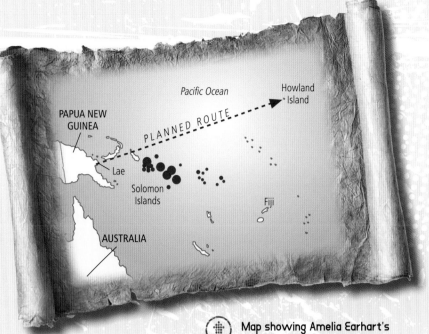

Map showing Amelia Earhart's planned route from Lae, New Guinea, to Howland Island, halfway between Australia and Hawaii, USA.

WHAT REALLY HAPPENED?

*Some have claimed that Earhart crash-landed on Japanese-occupied Saipan Island, and was later executed as a US **spy**. However, photographs showing Earhart as a prisoner turned out to be fake. Others believe Earhart is still alive somewhere under another name, but there is no evidence to support this.*

Over the years, many theories were put forward to explain Amelia Earhart's disappearance, but nothing was ever found that could be proved to be from her plane. Her case remains one of the great unsolved mysteries of the twentieth century.

What type of aircraft was Earhart flying?

Who was Earhart's navigator?

Which island was Earhart heading for when she vanished?

THE LOST COLONY

In sixteenth-century America, many **settlers** lost their lives in the struggle to build a future in the 'New World'. But could a whole community of 115 people really disappear without leaving any trace?

ON ROANOKE ISLAND

In 1585, English settlers arrived to found a colony on Roanoke, a small island off the coast of North Carolina. Life was hard, and the small community suffered many setbacks. But when the colony's governor left and returned three years later, he was shocked by what he found. Everyone had gone. The houses were empty, and the paths overgrown with weeds. The only clue to what had happened was a single word, 'CROATOAN', carved on a wooden post.

This reconstruction of an early English settlers' village in Virginia shows how the Roanoke colony might have looked.

DISAPPEARANCE FILE

Subject The Lost Colony of Roanoke
Date 1587
Place Roanoke, Virginia
Status UNEXPLAINED

WHAT REALLY HAPPENED?

*One possibility is that the settlers ran out of food, tried to return to England but died on the journey. More likely, the survivors ended up living among nearby Native American tribes, who either adopted or **enslaved** them. Scientists and historians are now testing this theory.*

'CROATOAN'

Before he left, the governor had told the settlers that if anything went wrong, they were to leave a clue to what had happened. If they went to live with the nearby, friendly Croatoan tribe, they were to write 'CROATOAN' on a tree. If they were attacked or driven out against their will, they were to carve a cross instead.

For years afterwards, people tried to find out what had happened. Some reported seeing fair-skinned people on nearby Croatoan Island. Others reported seeing traces of settlements further along the North Carolina coast. To this day, no one can say for certain what happened to the Roanoke settlers.

 Archaeologists **excavate** the site of a fort close to where the original Roanoke colony is believed to have stood.

When was the Roanoke colony founded?

How many colonists disappeared?

What word was found carved on a post at Roanoke?

THE LINER THAT VANISHED

On 26 July 1909, the luxury steamer SS *Waratah* set sail from Durban in South Africa with 211 passengers and crew. Built to carry passengers emigrating from Europe to Australia, the *Waratah* was returning to England after her second voyage.

BRIGHT FLASHES

On the 27 July, a ship called the *Harlow* spotted a large steamer that looked like the *Waratah* some distance away. Later, the crew of the *Harlow* saw two bright flashes on the horizon, but they thought they were caused by fires on the shore.

The *Waratah* was due to reach Cape Town on 29 July. She never arrived. Naval ships searched the area where she was last seen, but no trace of her was ever found.

DISAPPEARANCE FILE

Subject	SS Waratah
Date	27 July 1909
Place	Indian Ocean
Status	UNEXPLAINED

Known as the 'Australian *Titanic*', the SS *Waratah* was only one year old at the time of her disappearance. The ship did not carry a radio, but this was not unusual at the time.

PUBLIC ENQUIRY

After the *Waratah* disappeared, a public enquiry was held in London. Some experts said the ship might have been top-heavy; others said she could have been the victim of a freak wave or a 'hole in the ocean', when winds and currents can drag even a large ship to the bottom.

Many theories were argued back and forth. The well-known writer of the *Sherlock Holmes* stories, Sir Arthur Conan Doyle, even held a **séance** to try and find out what had happened. But in the end, no one could explain how such a large ship could vanish without leaving either wreckage or survivors.

WHAT REALLY HAPPENED?

The Waratah *was carrying a heavy cargo of lead which could have shifted, causing her to capsize. But if so, where was the wreck? In 1999, the wreck of a big ship was spotted in the area where the Waratah vanished, but this was found to be a transport ship sunk by a German* **U-boat** *in 1942.*

Many ships have been lost in stormy seas off this rocky **headland**, known as the Cape of Good Hope, on the southern tip of South Africa.

How many people were on board the Waratah?

What famous ship was the Waratah compared to?

Which port was the Waratah bound for?

THE MARY CELESTE

DISAPPEARANCE FILE

Name Mary Celeste
Date November 1872
Place North Atlantic Ocean
Status UNEXPLAINED

In 1872, a small cargo ship was found drifting in the Atlantic Ocean. Everything on board seemed perfectly normal, except for one thing: the ship was deserted. No trace of the crew has ever been found. The case of the *Mary Celeste* remains one of the great unsolved sea mysteries of all time.

SHIP OF GHOSTS

On 5 November 1872, the *Mary Celeste* set sail from New York bound for Genoa in Italy with a valuable cargo of raw alcohol. On board were Captain Benjamin Briggs, his wife and daughter, plus a crew of seven men.

Ten days later, another ship, the *Dei Gratia*, set sail on a similar route under Captain David Morehouse, an acquaintance of Briggs. After a month at sea, Morehouse spotted the *Mary Celeste* drifting in the Atlantic. He immediately sensed that something was wrong and sent his **chief mate**, Oliver Deveau, to investigate. Finding the *Mary Celeste* deserted, Deveau and two others sailed her to Gibraltar.

In a final letter to his mother, the captain of the *Mary Celeste*, Benjamin Briggs, wrote: 'Our vessel is in beautiful trim and I hope we shall have a fine passage.'

WHAT HAPPENED NEXT?

At Gibraltar, an official enquiry was held. The crew of the *Dei Gratia* were questioned and the *Mary Celeste* was examined. All the crew's clothes and possessions were still on board. The cargo was intact. The hatch on the main cargo **hold** was closed, but two smaller hatches were open. The last entry in the log was dated 25 November.

A painting of the *Mary Celeste* in 1861. At this time, the ship was known as the *Amazon*.

WHAT REALLY HAPPENED?

Over the years many people have tried to solve the mystery of the Mary Celeste. Some even claim the crew were abducted by aliens! One theory is that alcohol fumes from the cargo may have made the captain think the vessel was about to explode, and this was why he and the crew left in such a hurry.

The enquiry found that Captain Briggs and his crew had abandoned the *Mary Celeste* in a great hurry and taken to the **lifeboat**. Why they had left the ship and what happened to them afterwards was never discovered.

Who was the captain of the Mary Celeste?

What cargo was the Mary Celeste carrying?

Who boarded the Mary Celeste when she was found?

THE LOST ARMY OF CAMBYSES

In the summer of 2000, scientists searching for oil in the Egyptian desert came across weapons, jewellery and human bones buried in the sand. Could these be the remains of the lost army of Cambyses?

After crossing the Sinai desert, Cambyses' army swept into Egypt, easily defeating the forces of Psamtik III at the Battle of Pelusium.

A MIGHTY RULER

In the sixth century BCE, the Persian ruler Cambyses II was one of the most powerful men in the ancient world. After successfully invading Egypt in 525 BCE, Cambyses sent an army of 50,000 soldiers from Thebes to Siwa in the desert west of the River Nile. The soldiers' orders were to attack the Temple of Amun, where rebel priests were refusing to accept his rule.

After marching for seven days across the desert, the army were resting at an **oasis** when a fierce wind sprang up. Soon columns of whirling sand descended on the troops, burying men and animals in clouds of dust.

DISAPPEARANCE FILE

Name	The Lost Army of Cambyses
Date	525 BCE or 524 BCE
Place	Western Egyptian Desert
Status	UNEXPLAINED

The story of Cambyses' army was first told by the Greek historian, Herodotus (484–425 BCE).

WHAT HAPPENED NEXT?

Hearing what had happened, Cambyses sent out riders to try to find his army. The trail led through the desert oasis of Bahariya, then southwest toward Siwa, but disappeared in the sand. The huge army had vanished without trace.

For many years, historians thought the story was just a **myth**. But over the last ten years, important finds have been made in Egypt's western desert. These are now being studied by experts. Many believe they could hold the answer to the mysterious fate of Cambyses' army.

WHAT REALLY HAPPENED?

Over the years many explorers and archaeologists have searched in vain for traces of Cambyses' army. The remains found in Egypt recently seem to be of Persian origin, and appear to belong to soldiers who became lost or stranded in the desert. Whether they belong to Cambyses' army is less certain.

Remains of the ancient temple of Amun at Siwa, in the western Egyptian desert.

When did Cambyses invade Egypt?

Which temple was Cambyses' army planning to attack?

Where have remains of an army been discovered?

19

Eilean Mohr off the west coast of Scotland is one of the most remote islands in the British Isles. According to local legend, it was haunted by ghosts who were determined to drive out intruders. Could this explain the mysterious case of the vanishing lighthousemen?

Eilean Mohr is the largest of the seven rocky Flannan Isles. It rises 87 metres above the Atlantic Ocean, on the west coast of Scotland.

DISAPPEARANCE FILE

Names James Ducat, Thomas Marshall and Donald McArthur
Date December 1900
Place Eilean Mohr, Scotland
Status UNEXPLAINED

DESERTED

On 26 December 1900, lighthouseman Joseph Moore was returning to Eilean Mohr by boat after a fortnight's leave. As Moore approached the island and looked for the usual signs of welcome, he was puzzled to see that there was nobody waiting at the **landing stage** to greet him.

Inside the lighthouse, Moore found the living quarters deserted. On the kitchen table were the remains of a half-eaten meal. An upturned chair lay on the floor. The lighthouse was empty, and its three occupants had disappeared without trace.

WHAT HAPPENED NEXT?

Alarmed, Moore returned with four others to make a full investigation. They discovered that two of the keepers must have left the lighthouse dressed for stormy weather. A third set of oilskins was still hanging on the hook.

The west landing stage had been lashed by gales. A lifebelt had been ripped from its mountings. But no trace was found of the lighthousemen, nor any sign of what could have happened to them. To this day, the mystery of their disappearance remains unsolved.

The job of the lighthousemen was to keep the lamp lit to guide ships away from the rocks at night.

WHAT REALLY HAPPENED?

Some claim that the three men were carried off by a giant bird or sea creature. It is more likely that during a storm, two of the men went to check the crane on the west landing. Meanwhile, the third man saw big waves approaching and rushed out to warn them. In the confusion, all three were swept out to sea.

When were the disappearances discovered?

Who discovered the disappearances?

How many men disappeared?

LOST ON EVEREST

DISAPPEARANCE FILE

Names   George Mallory
             Andrew Irvine
Date   8 June 1924
Place   Mount Everest, Nepal
Status   SOLVED

At the time of his disappearance Mallory was aged 38 and had many years' experience as a mountaineer. Both he and Irvine were well equipped for climbing at high **altitude**.

IN SIGHT OF VICTORY

On the day that Mallory and Irvine made their fateful attempt on the **summit** of Everest, thick clouds hid the mountain. But for a few minutes around lunchtime, the cloud lifted, and the two men were spotted within sight of the summit. Then they were once more hidden from view. It was the last time they were seen alive.

On 8 June 1924, British climbers George Mallory and Andrew Irvine set out to conquer Everest – and never came back. Nobody knew what had happened until Mallory's body was discovered in 1999. Could he have been the first man to climb the world's highest mountain?

At 8848 metres, Mount Everest in the Himalayas is the world's highest mountain.

WHAT REALLY HAPPENED?

Many believe that Mallory's attempt on the summit of Everest was successful, and that he died on the way down the mountain. However, there is no proof of this. The fact that the photograph of his wife was not found on his person when his body was discovered in 1999 does not prove that he reached the summit.

MEMORIAL

When Mallory and Irvine failed to come back, their friends waited several days. Then, accepting that they must both have died on the mountain, they built a memorial cairn and left. The mystery of what really happened that day, and whether the two men reached the summit, has never been solved.

These snow goggles, pocket knife and watch were found on Mallory's body in 1999.

WHAT HAPPENED NEXT?

In 1933, Irvine's ice axe was found on a slope at 8500 metres, but there was no sign of his body. It was not until 1999 that Mallory's frozen remains were found 300 metres further down the slope.

Rope marks showed that Mallory had fallen, been caught by the rope and then fallen again. A photo of his wife that he planned to leave on the summit was not in his pocket. Many people took this as a sign that Mallory and Irvine had reached the summit that day and that they were on the way down when the accident occurred.

On what date did Mallory set out for the summit?

When was Mallory's body found?

What did Mallory plan to leave on the summit?

23

INTO THE UNKNOWN

DISAPPEARANCE FILE
Subject   Percy Fawcett
Date   June 1925
Place   Mato Grosso, Brazil
Status   UNEXPLAINED

In 1925, the well-known British explorer Percy Fawcett disappeared in mysterious circumstances during an expedition to find an ancient lost city in the jungles of Brazil. His fate and that of his son Jack is still unknown.

LOST CITY

Fawcett was convinced that an ancient lost city that he called 'Z' existed somewhere in the Mato Grosso, a vast wooded region in western Brazil. He left behind strict instructions that, if he did not return, no one should try to rescue him in case they went missing too.

The legendary explorer Percy Fawcett was said to be the inspiration for the film character Indiana Jones.

On 29 May 1925, Fawcett sent a message to his wife that he had reached the Xingu River and was about to enter unexplored territory. The message ended: "You need have no fear of failure". Shortly after this, he headed north into the rainforest. Neither he nor his son Jack was ever seen again.

Atlantic Ocean
VENEZUELA
Amazon River
Mato Grosso
PERU
Xingu River
BOLIVIA
BRAZIL
Pacific Ocean

Map showing the Amazon Basin and the Xingu River region, where Percy Fawcett and his son Jack were last seen.

RUMOURS

After Fawcett disappeared, many rumours started to go around. Some said that Fawcett had been killed by tribespeople or wild animals; others said that Fawcett had lost his memory and was living among **cannibals**.

An explorer called Orlando Villas Boas claimed that Kalapalo tribespeople had confessed to murdering Fawcett and had handed the body over to him. But the bones were later found not to be Fawcett's.

In a BBC interview in 1998, an elder of the Kalapalo denied that the tribe had had any part in Fawcett's death. More than 80 years later, the mystery of his disappearance is as baffling as ever.

WHAT REALLY HAPPENED?

For a long time it was thought that Fawcett had been murdered by tribespeople of the Upper Xingu River. But Fawcett took care to stay on friendly terms with local people and always took gifts for them. It is most likely that he simply got lost or died of natural causes in the jungle.

 The Mato Grosso region of Brazil has often been visited by explorers searching for lost cities.

What was Fawcett looking for in Brazil?

Whom did Fawcett contact in May 1925?

Who claimed to have been given Fawcett's body?

Between 250 BCE and 900 CE, southern Mexico was home to one of the greatest civilizations the world has ever known. Then the huge stone buildings of the Mayan people mysteriously crumbled and their cities were reclaimed by the jungle. What happened?

DISAPPEARANCE FILE

Subject	Mayan Civilization
Date	780 CE onwards
Place	Southern Mexico
Status	UNEXPLAINED

Mayan texts have been found inscribed on stone monuments and pottery. Some texts were also painted on a type of paper made from tree bark.

A THRIVING CIVILIZATION

Mayan civilization thrived for nearly 2000 years. The Mayans were great builders, mathematicians and scientists. From **observatories** like the one at Chichen Itza, they even tracked the movements of the planets. Then something happened that turned their world upside down.

From about 780 CE, the Mayan cities were suddenly abandoned. It was as if the inhabitants had left and never returned. When people learned to read Mayan symbols in the 1970s, experts hoped the inscriptions would explain what had happened. They did not.

FAMINE AND DROUGHT

The mysterious decline of the great Mayan civilization has always puzzled historians. Several Mayan cities have been excavated, but no signs of warfare or violent conflict have ever been found.

For a long time it was believed that a terrible sickness attacked the population, or that a disease killed off their crops and caused the people to starve. Recently, it has been suggested that the Mayans suffered a catastrophic drought that caused famine and loss of life on a huge scale.

The Kukulkan Pyramid at Chichen Itza is one of the most important surviving remnants of Mayan civilization. Like all Mayan structures, it was built by armies of labourers without the help of machines or metal tools.

WHAT REALLY HAPPENED?

It now seems very likely that a large-scale drought could have caused the sudden collapse of the Mayan world. Scientists have looked at soil samples taken from Mexico's Lake Chichancanab. These show that in the ninth century when Mayan civilization disappeared, the region was at its driest for 7000 years.

Where was the lost world of the Maya?

When did the Mayan civilization collapse?

When did people first learn to read Mayan symbols?

In the 1920s, the SS *Baychimo* was a small cargo steamer that sailed around the northern coast of Canada, delivering supplies and trading furs with local people. Then one cold day in 1931, the Arctic ice closed in. The *Baychimo* was trapped!

DISAPPEARANCE FILE

Subject   SS Baychimo
Date   24 November 1931
Place   Arctic Ocean
Status   UNEXPLAINED

ARCTIC RESCUE

Realizing he and his crew were in danger, the captain radioed for help. Soon after, the first-ever **airlift** from the Arctic took place. Twenty-two of the ship's crew were rescued. The rest decided to shelter nearby for the winter and re-board the ship in the spring when the ice melted.

Since the *Baychimo* first drifted free of the ice, people have managed to board her several times, but nobody ever succeeded in rescuing her or towing her safely back to harbour.

It never happened. After a severe blizzard in late November, the crew emerged from their wooden huts to find that the pack ice had loosened – and the *Baychimo* had floated away!

GHOST SHIP

Since then, the *Baychimo* has often been spotted drifting across the Arctic Ocean. In 1932, an explorer caught sight of her while sledding across the Arctic. The next year, Inuit hunters saw the ship and boarded her, but had to leave when they saw a storm approaching. In September 1935 and November 1939, the ship was spotted again near Wainwright, Alaska. In 1962, another group of Inuit people sighted her on the Beaufort Sea.

 Inuit people live throughout the Canadian and Arctic regions where the *Baychimo* has been seen.

The last recorded sighting was in 1969 – 38 years after the *Baychimo* had first been abandoned.

In the early 1990s, the company that originally owned the *Baychimo* was unable to say whether the little ship was still afloat. Perhaps she is still adrift somewhere in the Arctic….

WHAT REALLY HAPPENED?

The Arctic Ocean has a pattern of circular currents that are driven by wind and by oceanic flows. These flows come in via the Bering Straits and the Greenland Sea. Once the Baychimo was caught in these unpredictable currents, it could have drifted in and out of inhabited areas, ending up almost anywhere.

What type of ship was the Baychimo?

When was the Baychimo last seen?

When did the Baychimo first become trapped in the ice?

29

GLOSSARY

Airlift An operation to rescue people by plane or helicopter.

Altitude Height above sea level. On high mountains, climbers need breathing equipment to cope with the effects of altitude.

Aluminium A type of metal.

Analyze To examine something very carefully.

Baffling Hard to explain, puzzling.

Bizarre Strange or unusual.

Cairn A pile of stones built as a landmark or to mark a grave.

Cannibals Tribal people who eat the flesh of humans for food or as part of a ritual.

Cargo Goods carried on a ship.

Chief mate A senior officer on board a ship.

Colony A community of settlers.

Drought A time when there is no rain and crops do not grow well.

Enslave To force a person to work very hard without being paid.

Excavate To dig up remains of a civilization.

Famine A time when there is not enough food to eat.

Headland A piece of land that sticks out into the sea.

Hold The part of a ship where the cargo is stored.

Landing stage A place where a ship or boat can tie up safely.

Lifeboat A vessel that passengers and crew can use to escape from a sinking ship.

Lighthouse A tall building with a light at the top to guide ships at night.

Logbook A written record of events.

Myth (a) An ancient story, often about gods or heroes; (b) a story that is found not to be true.

Oasis A fertile area in the desert where water can be found.

Observatory A building from which scientists can study the night sky.

Oilskin A type of thick, waterproof jacket.

Ore Raw material from which metals can be extracted.

Plaque A memorial stone or plate.

Sandstorm A strong wind in a desert carrying clouds of sand.

Séance A meeting where people try to make contact with the spirits of dead people.

Settler A person who goes to start a new life in another country.

Spy A person who secretly tries to find out information.

Steamer A type of ship with a coal-fired engine.

Summit The highest point of a mountain.

Telegram A type of message that is sent by telephone wires but is delivered in printed form.

Torpedo A missile that travels through water and can be launched from the air

U-boat A German submarine.

Unstable Unbalanced, liable to tip over.

Wreckage Debris left after an accident or sinking.

ANSWERS

Page

6-7   Lieutenant Charles Taylor; Avenger torpedo bombers; 'Cause Unknown'.

8-9   306; Germany; a cargo of ore.

10-11 An Electra 10E; Fred Noonan; Howland Island.

12-13 1585; 115;; 'Croatoan'.

14-15 211; the Titanic; Cape Town.

16-17 Benjamin Briggs; raw alcohol; Oliver Deveau.

18-19 525 BCE; the Temple of Amun at Siwa, in the western Egyptian desert.

20-1   26 December 1900; lighthouseman Joseph Moore; three.

22-3   8 June 1924; 1999; a photograph of his wife.

24-5   An ancient lost city which he called 'Z'; his wife; the explorer Orlando Villas Boas.

26-7   Southern Mexico; the ninth century CE; in the 1970s.

28-9   A small cargo steamer; 1931; 1969.

WEBSITES

http://www.ameliaearhart.com/
A site dedicated to the memory of Amelia Earhart.

http://www.byerly.org/bt.htm
A site about the many strange events that have taken place in the Bermuda Triangle.

http://www.maryceleste.net/
All about the mystery of the Mary Celeste.

Website information is correct at time of going to press. However, the publishers cannot accept liability for any information or links found on third-party websites.

INDEX